Pentium™ Processor
Optimization Tools

*This book is dedicated to my wife, Phyllis,
and my daughter, Stephanie.*

Contents

Introduction

WHO IS THIS BOOK FOR?

This book is for programmers, not just any programmer, mind you, but for programmers who desire to learn advanced program optimization techniques for the Intel 80x86 family of chips, including the Pentium.

The first few chapters review the basics of 80x86 assembly language programming but an intermediate understanding of assembly or C programming is extremely helpful for the later chapters.

WHAT IS ON THE DISK?

The disk includes all the code listings in the book as well as a version of Quantasm's PentOpt Program (a Pentium Optimizer) and DEBUG32 (a 32-bit, protected mode, DPMI debugger). Most of the code will work with Microsoft's MASM 5.1 or above (MASM 6.0 or above preferred) or Borland's TASM (any version). A few of the Pentium code examples require MASM 6.11, the first Microsoft assembler to support the Pentium. (You can bypass this requirement by writing macros to generate the proper opcodes.)

WHY LEARN ASSEMBLY LANGUAGE FOR THE PENTIUM?

As the software world continues to turn toward object oriented and high level languages with more and more complex operating systems, so why should you learn all the details of assembly language for the Pentium. There is one simple answer: speed. There are other reasons why you might want to program in assembly language, but the overriding reason, I think, is speed. If it is not, then you can still program for the 8088 in assembly language. The Pentium contains two instruction pipelines, both somewhat equivalent to a 386 or 486 CPU. Keeping both of these pipelines busy is mostly what programming for the Pentium is all about.

If you program mostly in a higher level language, such as C/C++, knowing assembly language will help you understand the language, its quirks and its performance capabilities on the PC. In this book you'll see how easy it is to add small amounts of in-line assembly that result in large performance gains.

There are a number of tasks that are simply more conveniently done with assembly language. These tasks include writing portions of operating systems, system utilities, device drivers, VxD's and the like. Many of these programs also will benefit from the performance gains possible when optimizing for the Pentium.

Finally, you may want to learn and use assembly language because it is enjoyable and/ or a challenge. If these reasons fit you, then you won't be disappointed with the Pentium. Being the first CPU in the 80x86 family with more than one pipeline provides for many new and interesting challenges that were never an issue on previous 80x86 CPUs.

HOW TO PROCEED

Programmers who are new to assembly language (or new to assembly language on the Intel 80x86 family of CPUs) should start with Chapter 1 or 2. If you are comfortable with binary and hexadecimal numbers, you can skip Chapter 1.

Programmers who are knowledgeable about 80x86 assembly language should skip or skim Chapters 1 through 5.

Expert assembly programmers should start with Chapter 8 or 9, depending on any previous experience with the Pentium. Most of the material in the advanced topics (chapters 16–19) rely heavily on the information in Chapters 8–15.

The chapters are arranged in sections, as follows:

1–3	Review and historical context
4–7	80x86 family background
8–12	Introduction to Pentium and tools
13–15	Superscalar Pentium programming
16–19	Advanced topics
20	PowerPC vs. Pentium

ACKNOWLEDGMENTS

Writing a book such as this for an advanced technical subject is not an easy task. It would not have been possible without the help of a number of people. Those who helped with technical information are: Frank van Gilluwe, Dave Horn, Rob Larson, Terje Mathisen and Stuart McCarley. Harlan Stockman (hwstock@sandia.gov) provided much of the code and the benchmarks for the FPU chapter. Thanks to Shapeware Corp. for their Visio drawing package that I used to produce the figures in this book. And special thanks to my long-time friend Larry Conrad who kept my writing closer to the English language than a programming language.

—Mike Schmit

Review
and Historical
Context

Number Systems

1

> *"It's a poor sort of memory that only works backwards,"* the Queen remarked.
>
> —Lewis Carroll from *Alice's Adventures in Wonderland*

In this chapter we'll review binary, hexadecimal and decimal number systems. If you have a working knowledge of binary and hexadecimal, then skip to Chapter 2.

If you've never programmed a computer or used a higher-level language such as C, BASIC or Pascal, you may be familiar only with the concept of decimal (base 10) numbers. We all grew up with decimal numbers—for money, time, measurements and even television channels. Everything is based on decimal—except the internals of computers and other electronic devices. Decimal is easy for us because we grew up with it. And, of course, we have 10 fingers.

The binary number system is used internally in every computer. Binary, or base two, has two digits, 0 and 1. Decimal, or base 10, has 10 digits, 0 through 9. Computers use binary because the electronic circuits can have only two states, "on" or "off." Different devices may use different physical properties (a magnetic disk may store binary digits as magnetized or not magnetized or as north or south) but the effect is the same—on or off.

To become familiar with binary, we'll start by looking at whole integer decimal numbers (i.e., 0, 1, 2, 3 . . .). We form decimal numbers by combining a number of digits. Each digit has two factors that are multiplied together. The first factor is the digit (0

Figure 1.1   Example Decimal Number

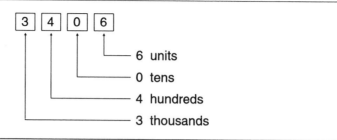

through 9). The second factor varies based on its position within the whole number. The far right digit has a multiplier of 1. The next digit to the left has a multiplier of 10, the next 100, and so on. Moving a digit's multiplier left increases its value by a factor of 10, making the numbers base 10.

For example in the number 3406, we say that the number is:

digit	×	multiplier	=	total	position
6	×	1	=	6	0
+ 0	×	10	=	00	1
+ 4	×	100	=	400	2
+ 3	×	1000	=	3000	3

3406

Of course, we already knew the value of 3406 was 3406. The real issue is how to convert numbers from one base to another. This same process can be performed for numbers in any base. Also notice the multiplier is the base raised to the power of the position. In the example above the 4 is multiplied by 100 and the 100 is 10^2 (10 raised to the power of 2).

Each digit in a binary number is called a bit, which is a binary digit. So when we have a binary number, say with 4 bits, the value of each of bit is progressively larger. The first bit (bit 0) has a value of 1, or 2^0. The next bit has a value of 2, or 2^1. The next bit has a value of 4, or 2^2. The last bit has a value of 8, or 2^3. Each bit has a value that is two times the value of the previous bit. In decimal, each digit has a value of 10 times the value of the previous digit to its right.

A byte is a binary number that contains 8 bits. If all the bits in a byte are 1, (the largest possible number), the base 10 value of the byte would be 255. So a byte can have a value from 0 to 255.

Figure 1.2   Example Binary Number

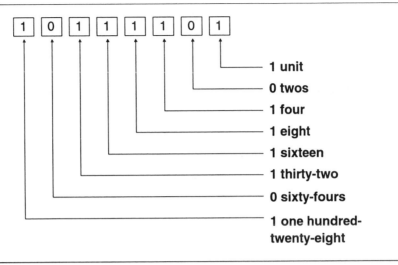

In the following example we'll convert the binary number to base 10.

binary digit	×	decimal multiplier	=	decimal total	position
1	×	1	=	1	0
+ 0	×	2	=	0	1
+ 1	×	4	=	4	2
+ 1	×	8	=	8	3

Addition in binary is very easy because there are only four possible combinations of numbers to add. By contrast, in base 10 there are 100 combinations. The following is a list of all possible single bit additions.

bit 1	bit 2	result
0	0	0
0	1	1
1	0	1
1	1	0 with a carry

To add two numbers in binary, we follow the same procedure as when adding in decimal. We'll add 01101001 to 00010001:

binary	decimal
0 1 1 0 1 0 0 1	105
0 0 0 1 0 0 0 1	17
0 1 1 1 1 0 1 0	122

HEX

Hexadecimal (usually shortened to "hex") is a number system based on 16 digits (base 16). Because there are only 10 symbols (0–9) for digits, this poses a small problem when working with number systems requiring more than 10 symbols. There could be many solutions to this problem. One would be to use the first 16 letters of the alphabet. Another would be to make up an entirely new set of symbols. However, the convention in general use is to use the digits 0 to 9 and then use the letters A to F for the values 10 to 15.

Here we'll convert a hex number to decimal and to binary. The hex number is 3A21h.

hex digit	×	decimal multiplier =	decimal total	position
1	×	1 =	1	0
+ 2	×	16 =	32	1
+ A	×	256 =	2560	2
+ 3	×	4096 =	12288	3
			14881	

Converting a hex number to binary is a completely different and much easier process. Each hex digit is just another representation for a combination of four binary digits (or bits). The reason that hex is commonly used is because of the fact that it is just a combination of four bits. Think of hex as a "shorthand" for binary. Table 1.1 is the conversion table.

So, to convert to binary, each hex digit is converted in sequence. Converting 3A21h goes as follows:

hex number:	3	A	2	1
binary:	0011	1010	0010	0001

Table 1.1   Decimal, Hex and Binary Equivalents

decimal	hex	binary
0	0	0000
1	1	0001
2	2	0010
3	3	0011
4	4	0100
5	5	0101
6	6	0100
7	7	0111
8	8	1000
9	9	1001
10	A	1010
11	B	1011
12	C	1100
13	D	1101
14	E	1110
15	F	1111

For easier reading, most examples in this book will use hex and decimal. Hex numbers are usually followed by the letter H for clarity. Memory addresses are always in hex and may be shown in the segment:offset format (4 hex digits, followed by a colon and then followed by 4 more hex digits). Later chapters will discuss the meaning of the segment:offset format.

```
1234:5678    segment 1234h, offset 5678h
123          decimal number
123h         hex number
```

In chapter 3 we'll discuss the use of an "assembler" to translate the code that you write into a machine readable format. Assemblers usually require hex numbers to begin with a decimal digit. This is because variable names and labels in programs usually start with an alphabetic character. Therefore, if a hex number starts with A–F, it must be preceded with a zero.

```
0FFh    ; hex for decimal number 255
FFh     ; error if the decimal value 255 is intended
        ; OK if the variable FFH is intended
```

SIGNED NUMBERS

We've seen how a byte can store any number from 0 to 255. However, we may wish to use negative numbers at some point. The same byte that can store numbers from 0 to 255 could also store signed numbers from −128 to 127. One way to think about this is to decide that the larger values (128 to 255) will be used for negative numbers: 255 is used for −1, 254 is used for −2 and so on. This may seem awkward or be confusing, so let's use an example.

Say we have a car with a five-digit odometer that goes from 0 miles to 99,999 miles (no tenths). Let's also assume that our car can go in reverse and the odometer will go backwards. If we start with a new car with an odometer reading of 00,000 and go backwards for one mile, it won't read −1, it will be 99,999. If we go backwards another mile it will read 99,998. If we go forward for 3 miles it will read 00,001. Clearly, 99,999 is the same as −1, 99,998 is the same as −2 and so on, when we have a five-digit decimal counter.

Now let's switch to binary. Let's install an eight-bit binary odometer. Start at 00000000 and go backward 1 mile. The reading will be 11111111 (or 255 in decimal). Go back another mile and it will read 11111110 (or 254 in decimal). Go forward for 3 miles and it will read 00000001 (or 1 in decimal).

The only remaining difficulty is determining if a number is signed or unsigned. How do you tell them apart? The answer is that you can't. In some high-level languages we declare certain variables to have a particular data type (i.e., integer, unsigned integer, etc.), and the compiler or interpreter keeps track of how to handle each variable. In assembly language the programmer must keep track. There are different instructions to handle signed and unsigned numbers, as we shall see in later chapters.

NUMERIC OVERFLOW

Even if you are only dealing with positive integers, you can run into problems. Suppose you have a byte variable (range 0–255) with a value of 255 and we add 1 to get 256. Wrong. Since a byte has a maximum value of 255, we must take this into account. This is the same as having a car with 99,999 miles on it and going one more mile. You can't fool anyone into thinking that you have a new car. When we see 00,000 on the odometer we immediately know that the car has 100,000 miles on it by looking at the rust and paint. We know that 100,000 miles have been logically subtracted from the real mileage because the odometer only goes up to 99,999. Note that the 100,000 value is the maximum odometer reading (99,999) plus one. Let's get back to adding 255 plus 1. Since the computer is only going to retain eight binary digits (255) we know that the real value will be off by 255 plus 1 or 256. So the computer will have a result of only 0. Since the computer registers have no rust or paint to clue them in that something is amiss, we need to have some other indication of overflow. Computers have a set of flags (or condition codes) that are set when various conditions occur, such as a numeric overflow. The "carry flag" is set when the result of adding two bytes is greater than 255. We'll discuss this more later on.

Let's say that we are dealing with signed bytes (−128 to 127). Start with 125 and add 10. We get 135 and it is stored as 135. But 135 is the same as −121. So all we have to do is check to see if we got a negative result and then we know that an overflow occurred. Wrong again. Actually, if we knew that we were adding two positive signed integers then a negative result would indicate an overflow. But what if we were adding two negative numbers? Here we expect a negative result. And what about adding a negative and positive number? As it turns out the computer has an "overflow flag" that takes all this into account. When adding two positive signed numbers or adding two negative signed numbers the overflow flag is set if the result has a different sign. When adding numbers with different signs there can be no overflow. (In a similar manner, the overflow flag is set when subtracting two numbers with different signs and an overflow occurs.) We'll discuss all the various flags in Chapter 4.

DATA SIZES

Depending on the purpose of a variable you may choose to have a small range of values or a larger range of values. In this section we'll discuss the various data sizes available on the 8088. We'll cover them in detail in the next few chapters.

A **byte** is the smallest addressable unit of storage in the computer memory. Each byte has its own address and may be read or written to individually by the CPU. If you want to read just one bit, you must read an entire byte or more into a register. (We'll discuss registers in Chapter 4.) If you want to write just one bit, you must read an entire byte, modify the bit, then write the entire byte back to memory. Each half of a byte (4 bits) is called a nibble. Data is sometimes arranged with one item per nibble, but must still be read and written one byte at a time.

Bytes can represent:

integers	8-bit signed or unsigned integers
characters	usually ASCII characters

A **word** is 16 bits, or two bytes. You can read or write words to or from memory as well as individual bytes. Words can be used for:

integers	16-bit signed or unsigned integers
segments	16-bit real mode segment or protected mode segment descriptor
offsets	16-bit offset address from start of segment

A **dword** is 32 bits, two words or four bytes. There are four common data types stored in dword formats:

integers	32-bit signed or unsigned integers
far ptrs	combination of offset then segment
float	single-precision floating point
offsets	32-bit offsets for large segments in protected mode

When we get to writing programs and declaring data we'll see that DB declares a byte, DW declares a word and DD declares a dword.

LITTLE ENDIAN VS. BIG ENDIAN

There is sometimes some confusion over the format in which values larger than 8 bits are stored in memory. On the 80x86 (i.e., 8088/86, 80286, etc.) computers a word is normally stored with the least significant byte in the lowest memory address and the most significant byte stored in the higher memory address. Other CPU architectures store multi-byte values in the opposite order, most notably the Motorola 680x0 family. You may have heard that the 80x86 method is backwards.

The Intel byte format is called "little endian" because values are stored in memory beginning with the little (least significant) end first. The other format is called "big endian" because values are stored in memory beginning with the big (most significant) end first.

Whether you are a novice assembly programmer or an expert, the little endian format will no doubt cause you some confusion at some point. So you should at least know that there are some good reasons why the little endian format is used. In our culture we read words from the left side of the page to the right. This is a completely arbitrary convention. Because of this we tend to write numbers in increasing values from left to right. If we were viewing a detailed street map we might see addresses shown as follows. (For this example I will ignore the normal addressing conventions of even numbers on one side of the street and odd numbers on the other).

	4	3	2	1
First Street				
Second Street	4	3	2	1

What I have shown is a single digit address for each house on a street and have shown the numbers increasing to the west. Now, for no real reason, let's paint a large 4 digit decimal number on each street, suitable for airplane viewing. Each digit will fill the street in front of one house lot. On First Street we'll put 8022 and on Second Street we'll put 3077.

First Street	4	3	2	1	←addresses
	8	0	2	2	←painted number
Second Street	4	3	2	1	←addresses
	3	0	7	7	←painted number

With north at the top of our book page, if the plane flies from south to north our numbers will appear right-side up. But if the plane flies from the north, east or west, it will be more difficult to read the numbers. The point being that how we choose to represent something on paper may have little to do with its actual practical use.

In the case of computers, there is one very practical use that makes the little endian format ideal. That use is one of the most very basic functions of computers: addition. Let's add the numbers on First Street and Second Street and put the answer on Third Street. We'll do this by adding the numbers at 1 First Street and at 1 Second Street and putting the answer at 1 Third Street, etc.

First Street		4	3	2	1	←addresses
		8	0	2	2	←value
Second Street		4	3	2	1	←addresses
		3	0	7	7	←value
Third Street	5	4	3	2	1	←addresses
	1	1	0	9	9	←value

You may have noticed that we ran into a small problem at 4 Third Street. The answer doesn't fit, so we needed to add another address on the street. The preceding method is the little endian process of adding any number of digits. (The same method can be used for subtracting.)

While exploring the little endian data format you've also learned how data is stored in the computer's memory. If we replace each of the digits in the preceding examples with a byte of data, we have a model of how data is stored in memory.

Here is how this same addition would be done with big endian format:

First Avenue		1	2	3	4	←addresses
		8	0	2	2	←value
Second Avenue		1	2	3	4	←addresses
		3	0	7	7	←value
Third Avenue	0	1	2	3	4	←addresses
	1	1	0	9	9	←value

Notice that we had to add a new address of zero on Third Avenue. Zero is OK, but addresses cannot become negative. When performing big endian addition you must be careful to have enough addresses available before the address where you start, whereas in little endian addition you must have addresses available at the end, which can be easier to provide. As you learned in grade school, you must start adding or subtracting digits with the least significant digit. Notice that in the case of the big endian format this means that we had to start at the highest address and work our way backwards. It is a poor sort of memory that only works backwards.

What Is Assembly?

*Genius is one percent inspiration and
ninety-nine percent perspiration.*
—Thomas Edison

INTRODUCTION

This book is about using assembly language programming to help produce efficient programs for the Intel 80x86 family of microprocessors more rapidly.

The goal is to help you become a knowledgeable assembly language programmer capable of efficiently producing optimized programs and/or subroutines. We will start with the basics of the 8088 and 8086 chips and then we will progress to the Pentium.

If you are already an advanced 80x86 assembly programmer, you'll probably want to skip the first four chapters. You should be able to tell from the first page or two of each chapter if you want to skip, skim or read the remainder.

What Is Assembly Language?

Assembly language is a language that is specific to each computer or family of computers. One of the goals of most high-level languages, such as C, BASIC, Pascal or Fortran, is to allow programmers to write statements that closely resemble the way we would describe the problem. Of course, we know that this is only a goal and it isn't always met.

In BASIC we might write the following:

```
IF BankBalance < 0 THEN PRINT "Bounced Check"
```

while in assembly language this would seem much more complicated and verbose:

```
CMP     BankBalance, 0
JA      OK
MOV     DX, OFFSET Bounced_msg
MOV     AH, 9
INT     21h
```

Don't worry if you don't understand all of the assembly statements—we'll learn all about them later. The point is that in assembly we must tell the computer every step to take. You might say that the difference between assembly language and a high-level language is like the difference between asking someone to calculate your gas mileage and having to tell them each key to press on a calculator to do the same thing.

So, if it requires so much detailed work, why program in assembly language at all? There are several reasons. First, computers can only understand machine language and assembly can (generally) be directly translated into machine language. All other languages must be compiled (into assembly) or run by an interpreter. So somebody has to write programs in assembly for every different computer. That "somebody" can be an assembly language programmer, or it can be a compiler (such as for the C language). But whoever wrote the compiler had to understand the machine at an assembly language level in order to translate the high-level language into its assembly language equivalent.

There are several other reasons for using assembly language. With assembly language we can write faster and smaller programs than most any compiler or interpreter can produce. Sometimes the speed or size difference is dramatic. In assembly, we also have access to every feature of the processor. For example, we can write programs to manipulate the system stack, communicate with devices such as modems and speakers, and utilize the floating-point math instructions. While many of these things can be done in various high-level languages, it is rarely done in an efficient manner without calling a function or subroutine written in assembly, which slows the process.

This is not to say that programming in assembly language is always at this low, detail-oriented level. Just as in any other language, projects of any significant size can be broken down into components. Low-level procedures can then be programmed to do common functions. You can also build or buy libraries that perform functions of similar nature to the standard C libraries, etc.

In practice, many people use assembly language to make parts of programs run faster. That is the primary purpose of this book. We will be studying ways to optimize subroutines or functions common to many programs. You can use these techniques and examples in projects written entirely in assembly language, or you can use assembly to optimize programs written in C, Pascal, Fortran or BASIC.

Faster and Smaller Programs

Why are assembly language programs faster and smaller? There are several reasons. First, when you write assembly code, you can select the minimum required instructions to perform an operation. Second, you do not need to select instructions based on any pre-defined patterns or rules (as do most compilers). Instead you use the best compiler available—your brain. In addition, you can select the best instructions for each situation. The best may be the fastest or the most compact or both. The point is that you get to decide what is "best" for every instruction.

So using assembly is a trade-off. Compilers cannot do better than humans (at least not yet), but they are much faster in generating the code. You must decide if speed and/or code size is more important than rapid development or a quick re-compile for another target machine. In general, compilers have only a few options to control the way code is generated. For example, in Microsoft C, you can choose to optimize for speed or size. Other than this you can globally enable or disable certain specific optimization techniques. The only way that you can selectively optimize some parts of a program for size and other parts for speed is to compile them as separate files (or modules).

Tools and Terminology

In the rest of this chapter we'll discuss some of the various terminology and tools that you may encounter when developing software. This is intended as general background material since a thorough examination of software tools would be a book unto itself.

WHAT ARE COMPILERS, INTERPRETERS AND ASSEMBLERS?

Collectively compilers, interpreters and assemblers fall into a class of tools known as translators. A human translator may listen to someone speak in Spanish, then repeat what they heard in English. The idea is that the translator is acting as an agent or a middleman. Although the two people trying to communicate may know some of the other language, they do not know enough to communicate effectively without the translator.

In the case of computers, you may know something about the machine language (see below), but the machine certainly knows nothing about the language you speak. The translator program provides this service for you. You write a program in a language that you understand, and the translator converts it for you so the machine will understand it.

Machine Language

Machine language is the language understood by a computer. It is very difficult to understand, but it is the only thing that the computer can work with. All programs and programming languages eventually generate or run programs in machine language. Machine language is made up of instructions and data that are all binary numbers. Machine language is normally displayed in hexadecimal form so that it is a little bit easier to read. Assembly language is almost the same as machine language, except that the instructions, variables and addresses have names instead of just hex numbers.

Assemblers

An assembler is a translation program that takes an assembly language source code file and converts it to object code. Object code is basically the same as machine language, but is structured in logical units called object records so that it may be relocated and combined with other object code files. In most cases one assembly language source code instruction translates into one machine language instruction. We will be using Microsoft MASM and Borland TASM assemblers for the examples in this book.

Compilers

A compiler is a translation program that takes a high-level language, such as C, BASIC or Pascal, and converts it to object code. In essence, a compiler translates each source code statement or instruction and generates the machine language equivalent. Each high-level language instruction may generate one machine language instruction, or it may generate dozens of machine language instructions. We will be using Microsoft C/C++ and Borland C/C++ compilers for the examples in the book.

Editors

Editors, or text editors, are programs that allow you to create and edit text files. The source code files for your programs are text files. There are many different text editors available, including EDIT that comes with DOS 5.0 and above. You can also use a word processor to create text files. An extra step is required to save word processing files as text files. My personal favorite is KEDIT from Mansfield Software.

Object Modules and Libraries

An object module is the file created by compiling or assembling a single program file. These files are called object files. You can combine commonly used object modules in libraries for convenience. Most every compiled high-level language comes with a pre-built library of functions that are used to perform useful functions by the compiler and/ or for programmer use. For example, the C runtime libraries contain functions such as printf, scanf and strcpy.

There is a big difference between the concepts of "object code" and all the other "objects" bouncing around the computer industry. The terms "object code," ".OBJ files," etc., refer to formats of machine language stored in a particular manner so they may be linked together or run by the computer. On the other hand, object-oriented programming is a term that refers to techniques and capabilities that allow a programmer to write functions that are easily re-used and/or extended in capabilities by other programmers. You'll often hear the words inheritance, polymorphism and encapsulation associated with object-oriented programming. These have nothing to do with object code.

Linker

A linker is a program that links or combines one or more object files and (optionally) object modules from a library to produce an executable file. These files have extensions of .EXE or .COM for DOS. For Windows there are no .COM file formats. Windows supports a special executable file format called Dynamic Link Libraries, .DLL files. We will be using Microsoft's LINK and Borland's TLINK.

Interpreters

Interpreters are programs that read high-level language programs, determine what actions need to be performed, and then execute the instruction. Some interpreters translate programs to an intermediate form (not machine language) and then execute from this format. Some call this semi-compiled and some call it p-code. Many versions of BASIC are interpreted. In addition, languages such as PostScript and REXX are interpreted.

Disassemblers

A disassembler is a program that reads a machine language program and attempts to reconstruct the assembly language source code that produced it. This task is especially difficult because there is no explicit difference between code and data in a binary program file: They are all just plain bytes.

Sophisticated disassemblers, such as V Communications' Sourcer, perform a complex analysis and simulation of the program to separate code and data. Using a disassembler is very useful in understanding how other programs operate, to learn skills and techniques to increase your knowledge, and to duplicate what a program does.

Disassembly is quite legal, but what you do with the resultant code can run afoul of copyright laws. In general, use of code from a product you own is acceptable for your own personal use or to gather understanding of program operation. You will violate a copyright if you include code from another copyrighted program and distribute the code in any form to others for money or for free. If you have any doubts, contact a lawyer versed in the current copyright laws.

Debuggers

Debuggers are special programs that allow you to run and monitor programs you have created to help you find errors, or bugs. They do this by allowing you to stop your program at any point (called a breakpoint) and to examine or change the values of variables and registers. The DOS debugger is DEBUG. Microsoft's CodeView and Borland's Turbo Debbuger are much more advanced in that they allow viewing your source code while your program executes. Other advanced debuggers such as Nu-Mega's Soft-ICE use the special features of the 80386 (and above) to perform hardware breakpoints. DEBUG32, an advanced, DPMI-compatible, 32-bit protected-mode debugger, is provided on the disk with this book. See Chapter 6 for a description.

In-Circuit Emulators

An in-circuit emulator (ICE) is a hardware device that plugs into the CPU socket of a computer. The ICE then monitors various hardware events while emulating the CPU, by using an actual CPU chip connected to additional circuitry. The advantage of using an ICE is that various portions of the system memory may be re-mapped, complex breakpoints can be used and an execution trace history can be collected. All this can be done at or near real-time execution speed. The disadvantage is that they range in price from several thousand dollars to the tens of thousands. As a software developer you can get most of the capabilities of an ICE with a product called the Periscope Model IV from Periscope.

The 8086 Family History and Architecture

I know no way of judging the future but by the past.
—Patrick Henry

History is more or less bunk.
—Henry Ford

"Those who cannot remember the past are condemned to repeat it." While I'm not sure if that quote applies to the history of computer chips, the history of the 80x86 chip family explains a lot about the current and future Intel products. This chapter contains a brief history of the Intel 80x86 family microprocessors and the major operating systems used on these processors.

The basis of the 80x86 family of microprocessors began in 1972 when the Intel Corporation began selling an 8-bit microprocessor, the 8008. The design was basically intended as a controller chip for computer displays.

When computer designers speak about a microprocessor having an 8-bit design they are referring, in general, to the size of the address and data paths. However, many use the term to refer only to the size of the internal general-purpose registers, because this directly affects the design of the software written for the chip. The number of address lines is also very important to the design of software, because the number of address lines is directly proportional to the number of bytes of addressable memory. However, there have been many 32-bit processors with virtual memory capabilities that have had fewer than 32 address lines.

In 1973 Intel announced the 8080 microprocessor, another 8-bit chip. This chip ran at a speed of 2 megahertz (megahertz or MHz is a million cycles per second). The 8080 was used in many early computers, including the IMSAI, Altair and others, in the mid-1970s. The 8080 has an 8-bit data bus and a 16-bit address bus, allowing it to address a total of 64K of memory.

Of course, these early microcomputers required software to make them useful. In the mid-1970s Digital Research Inc. (DRI) began selling the CP/M operating system. This was the first commercial microcomputer operating system designed to run on machines built by many companies. CP/M stands for Control Program for Microcomputers. (In the late 1980s DRI came out with DR-DOS, an MS-DOS work-alike. DRI is now part of Novell.)

One of the 8080 designers left Intel to start Zilog, where he designed the Z-80, another 8-bit chip. The Z-80 is a superset of the 8080 and ran at twice the speed, 4 MHz. Intel came out with the 8085 in 1976, but it never had the success of the Z-80 in general-purpose computers, although it is still being sold today for embedded systems use. Most Z-80 programs were written for the CP/M operating system and were still written to be compatible with the 8080. Because of the compatibility issue they just used the Z-80 as a fast 8080, using few (if any) of the Z-80's new features. Programmers and customers wanted (and often required) compatibility with all 8080 and Z-80 computers previously sold. The successes and failures of the Z-80 are a great lesson. It took market share quickly because of its speed and compatibility. It also failed to get many applications to be Z-80 specific, leaving the 8080 as the least common denominator.

In 1978 Intel announced the 8086 microprocessor. This is a 16-bit chip with a 16-bit data bus and a 20-bit address bus. To help programmers make the transition to the new chip, the 8086 could do everything that the 8080 could, but it was not source code or executable code compatible. However, programs written for the 8080 could be easily translated to the 8086 assembly language because it had all the same or similar instructions. When programs were translated, in general, they would still be able to address only 64K of memory, although the 8086 could address 2^{20} or a megabyte (1,048,576 bytes) of memory. Intel even had a program that would automatically translate 8080 assembly language into 8086 assembly language. In 1979 several companies had add-on boards and computers with 8086 chips. The only problem was that there were few programs available for the 8086.

Tim Patterson had written a CP/M work-alike for the 8086. This product was known as 86-DOS and was being sold with systems from Seattle Computers Products. Microsoft purchased 86-DOS, which became MS-DOS for the IBM PC, and the rest is history. But it wasn't quite that simple. In 1981 IBM announced the original IBM PC. At the time, IBM announced the availability of three operating systems: PC-DOS (IBM's version of MS-DOS), CP/M-86 (from DRI) and the UCSD p-system.

All three operating systems attempted to be compatible with the past systems. The UCSD p-system was source-code compatible with all operating systems that they supported. But being a p-code system (compiled to tokens) it was much slower than the competitors.[1]

Both CP/M-86 and MS-DOS (PC-DOS) had high compatibility with CP/M. The only real disadvantage for MS-DOS was that it used a different disk file format. This meant that 8080/Z-80 computers with CP/M programs could easily share data with 8086 computers CP/M-86 programs. This was only a real factor for the first year on the IBM PC. After that the installed base of the IBM PC was so large that the older CP/M machines did not matter as much. The fact that MS-DOS used a different file format was actually an advantage because it was dramatically faster.

The IBM PC uses the 8088 CPU, not the 8086. The 8088, introduced in 1979, has the same internals as the 8086, but it has only an 8-bit data path. Software can still read and write 16 bits of data at a time, but the hardware that interfaces to the memory chips splits the data access into two 8-bit operations. Intel did this so that hardware designers could continue to use all the 8-bit components that they were already familiar with and that were less expensive. IBM probably chose the 8088 to keep the price of the system as low as possible.

Some computer historians belittle IBM for choosing the 8088 instead of the 8086. However, this makes no sense because the software to operate an 8088 is exactly the same as that for the 8086. Both the 8088 and 8086 have 16-bit general-purpose registers and 20 address lines. The 8086 has a 16-bit data bus and the 8088 has an 8-bit data bus. In my opinion, there is no reason to call the 8088 an 8-bit machine. The only difference is in the hardware design, and this has gone through several major changes in the last decade. For example, the IBM PC-AT has a new bus design, as do the PS/2 series of machines, which use the Micro-channel architecture (MCA). The EISA machines have another bus design that is faster but still accepts add-on boards for the PC-AT bus. Newer machines have what is called a local bus (VESA or PCI) as well as one of the older bus designs.

COMPATIBILITY LESSONS

The lessons so far are clear. Customers want to have compatibility with all previous software. Binary compatibility, where programs do not need to be re-assembled or re-compiled, is preferred. Data format compatibility is also a preference, but not an overriding

---

1. Compiling to tokens is completely different from compiling to object code. A system that compiles to p-code has an interpreter that reads and executes the p-code; therefore, compiled languages are usually much faster than a language that is interpreted.

consideration for most people. Another lesson is that some compatibility can be sacrificed if significant speed improvements are provided.

MATH CO-PROCESSORS

One of the best marketing ploys of the original IBM PC was that it came with an empty socket for the 8087 math co-processor chip. Although only a small percentage of customers ever upgraded their systems to include this option, the fact that it was available made the systems much more desirable.

The 8087 math co-processor is a completely independent device that can perform floating-point math operations much faster than they can be emulated in software with integer operations. Because the 8087 FPU is connected directly to the 8088 or 8086 CPU, it can decode instructions in synchronization with the CPU. The FPU then recognizes and executes only those instructions that are meant for the FPU. While the FPU is executing an instruction, it signals the CPU that it is busy. The WAIT instruction causes the CPU to pause until this busy signal is terminated. If a floating-point exception occurs, the FPU can interrupt the CPU. The 8087 performs 80-bit arithmetic and comparison operations on a number of data formats. The floating-point data formats conform to the IEEE format for single- and double-precision floating-point numbers.

In 1982 Intel announced the 80186 and 80188. These CPUs were never used in large numbers in desktop computers. They are used primarily for embedded systems. The 80188 is the same as the 80186, except that is has an 8-bit data bus just like the 8088. The 80188 and 80186 have some additional features commonly used in embedded systems. These features include three internal timers, an interrupt controller, a DMA controller and a clock generator. The 80188 and 80186 also added about 10 new CPU instructions and improved the speed of most instructions.

THE 80286

In 1982 Intel announced the 80286. The 286 was first used by IBM in 1984 when they announced the 6 MHz IBM PC AT. The AT stood for advanced technology. The 286 could still run all the older software, but it had an additional programming mode—the protected mode. In protected mode, each program segment is not addressed with a physical address, but rather through a segment selector. This change allowed the maximum addressable memory to go from 1 MB (megabyte) to 16 MB.

Protected mode is especially beneficial in multi-user operating systems because it "protects" the code and data in one program from being read or written to by another program. Protected mode also tends to keep a single program from accidentally damaging itself.

The downside of protected mode is that it completely prevents (or makes it very difficult) for programs to do a lot of tricky things that had become very common. For example, to make data appear on the screen faster, most programs wrote the data directly to the memory-mapped screen. Under a protected-mode operating system, with multiple programs running, this is a disaster.

A multi-user protected-mode operating system should also provide some security. In the mainframe and minicomputer markets, two or more users would be using a computer at the same time. For security purposes it is essential that one user not be able to read or write the data or code from another program. The 286 was designed to start up in real mode (emulating an 8086), and once it was switched to protected mode it could not be switched back. If it could be switched back and forth, then any programmer could write such a program and be allowed access to another program. For this reason it was very difficult to write a protected-mode operating system that could support new protected-mode programs and still run older DOS programs.

Brain-Dead?

Because of a fairly obscure feature of the original IBM PC-AT, it turns out that the 286 could be switched from protected mode to real mode by some of the external circuitry. This was done, in effect, by turning off the CPU and then having the keyboard controller send a hardware reset signal that essentially turns the CPU back on. When the CPU was on again, the code left in memory would detect that it was back in real mode and could then run a DOS program. The entire process is extremely slow, taking several orders of magnitude more time than a mode switch on the 80386.

The first versions of OS/2 used this trick to run DOS programs. Because the 80286 cannot directly switch modes, some have said it is brain-dead. However, this criticism is based on the 20/20 hindsight after personal computers had become extremely popular and inexpensive in a very short time. The Intel engineers had probably finished most of the requirements for the 80286 design at the same time that the original IBM PC began shipping. IBM's market research predicted that they would sell about 50,000–100,000 PCs in the first couple of years. Instead it was millions.

The 286 provided a number of new instructions. Most of them are related to setting up and controlling protected-mode operation. In addition, many instructions were optimized to take fewer machine cycles. Instructions reading or writing memory were sped up two to three times.

32-BIT 80386

In 1985 Intel announced the 80386. And in the fall of 1986, Compaq announced the first IBM compatible based on the 80386. IBM's first 386 machine was announced in the spring of 1987 with the new PS/2 series machines (along with OS/2 a new protected-mode operating system). There are several significant new features on the 386:

- 32-bit addressing and data
- virtual 8086 mode
- virtual memory
- built-in debugging support
- new instructions
- faster cycle times
- higher clock speeds

During the next few years the compatibility issue became even more apparent. IBM's MCA systems (PS/2s) did not sell as well as expected. Although all the software was still compatible, hardware add-on boards weren't as plentiful and were more expensive. These were also the first IBM PC's with 3.5-inch disks. All previous machines used one of several 5.25-inch floppy disk formats. Although there had been some problems, every new drive type could read data from all previous formats. This was not possible with the new 3.5-inch floppies. The PS/2 design did not allow for a 5.25-inch floppy drive to be built into the system. IBM had an external 5.25-inch drive but it was not available immediately when the PS/2s were announced. Today most users have switched to the superior 3.5-inch format because it is more reliable and more portable. But the switch-over has taken many years. However, the marketplace rejected the wholesale conversion to a new system bus (the MCA machines). In 1988 a consortium of hardware makers created the EISA bus. This was successful only for high-end machines—in other words, customers that wanted the most powerful machines would buy whatever it took to get the power. Everyone else wanted compatibility and low cost.

At the end of 1987 IBM and Microsoft shipped OS/2 version 1.0. Over the next few years versions 1.1, 1.2 and 1.3 were also shipped. None of these met with much success. There are many possible reasons. OS/2 1.x could only run some DOS programs and only one at a time. The DOS programs ran more slowly than when just DOS was being run. Although new OS/2 programs could be multitasked, these programs had to be rewritten for OS/2. There were not many device drivers and printer drivers available for the wide array of add-on products on the market. In the meantime, a number of utility products appeared on the market that worked with DOS programs to make more memory available to them and/or allow several DOS programs to be run at once. Some, such as Quarterdeck's DesqView, had been around for a few years, but now became popular because of the more reliable 386 platform to run them on.

The 386 also made another new class of products available—protected-mode debuggers. The first popular one of these was Soft-ICE, by Nu-mega Technologies. The Soft-ICE debugger can set breakpoints using the debug registers on the 386. Previously, this type of breakpoint was available only by using an expensive in-circuit emulators (ICE).

Intel announced the 386SX in 1988. The 386SX is the same as a regular 386 (renamed to 386DX), except that the external data bus interface is 16 bits wide instead of 32 bits. The 386SX also has only 24 address lines instead of 32, making it easier to redesign 80286 motherboards to accept the 386SX. The 386SX machines are slower than 386DX machines, but cheaper to build (being very similar to the 286). But the 386SX can run all 386 software, including the powerful memory managers and debuggers.

RISCy 80486

In 1989 Intel announced the 80486 processor. The good news about this chip was that it was faster and didn't require any re-programming. There are only six new instructions on the 486, none of which are of much use for applications programs. The 486 is the first x86 chip with an on-chip memory cache. Internally, the 486 is a much different design than the previous x86 chips. The core CPU functions are implemented in a manner much like RISC chips. Because of this, the balance of optimization between the more powerful complex instructions and the simple (but now fast) instructions began to shift. The 486 also has a built-in floating-point processor that is much faster than the equivalent 386 plus 387 math co-processor.

THE 80586

In 1993 Intel announced the Pentium. For marketing and legal reasons Intel decided to not use the expected 80586 name. The Pentium is pretty much the same as the 486, but with two instruction pipelines, a bigger cache and other hardware features to improve performance. There are a few new instructions, primarily of use within an operating system. However, the ability to optimize older programs or write new programs with very high performance has been greatly expanded because the Pentium has two pipelines.

THE COMPETITION

In 1994 a joint effort of IBM, Motorola and Apple began shipping systems with PowerPC CPUs. The new PowerPC family of chips is a competing product line to the Intel chips. See Chapter 20 for a description of this chip and a comparison to the Pentium.

THE P6

Intel has stated that the next CPU in the 80x86 family will be announced in 1995. This chip is coded-named the P6. It doesn't really take a rocket scientist to figure out what P6 is (the Pentium was code-named P5). Maybe they'll be more secretive and call the next one P007.

Table 3.1 Increasing x86 CPU power

	Year	MIPS	Initial MHz	Transistors
8088	1979	0.33	4.77	29,000
80186	1981	0.7	5.0	100,000
80286	1982	1.5	6.0	134,000
80386	1985	5.0	16	275,000
80486	1989	20	25	1.2 M
Pentium	1993	100	60/66	3.1 M
*P6	1995	200	133	6.0 M
*P7	1997/98	500	250	12 M

Notes:
* = estimates/guesses
MIPS = millions of instructions per second
MHz = clock speed in millions of cycles per second
Transistors = number of transistor circuits in the CPU design

80x86 Family Background

8086 Architecture and Instruction Set

4

> The physician can bury his mistakes,
> but the architect can only advise
> his client to plant vines.
> —Frank Lloyd Wright

In this chapter we will review the 8086/8088 instruction set and internal architecture. The architecture of a CPU is a combination of the internal registers, how they are used, how memory is accessed and how the instructions are encoded. But before we get started I have to tell you about a friend of mine.

Jeff was an usher at my wedding and we spent many summers and weekends rock-climbing and backpacking together. We were always challenging each other, physically, to perform our best. We'd been caught in August snowstorms on Half Dome and had all our expensive camera gear stolen by bears. After being out of touch for several years Jeff and his wife flew out to ski with my wife, Phyllis, and me at Tahoe for a week. Jeff was clearly the best skier on the mountain. But the biggest surprise was that Jeff had become interested in triathlons and had recently placed 95th in the two-mile swim, a 100-mile bike ride and then a regular 26-mile run of the Iron Man triathalon in Hawaii.

This chapter may seem like a marathon if you are not prepared for it. If you've used 80x86 assembly before you are in good shape. If not, take it slow and I'll show you some shortcuts.

8088 Architecture

For a programmer, the 8086 and 8088 are identical, except for some minor timing differences. Moving bytes to or from memory are the same on the 8088 and 8086, but moving a word to or from memory requires four additional cycles on the 8088 because the move is split into two byte-sized moves.

The predominant chip in use is the 8088—the engine for the original IBM PC, and the focus of this chapter. This book will concentrate on the most commonly used instructions and their optimized use. A complete assembly-language guide containing every CPU instruction and all assembler directives would be unwieldy and defeat the intention of this introductory text.

REGISTERS

The 8088 holds data in 16-bit containers called registers. I think of registers as a box that holds a fixed number of digits. The 8088 has 14 of these registers: AX, BX, CX, DX, DI, SI, BP, SP, IP, CS, DS, ES, SS and a flags register. (See Figure 4.1.)

"So, Mike," you may wonder, "what is so important about registers?" Registers are the only places where any CPU operations take place. All addition, subtraction, comparison, etc., must take place in a register. To perform an addition to a memory location, for example, the CPU must read from memory, perform the addition, then write the data back to memory. Although in some respects registers are simply variables (16-bit variables in the 8088 and 8086), it is clear that operations on variables already in registers are much faster than on variables in memory needing to be moved in and out of registers.

A final subtlety is that some instructions use an additional unnamed register within the CPU and do not require loading data into a named register.

SEGMENTATION

The 8088 memory-addressing scheme is based on the use of two registers to provide a single memory address. Many computers use just a single register for an address. There are advantages and disadvantages for both methods that I will not go into. Here we will just discuss how it works. The total address space, in bytes, of a CPU is based on the number of address lines that are physically connected from the CPU to the memory chips. In the case of the 8088 there are 20 address lines. Taking 2 to the 20th power yields a total of 1,048,576 or 1 megabyte (MB). Since the registers in the 8088 are only

Figure 4.1 8088 Registers

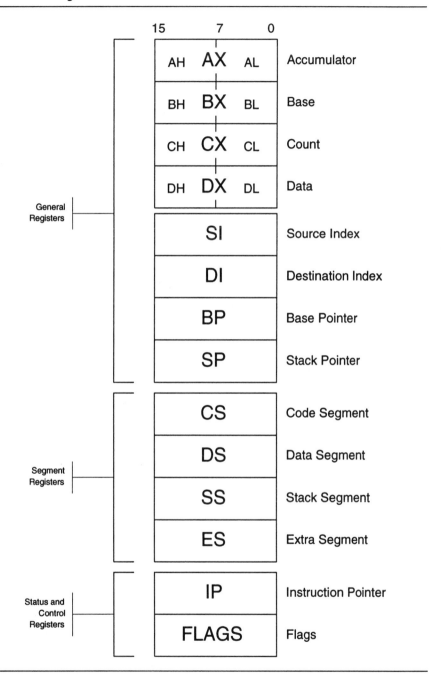

16 bits wide (a maximum range of 0 to 65,535, or 64K) the designers of the 8088 had to provide a method to address the entire 1 MB data space. The solution was to use the combination of two registers, one providing the high 16 bits of the 20-bit address and another to provide the low 16 bits of the 20-bit address. (Yes, the 12 bits in the middle do overlap.)

To point to a particular address, the 8088 combines the value in a segment register (see below) with an offset value. The source of the offset value will be discussed in more detail later, but can be any combination of a displacement (a constant), a base register (BX or BP) and an index register (SI or DI).

A paragraph of memory on the 8088 is defined as a contiguous block of 16 bytes on an even 16-byte boundary. So the segment registers provide the beginning paragraph number of a segment of memory. The offset address is the location beyond the beginning of the segment. (See Figure 4.2.)

Each segment can be only 64K in length (because of the limitation of 16-bit registers used for offsets). There are a number of techniques available for writing programs with more than 64K of code or more than 64K of data. We'll discuss some of these later. Also, on the 80386 and above there are modes that allow segments to be addressed with offsets of 32 bits, providing up to 4 gigabytes in a segment.

Table 4.1 shows which segments are used for various operations on the 8088.

Figure 4.2 Physical Address Generation

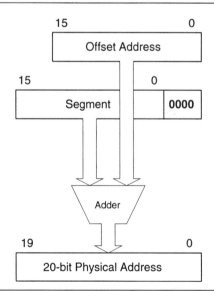

Table 4.1 Segment Register Selection

Operation	Default Segment	Other Segments	Offset
Instruction fetch	CS	none	IP
Stack	SS	none	SP
String source	DS	CS, ES, SS	SI
String destination	ES	none	DI
BP as base register	SS	CS, DS, ES	any EA
BX as base register	DS	CS, ES, SS	any EA
SI or DI as index	DS	CS, ES, SS	any EA
Other memory variables	DS	CS, ES, SS	any EA

Notes: EA = effective address

Effective Addresses

Offsets and effective addresses are pretty much the same thing. The term effective address is usually used when referring to the process of calculating an address from the component parts in an instruction: the sum of a displacement (a constant), a base register and an index register. The offset is the resultant 16-bit number that specifies a memory location relative to the beginning of a segment. See the MOV instruction later for some examples.

Segment Overrides

When you wish to perform an operation that uses a segment other than the default segment (as shown in Table 4.1), you must use a segment override. As can be seen from the table, only some operations allow other segments. See the MOV instruction later for some examples.

STACKS

A stack is a data structure consisting of a block of memory that is used in a first-in, last-out fashion, similar to the spring-loaded stack of plates at the start of a cafeteria line. The last plate placed on the stack is the next to be used. The stack on most every CPU is designed to be used from high addresses to lower addresses; i.e., the first address used the highest address in the stack. Other memory for a program's use is then allocated in the opposite direction (low to high). There is no particular reason why it has to be done in this manner, but this is the accepted convention and the way the hardware is built.

A pointer is kept that points to the last-used item on the stack. On the 8088, stack space is always allocated one word (16 bits) at a time. Putting a word on the stack is referred to as PUSHing. Taking a word off the stack is called POPping. A word is pushed onto the stack by decrementing (subtracting from) the stack pointer by two and then writing the item at the stack pointer address. A word is popped off the stack by copying it from the stack pointer address and then incrementing (adding to) the stack pointer by two. The stack pointer is always SS:SP, where SS is the stack segment and SP is the stack pointer. The SS (stack segment register) is never changed by stack operations.

A system may have many stacks, but only one is active at a time. SS:SP always points to the top of the stack. The stack is changed by loading new values into the SS and SP registers. This is done by the operating system, and you normally do not need to worry about it. See the **CALL** and **RET** instructions in Figure 4.3 and the PUSH and POP instructions in Figure 4.7 for examples of stack operations.

Figure 4.3 Stack operation diagram

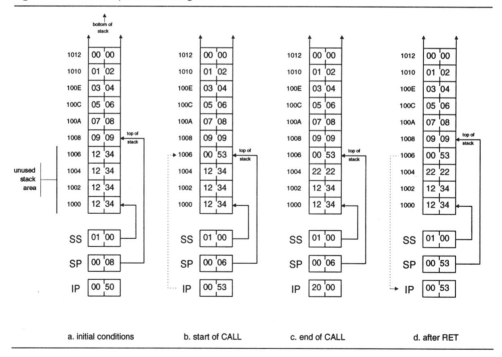

GENERAL-PURPOSE REGISTERS AX, BX, CX, DX

These four registers are general purpose 16-bit registers. Most of the basic instructions (add, subtract, compare, etc.) can operate on any of these registers. These registers also have the ability to be operated on only 8 bits at a time, giving you eight 8-bit registers. When referring to the low byte, the "X" is replaced with an "L," and when referring to the high byte, the "X" is replaced with an "H." For example, AX is made up of AL and AH. Each of these registers have some special uses as follows:

AX is the accumulator. Many instructions have a shorter format when using the AL or AX register. Other instructions operate with AL or AX as an implied register, such as multiplies and divides, string instructions and binary-coded decimal (BCD) math instructions. Implied registers are registers that are automatically used without explicitly naming them. Each implied register, if any, is noted with the description of an instruction. The name accumulator (from the word accumulate, to amass or collect) was originally used in place of the word register on many computers. This was probably because of the evolution of mechanical adding machines into electronic computers.

BX, a base register, can be used as an offset in a memory address. For example, to move the contents of the byte at address 6 into the AL register:

```
mov    bx, 6
mov    al, [bx]
```

The use of the square brackets surrounding BX means that the value in BX (a 6 in this case) is to be used as an address in memory. When these two instructions are completed, AL will contain a copy of what was in memory location 6 within the current data segment.

The CX register is used as a counter for loops and string operations. For example, to add 5 bytes starting at address 6 into the AL register:

```
    mov bx, 6           ; starting address
    mov al, 0           ; initialize count to 0
    mov cx, 5           ; load CX with number of loops to do
adder:
    add al, [bx]        ; add a byte
    add bx, 1           ; point to next byte
    loop adder          ; subtract 1 from CX and loop back
                        ; up if CX is not zero yet
```

The DX register is used as the high word in 32-bit multiplies and divides. When multiplying two 16-bit values, the result can be as large as 32 bits. This requires two 16-bit registers to hold the result. The combination of DX and AX is always used for this purpose. For example, to multiply 1000 by 2000:

```
mov    bx, 1000
mov    ax, 2000
mul    bx                    ; (AX is always assumed)
```

The answer, 2,000,000 decimal (1E8480h), is now held with the high-order word in DX (001Eh) and the low-order word in AX (8480h).

BASE AND INDEX REGISTERS BP, DI, SI

These three registers are 16-bit base or index registers and are also general-purpose registers. Although they can only be accessed 16 bits at a time, they can be used in much the same way as the other general-purpose registers. The BP register, a base register, is often used as an offset into the stack. Typically, high-level language (HLL) compilers will set BP to point to the stack to retrieve parameters passed by a calling procedure. In addition, space can be allocated in the stack to store local variables. Index registers DI and SI are used as pointers to the source and destination memory areas for string operations.

The use of the words base and index is only meaningful in the sense that when accessing memory you can combine the contents of one base register and one index register. Other than that, the concepts of using them are nearly the same. The other difference is that the BP register has the stack segment as its assumed segment.

SPECIAL-PURPOSE REGISTERS

There are several groups of registers that have special uses. Certain CPU operations automatically use these registers for their intended purpose with no action required on your part.

Segment Registers DS, ES

The segment registers are used to store the starting address of a segment of memory. The data segment (DS) register has the starting address of the data segment. The extra segment (ES) register has the starting address of the extra segment. The extra segment can be used for any data and must be used for some string operations that will be explained later.

Remember that the *value* stored in the segment register is not really the starting address, but only the highest 16 bits of the entire 20-bit address. To convert the value in a segment register to a physical address, it must be multiplied by 16 (or shifted left by four bits).

Code Segment Register and Instruction Pointer CS:IP

The code segment (CS) register points to the segment that holds the currently executing code. The instruction pointer (IP) register contains the offset in the code segment that points to the currently executing instruction. The combination of the CS:IP registers (Figure 4.4) is always used to point to the next instruction to be executed. I think of them as a bookmark pointing to the next section in a book to be read.

Stack Segment Register and Stack Pointer SS:SP

The stack segment (SS) register contains the starting address of the stack segment. The stack pointer (SP) register contains the offset in the stack segment that points to the top of the stack. Together with the stack segment register, SS:SP point to the top of the stack. The stack is used to store the return addresses to procedures, saved registers and local variables. See the stack section earlier.

Figure 4.4 CS:IP Operation

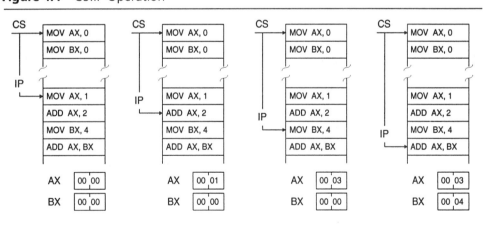

CS = Code Segment
IP = Instruction Pointer
CS:IP Point to the next instruction to execute

Flags Register

The flags register (also known as the status word or condition codes) consists of 16 individual bits, each of which has its own purpose (see Figure 4.5). Some of these may be set, cleared or tested individually or in groups. On the 8088 and 8086 only 10 of them are used. Other 80x86 CPUs use other bits. Table 4.2 describes, in general terms, the purpose of each of the flags. Understanding and using the flags is one of the primary differences between assembly language and HLLs. Compilers automatically handle all the details of setting and testing the flags. For example, when adding two numbers, the overflow flag is set if the result is too large for the destination. The conditional jump instruction "jo" (jump on overflow) can be used to branch to an error-handling routine.

Not all instructions affect the flags. And after studying the instruction set, you may believe that the instructions that change the flags and the ones that don't have been somewhat randomly chosen. For example, if you add two numbers and the result is zero, then the zero flag (ZF) is set. But if you move a zero into a register the zero flag (ZF) is not changed. Some instructions change only some of the flags and not others. There is a crafty method to this madness that I'll cover later in this chapter.

Figure 4.5   Flags Diagram with Bit Locations

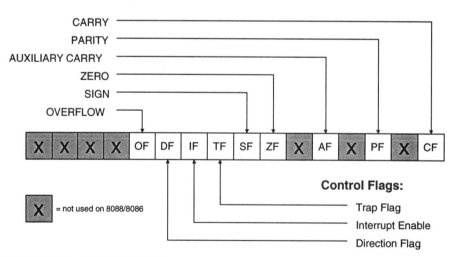

Table 4.2 8088/8086 Flags

bit 0	**CF carry flag.** The CF is set when there has been a carry out of or borrow into the high-order bit of the result. Shifts and rotates may set or clear the carry. May be directly set (STC), cleared (CLC) or complemented (CMC).
bit 1	(reserved, always 1)
bit 2	**PF parity flag.** The PF is set when a result has even parity. Parity is checked only for the low-order byte.
bit 3	(reserved)
bit 4	**AF auxiliary flag.** The AF is set when there has been a carry out of the low-order nibble into the high-order nibble or a borrow from the high nibble to the low nibble. This flag is set or cleared by the various arithmetic instructions and is used by the BCD arithmetic instructions.
bit 5	(reserved)
bit 6	**ZF zero flag.** The ZF is set when the result of an operation is zero.
bit 7	**SF sign flag.** The SF is set when the result of an operation has the high-order bit set. Signed numbers are negative when the high-order bit is set.
bit 8	**TF single step flag (trap flag).** Setting the TF puts the processor into single-step mode. Debuggers use this to single-step through the program being debugged.
bit 9	**IF interrupt enable flag.** Setting the IF allows the processor to respond to external interrupts. Clearing the IF disables these interrupts. Non-maskable interrupts (NMI) are not affected by this flag.
bit 10	**DF direction flag.** Setting the DF causes string instructions to auto-decrement. Clearing the DF causes string instructions to auto-increment.
bit 11	**OF overflow flag.** The OF is set when an arithmetic instruction has lost a bit of significance due to overflow.
bit 12	(reserved)
bit 13	(reserved)
bit 14	(reserved)
bit 15	(reserved)

The 8088 Instruction Set

This section is a review of the commonly used 8088 instructions. Keep in mind that this is a brief description of *what* the instructions do, rather than *how or why* to use them to perform a desired result. The last section of this chapter contains a few examples on how to use various combinations of instructions for specific purposes. From the few short examples shown earlier you may have noticed that there is a common notation used for the various assembly instructions.

The Intel processors use an assembly language notation as follows:

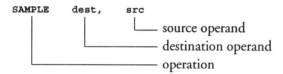

```
SAMPLE    dest,    src
                          └── source operand
                    └── destination operand
          └── operation
```

Not all instructions have both a source and a destination. Some instructions have only one operand that is both the source and the destination. Other instructions have no operands in the instruction and instead have implied operands. This "irregularity" is both a cause for disdain and a source of great optimization opportunities for all of the 80x86 processors. The main point to remember is that if there are two operands, the one on the left is the destination. We will cover each type of instruction in the next section.

SHORTCUT
MOV and ADD are important; no shortcuts yet.

MOV

The MOV instruction copies the value in the source operand to the destination operand. You can think of it as moving a copy of the data.

For example,

```
MOV ax, 1
```

This instruction moves a one into the AX register. You may want to think of it as

```
MOV ax, 1     ; ax= 1
```

There are many different combinations of sources and destinations. The source can be an immediate value (a constant), a register or a memory address. The destination can be a register or a memory address. This gives us five general combinations of sources and destinations, commonly described as follows:

```
mov    reg, reg
mov    reg, imm
mov    reg, mem
mov    mem, reg
mov    mem, imm
```

where

reg = register: any 8-bit register or 16-bit general-purpose register
imm = immediate: 8-bit or 16-bit constant value
mem = memory: the address of a byte or word in memory

The term "immediate" is always used to describe a constant that you provide as part of an instruction. Memory addresses can be a specific offset within a segment or can be based on an address stored in a register. If an address is stored in a register, then a displacement (constant) may be added to it. Registers that may be used to store an address are BX, BP, SI and DI.

Register to register:

```
MOV    ax, bx
MOV    al, bh
```

Immediate to register:

```
MOV    ax, 2
```

Immediate to memory:

```
MOV    memory_data, 0
MOV    byte ptr [bx], 1
MOV    word ptr [si+1], 2
```

Memory to register:

```
MOV    ax, [bx]
MOV    al, [di-1]
MOV    cx, memory_data
```

Register to memory:

```
MOV     [bx], ax
MOV     [di-1], al
MOV     memory_data, cx
```

You may have noticed that in the immediate-to-memory category there are two new terms: byte ptr and word ptr. These are not instructions for the CPU, but rather instructions for the assembler. These are data type overrides. By itself, the instruction MOV [BX], 1 is ambiguous. Does it mean to move a byte with a value of 1 into the address in the BX register? Or does it mean to move a word with a value of 1 into the address in the BX register? There is no way to tell, so the assembler will generate an error if the data type is not specified.

You may now be wondering, "But why is there no data type required on the instruction MOV memory_data, 0?" The answer is that the variable named memory_data had to have been defined (or declared) somewhere else in the program. The assembler can determine the data type from this declaration. This will be covered in detail in Chapter 6.

MOVING INTO SEGMENT REGISTERS

Moving a value into a segment register is a little different from moving data in the other registers because there is no way to move an immediate value into a segment register. Our only MOV options with a segment register (sreg) are

```
mov     sreg, reg
mov     sreg, mem
mov     mem, sreg
mov     reg, sreg
```

where

    sreg = segment register: DS, ES or SP
    reg   = register: any 16-bit general purpose register
    mem= memory: the address of a word in memory

I've heard various explanations of why immediate values cannot be used, but they usually make no sense. I think that it was just a design trade-off and it has stayed this way. Here are some examples:

```
mov    ax, 40h
mov    ds, ax
mov    es, [bx]
```

ADDRESSING MODES

All the different methods of reading and writing to memory are called addressing modes. The 8088 allows you to specify an address by using a combination of three items. To be more precise, the address used is a segment base (segment register times 16) plus the sum of three other components:

a displacement (constant)
a base register (BX or BP)
an index register (SI or DI)

An address may have any combination of these three components, but must have at least one of them. Here are some examples:

```
mov ax, [1234]       ; displacement
mov ax, var1         ; displacement (assembler determines
                     ; the displacement value from the label var1)
mov ax, [bx]         ; base
mov ax, [si]         ; index
mov ax, [bx+1]       ; base  + displacement
mov ax, [si+2]       ; index + displacement
mov ax, [bx+si]      ; base  + index
mov ax, [bx+si+3]    ; base  + index + displacement
```

These are the only combinations that the assembler can generate for the 8088 to execute. However, you will see some memory address expressions that appear to be different or more complex. These are always just different ways of generating the displacement (or constant) portion of the address. Note: On the 386 and above there are additional addressing modes. See Chapter 7.

ADD   ADDITION

The ADD instruction performs binary addition on two operands, overwriting the result on top of one of the operands.

```
add    ax, bx
```

Table 4.3   The Arithmetic Flags as Modified by ADD

The *carry flag* (CF) is set when there has been a carry out of the high-order bit of the result.

The *overflow flag* (OF) is set when a bit of significance is lost because of overflow. (This is different from a carry in that signed operations lose a bit of significance before a carry occurs.)

The *zero flag* (ZF) is set when the result of an operation is zero.

The *sign flag* (SF) is set when the result of an operation has the high-order bit set, signifying a negative result.

The *auxiliary flag* (AF) is set when there has been a carry out of the low-order nibble into the high-order nibble. (This is for BCD instructions, described later.)

The *parity flag* (PF) is set when a result has even parity in the low-order byte. Parity is the least significant bit of the sum of the number of bits set, plus 1.

adds AX and BX and stores the result in AX. You can think of it like this:

AX = AX + BX

So although there are only two operands for the ADD instruction, both are considered source operands, and the first operand is also the destination. The ADD instruction can use all the same memory addressing modes as the MOV instruction.

Many arithmetic instructions affect special bits stored in the Flags register. For example, an ADD instruction will change the flags as described in Table 4.3.

ALU Instructions

The ADD instruction described earlier is just one of a group of instructions known as the ALU instructions. (The ALU is a portion of a CPU called the arithmetic logic unit.) The flags in Table 4.3 are changed by many of the ALU operations. I will refer to this subset of the flags as the arithmetic flags. The ALU operations include ADD, SUB, ADC, SBB, INC, DEC, NEG, CMP, AND, OR, XOR, NOT and TEST. These instructions are described next.

SHORTCUT
If you fully understand the MOV and ADD instructions, the next 12 instructions are easy. Just skim the comments in the examples to see what each instruction does.

ADC   ADD WITH CARRY

ADC is add with carry. This is how you can use a computer with only 16-bit registers to perform arithmetic on any size of integers.

```
adc ax, bx     ; AX = AX + BX + CF (carry flag)
```

To add two 32-bit numbers in four 16-bit registers:

```
                ; equivalent to: DX:AX = DX:AX + CX:BX
add ax, bx      ; AX = AX + BX
adc dx, cx      ; DX = DX + CX + CF
```

SUB   SUBTRACTION

The SUB instruction performs binary subtraction on two operands, overwriting the result on top of one of the operands.

```
sub  ax, bx    ; AX = AX - BX
```

SBB   SUBTRACT WITH BORROW

The SBB instruction performs binary subtraction with borrow on two operands, overwriting the result on top of one of the operands. If the carry flag (CF) is set, then an additional one is subtracted.

```
sbb  ax, bx    ; AX = AX - BX - CF
```

To subtract two 32-bit numbers in four 16-bit registers:

```
                ; equivalent to: DX:AX = DX:AX - CX:BX
sub            ax, bx ; AX = AX - BX
sub dx, cx     ; DX = DX - CX - CF
```

INC   INCREMENT

INC adds one to the operand (which is both the source and the destination). The operand is always treated as an unsigned number. This instruction does not affect the carry flag (CF).

```
inc ax        ; AX = AX + 1
```

DEC   DECREMENT

DEC subtracts one from the operand (which is both the source and the destination). The operand is always treated as an unsigned number. This instruction does not affect the carry flag (CF).

```
dec ax        ; AX = AX - 1
```

NEG   NEGATE

The NEG instruction, in effect, subtracts the operand from zero. This is known as a twos complement negation. (What really happens is that each bit is reversed, then the entire operand is incremented.)

```
neg ax        ; AX = 0 - AX
```

CMP   COMPARE

CMP can be thought of as a comparison instruction, but what it really does is a subtraction, except that it does not store the result. Instead only the flags are affected. The outcome is a comparison. This example compares AX to 5:

```
cmp ax, 5     ; compare AX to 5
jl  small     ; jump if AX is less than 5 to small
```

BIT OPERATIONS: AND, OR, XOR, NOT, TEST

The arithmetic bit instructions perform bitwise operations on registers or memory operands. These instructions are AND, OR, XOR, NOT and TEST. The table shows the operation of AND, OR and XOR (eXclusive OR) on two bits.

bit 1	bit 2	AND	OR	XOR
0	0	0	0	0
0	1	0	1	1
1	0	0	1	1
1	1	1	1	0

The TEST instruction performs an AND operation but affects only the flags and does not write the result to any operand (similar to CMP and SUB). The NOT instruction toggles, or reverses, each bit of an operand.

Shifts and Rotates

There are two types of shifts and two types of rotates. Each type can be left or right. For each type, the destination is shifted or rotated by the number of bits in the second operand, or the count. The count may be 1 or contained in CL. (On the 80186 and above an immediate shift count of 1 to 31 may be used.) The shift instructions affect all the arithmetic flags except the auxiliary flag (AF). The rotate instructions affect only the carry flag (CF) and overflow flag (OF). The flag of primary interest for both shifts and rotates is the carry flag (CF). When a bit is bumped off either end of an operand, it ends up in the carry flag (CF); see Figure 4.6 for examples.

SHR   SHIFT LOGICAL RIGHT

SHR (shift logical right) shifts the destination operand to the right by the count. Zeroes are shifted into the high-order bit. The overflow flag (OF) is set if the high-order bit changes values, else it is cleared. The original low bit is copied into the carry flag (CF). Shifting right in binary is the same as dividing by 2 (and discarding the remainder).

```
shr ax, 1    ; AX = AX / 2
```

SAR *Shift Arithmetic Right*

The arithmetic shift is slightly different from other shifts in that the value in the most significant bit retains its original value. The effect is that the result has the same sign (positive or negative) as the input value.

```
sar ax, 1    ; AX = AX / 2
```

SHL/SAL *Shift Left*

SHL (shift logical left) and SAL (shift arithmetic left) are the same instruction. The destination operand is shifted to the left by the count. Zeroes are shifted into the low-order byte. The overflow flag (OF) is set if the high-order bit changes values, else it is cleared.

```
shl ax, 1    ; (CF +) AX = AX * 2
```

ROR/ROL *Rotate Right, Rotate Left*

The rotate instructions do exactly what they say. Bits that come off one end of an operand just rotate around and are moved into the other end. In addition, the bit that rotates around is copied into the carry flag (CF).

RCR/RCL *Rotate Carry Right, Rotate Carry Left*

The rotate with carry instructions are the same as the other rotates, except the carry flag is included as part of the operand. For example, when working with a 16-bit register, the rotate is really working with a 17-bit value, the high bit being the carry flag.

PUSH

The PUSH instruction pushes a word onto the stack. The SP register is decremented by two and then the source operand is copied to the stack. The word to be pushed can be a 16-bit register or a memory location.

Figure 4.6 8-bit Shift and Rotate Bit Diagram

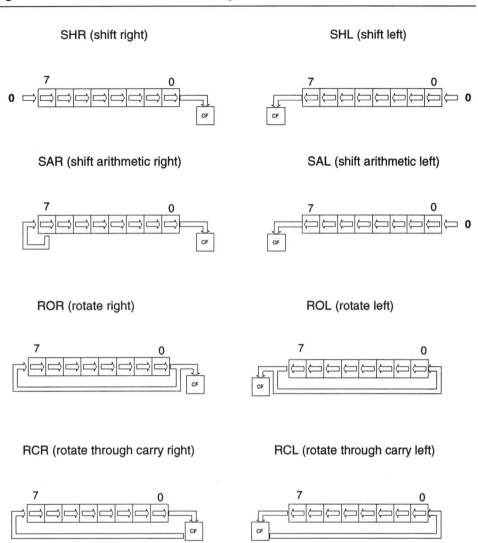

POP

The POP instruction pops a word from the stack. The word is copied from the stack to the destination operand, then the SP register is incremented by two. The word can be popped into a 16-bit register or a memory location. See Figure 4.7.

Figure 4.7 Push/Pop Stack Operation

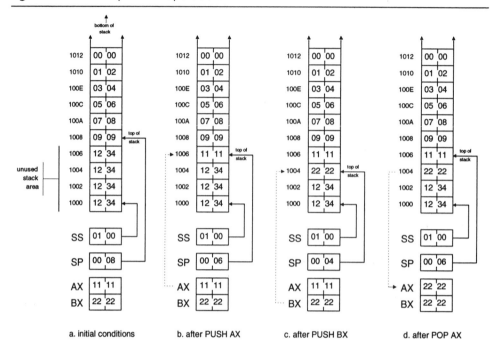

stack operations shown for:

```
PUSH      AX ; b
PUSH      BX ; c
POP       AX ; d
```

Now that we've covered a number of instructions, it is time to show a few of them combined together.

```
push   bx        ; save BX on stack
push   cx        ; save CX
push   dx        ; save DX

mov    ax, 10    ; AX = 10
mov    cl, 3     ; CL = 3
mov    bx, 2     ; BX = 2
push   bx        ; AX (10) on stack
pop    dx        ; DX = 10 (from stack)
```

```
shl    ax, cl   ; AX = AX * (2 * 2 * 2) --> AX = 80
                ;    (three 2's because CL = 3)
inc    ax       ; AX = AX + 1  --> AX = 81
add    ax, bx   ; AX = AX + BX --> AX = 83
sub    ax, dx   ; AX = AX - DX --> AX = 73

pop    dx       ; restore DX from stack
pop    cx       ; restore CX
pop    bx       ; restore BX
```

This short section of code demonstrates several instructions, but we still need several others before we can write programs that are very useful.

Program Control
And Branching

The CALL, RET and JMP instructions change a program's operation by transferring control to various procedures and subroutines.

CALL

The CALL instruction operates nearly the same as the JMP except that in addition to transferring control to a new destination, the current location is saved on the stack. This is a call to a subroutine. When the subroutine ends it performs a RET, and control returns to the instruction immediately following the CALL instruction. For a near call only IP is pushed on the stack. For a far call IP and CS are pushed. CALLs must be coordinated with a matching return instruction.

```
mov    ax, 5    ; setup AX for call
mov    bx, 2    ; setup BX for call
call   func1    ; call subroutine
```

RET

The RET instruction returns to the instruction immediately after the most recently executed CALL instruction. It does this by popping the address off of the stack. Far calls must be matched with a far return (RETF) and near calls must be matched with a near return (RETN). The assembler usually does this automatically when you use the RET instruction. A procedure that calculates $2 * X + Y + 1$ (AX = x and BX = Y) would be

```
func1 proc near
  shl  ax, 1      ; multiple AX by 2
  add  ax, bx     ; add BX
  inc  ax         ; add 1
  ret             ; return with result in AX
func1 endp
```

JMP

JMP is a jump to a new address. There are several formats for JMP instructions. The simplest form is:

```
  inc  ax
  jmp  dest
  . . .
dest:
  mov  bx, ax
```

This is a near jump (near means the destination is in the same segment). There is also a short jump format. This is a special form of the jump where the destination is within +127 or –128 bytes and so it takes up less space (2 bytes of code instead of 3). You can also perform FAR jumps. These are jumps to other code segments. There are also two types of indirect jumps. The first is where the new code segment offset is stored in a register:

```
  jmp  bx
```

The other type is where the new offset (or segment and offset) are stored in a memory variable:

```
  jmp  [bx]
  . . .
  jmp  word ptr dest
  . . .
new_dest:
  . . .
dest dw new_dest
```

The advantages of these types of jumps is that you can write a program that reconfigures itself. These are powerful techniques, as the following example shows:

```
    mov     bl, [si]       ; read char from a previously loaded string
                           ; assume char is an "A", "B" or "C"
    mov     bh, 0          ; zero high byte of BX
    sub     bl, 'A'        ; subtract ASCII value of 'A'
    jmp     jmp_tbl[bx]    ; jump to code for processing
    jmp_tbl dw lbl_A       ; this data table contains an array
            dw lbl_B       ; of three near pointers to the labels for
            dw lbl_C       ; processing "A", "B" or "C"

lbl_A:
    ...                    ; code here for "A", etc.
lbl_B:
    ...
lbl_C:
    ...
```

The preceding example is how to construct a simple CASE statement in assembly language. There is only one assembly instruction to this construct. And this is why it is very fast and efficient in assembly language. For most applications you will want to check the range of the parameter that controls the jump destination (in this example it is BX). For this type of operation we will need to use conditional jumps.

CONDITIONAL JUMPS

Conditional jumps are the decision-making instructions in the computer. You might think of these as somewhat like IF..THEN statements in other languages. However, conditional jumps are more primitive. Conditional jumps only test the state of one or more bit flags in the Flags register. The flags must be set with any one of a number of other instructions. To compare to integers you would use the CMP instruction:

```
    cmp  ax, bx      ; compare AX and BX (set up flags)
    jne  dest        ; jump if not equal
    mov  cx, 1       ; CX = 1
dest:
```

This code sequence is the same as saying

```
    IF AX = BX THEN CX = 1
```

The JNE is "jump if not equal." The CMP instruction sets the zero flag (ZF) if AX and BX are equal. Actually, CMP performs a subtraction, but just doesn't store the result anywhere; it just sets some of the bit flags in the Flags register.

```
    cmp   ax, bx      ; compare AX and BX (set up flags)
    jge   dest_1      ; jump if greater or equal
    mov   cx, 1       ; CX = 1
    jmp   dest_2
dest_1:
    mov   cx, 2 ; CX = 2
dest_2:
```

This code sequence is the same as saying

```
IF AX < BX THEN CX = 1 ELSE CX = 2
```

SIGNED VS. UNSIGNED COMPARISONS

Referring back to Chapter 1, it is important to note that there is a difference between signed and unsigned numeric values. However, this difference is only based on the way that you use the data. For example, the byte 0FFh can be treated as 255 or −1. Conditional jumps are the main tool used to differentiate between signed and unsigned numbers. In the previous example, AX and BX were treated as signed values. This is because the conditional jump, JGE, was used. If JAE was used, then AX and BX would have been treated as unsigned values. The use of the word greater (signed) and above (unsigned) by Intel was a somewhat arbitrary choice. See Table 4.4 for a complete list of conditional jumps.

LOOP

The LOOP instruction allows you to easily repeat sections of code a given number of times. The number of repetitions is placed in the CX register before the loop starts. For example, to repeat a block of code 50 times you would do this:

```
    mov   cx, 50     ; CX = number of loops
loop1:
    . . .
    . . .
    loop  loop1      ; CX = CX - 1, if CX = 0 jump to loop1
```

The LOOP instruction decrements CX by 1 and then jumps to the specified destination if CX is not zero.

Table 4.4   Conditional Jumps

Jump (alt)		Explanation	
Unsigned comparisons			
ja	jnbe	jump if above	/ jump if not below or equal
jae	jnb	jump if above or equal	/ jump if not below
jb	jnae	jump if below	/ jump if not above or equal
jbe	jna	jump if below or equal	/ jump if not above
Signed comparisons			
jg	jnle	jump if greater	/ jump if not less or equal
jge	jnl	jump if greater or equal	/ jump if not less
jl	jnge	jump if less	/ jump if not greater or equal
jle	jng	jump if less or equal	/ jump if not greater
Other			
jc		jump if carry	
jnc		jump if not carry	
je	jz	jump if equal	/ jump if zero
jne	jnz	jump if not equal	/ jump if not zero
jo		jump if overflow	
jno		jump if not overflow	
js		jump if sign	
jns		jump if not sign	
jnp	jpo	jump if no parity	/ jump if parity odd
jp	jpe	jump if parity	/ jump if parity even

Notes: Some conditional jumps have an alternate form, such as JA and JNBE. Both forms are two ways of describing the same condition.

CONDITIONAL LOOPS

There are also two types of conditional loops. LOOPZ is loop while zero and LOOPNZ is loop while not zero. LOOPZ has a synonym, LOOPE or loop while equal. LOOPNZ has a synonym, LOOPNE or loop while not equal. Here is a simple example that scans a string until a zero (null) byte is found:

```
    lea   bx, string   ; load offset of string not shown
    mov   cx, 100       ; maximum string length of 100
loop_1:
    mov   al, [bx]      ; read a character from memory
    inc   bx            ; point to next character
    cmp   al, 0         ; compare with zero
```

```
        loopneloop_1        ; loop back if null not found
        je    found
        ...                 ; no null in 100 bytes
        ...
    found:
        dec   bx            ; found null, return bx to point to null
        ...
```

Here is an example of searching a string to skip by all leading spaces:

```
    lea   bx, string        ; load offset of string not shown
    mov   cx, 100           ; maximum string length of 100
    loop_1:
    mov   al, [bx]          ; read a character from memory
    inc   bx               ; point to next character
    cmp   al, 0            ; compare with null
    je    found_null
    cmp   al, 32           ; compare with ASCII space
    loope loop_1           ; loop back if still a space
    jne   found
    ...                    ; no space in 100 bytes
    ...
    found:
    ...                    ; bx points to first non-space
    ...
    found_null:
    ...                    ; found null, string must be all spaces
    ...                    ; or has a zero length
```

JCXZ

JCXZ is another conditional jump, but it does not use any of the flags. Instead, JCXZ jumps if CX is equal to zero. This is an easy way of testing CX before the start of a loop if the loop should not be executed at all if the count is zero. Remember that the LOOP instruction decrements CX before testing to see if it is zero. If CX starts at zero then the loop will execute 65,536 times. Of course, when loading CX with a constant this is not needed. But when CX is loaded as a variable it is wise to do this test.

```
    jcxz loop_skip; skip the loop if CX = 0
    loop_1:
    ...
    loop  loop_1
    loop_skip:
```

Flag Manipulations

The following nine instructions are used to save and restore flags or change an individual flag.

LAHF *LOAD AH FROM FLAGS*

LAHF copies the low byte of the flags register to the AH register. This instruction is provided for 8080/8085 compatibility. The following flag bits are copied: SF, ZF, AF, PF and CF.

SAHF *STORE AH TO FLAGS*

SAHF copies the contents of the AH register to the low byte of the flags register. Only bits 0, 2, 4, 6, and 7 are copied, because the others are undefined. These correspond to the CF, PF, AF, ZF and SF. This instruction is provided for 8080/8085 compatibility.

PUSHF PUSH FLAGS
POPF *POP FLAGS*

These instruction push and pop the flags register. PUSHF copies all bits from the flags register. POPF does not copy the undefined bits in the flags register.

STC *SET THE CARRY FLAG*
CLC *CLEAR THE CARRY FLAG*
CMC *COMPLEMENT (OR REVERSE) THE CARRY FLAG*

These instructions directly change the state of the carry flag (CF).

CLD *CLEAR DIRECTION FLAG*
STD *SET DIRECTION FLAG*

These instructions directly change the state of the direction flag (DF). The direction flag controls whether string operations increment or decrement the source and destination registers. When DF is set the string operations decrement.

Multiply and Divide

Multiply and divide are a little bit trickier than you might think because when you multiply two numbers together, the result can have more digits than when you started. When multiplying two 16-bit numbers, the result can require up to 32 bits. Conversely, when dividing two numbers, the dividend (the number being divided) can have more digits than the divisor or the quotient. Both multiply and divide automatically use AL, AX or DX:AX for one of the operands. The other operand can be a register or memory operand.

MUL AND IMUL   MULTIPLY AND INTEGER MULTIPLY

MUL and IMUL are the same, except that MUL is for unsigned multiplies and IMUL is for signed multiplies. One of the numbers to be multiplied must be moved into AL or AX. The other operand can be in a register or in memory. AL or AX is an implied operand of the multiply instruction. For example:

```
mov    bl, 10
mov    al, 50
mul    bl          ; AX = AL * BL
```

For larger values, use

```
mov    bx, 100
mov    ax, 500
mul    bx          ; DX:AX = AX * BX
```

In this case 16-bit registers are required because at least one of the values to be multiplied is larger than 255. Notice that the results are automatically stored in the implied destination of AX (8-bit × 8-bit) or in DX:AX (16-bit × 16-bit).

Signed multiplication works the same. The carry flag (CF) and overflow flag (OF) are cleared if the upper half of the result is 0; otherwise, they are set. The other arithmetic flags are undefined.

DIV AND IDIV   DIVIDE AND INTEGER DIVIDE

Division works like this:

```
mov    ax, 500
mov    bl, 10
div    bl                  ; AL = AX / BL, AH = remainder
```

The preceding 16/8-bit example divides AX by BL. The result is always returned in AL and the remainder is returned in AH. The following is an example of a 32/16-bit division:

```
mov    ax, [bx]        ; load low word
mov    dx, [bx+2]      ; load high word
mov    cx, [si]        ; load divisor
cmp    cx, 0           ; check for division by zero
je     div_by_0_err    ; (must handle this somewhere else)
cmp    dx, cx          ; check to prevent overflow
jae    div_ovfl        ; (must handle this somewhere else)
div    cx              ; AX = DX:AX/CX, DX = remainder
```

This example is a full-fledged 32/16-bit division. A 32-bit dividend is loaded into DX:AX and a 16-bit divisor is loaded into CX (which could be any other 16-bit general-purpose register or a memory operand). Because division by zero is undefined, the 8088 will generate an interrupt 0 if an attempt is made to divide by zero. When the divisor is not loaded as an immediate constant, it is a good idea to insure that it is not zero. However, that is not all that can go wrong. Try dividing 10 million by 10. Of course, the answer is one million. The problem is that this number is too big to fit into the AX register. This is a divide overflow error and generates the same interrupt 0 as a divide by zero. You can see that it is easy to check for a possible overflow because if the high word of the dividend is above or equal to the divisor, an overflow will occur. The states of all the flags are undefined after a division.

Note that, in general, an interrupt 0 will terminate your program. You can install your own interrupt 0 handler, but it is easier to properly check for errors and handle them in the main part of your program.

SHORTCUT
I find the BCD instructions to be interesting and useful, but they are not required knowledge for understanding most topics in this book.

BCD Instructions

The BCD (binary coded decimal) instructions operate on special data formats. There are two BCD data formats: packed BCD and unpacked BCD. Packed BCD data consists of one decimal digit (0–9) per nibble. Unpacked BCD data consists of one decimal digit (0–9) per byte. Integer data operations are always corrected within a given range of values. However, operations that include a decimal point (such as point floating-point operations) are not always exact within their upper and lower limits. Because of the inaccuracies of binary arithmetic it is sometimes advantageous to used BCD data. BCD arithmetic is performed by combining the integer arithmetic instructions with the BCD instructions. All BCD instructions operate on AL or AH registers. BCD instructions are used to

- Adjust the results of an integer arithmetic operation to generate proper BCD data.
- Adjust inputs to a subsequent integer arithmetic operation to insure that the operation will generate proper BCD data.

DAA   Decimal Adjust after Addition

Use DAA after adding two pairs of packed BCD digits, as follows:

```
mov   al, 12h        ; load 12h, or packed BCD 12 decimal
add   al, 39h        ; add 39, binary result is 4bh
daa                  ; adjust, result is 51h or 51 packed BCD
```

As you can see from this example, DAA checks the low nibble of AL to see if it is above 9. (In this case it is 4bH.) If it is, then 10 is subtracted from the low nibble and 1 is added to the high nibble. The same process is then applied to the high nibble. The carry flag (CF) is set if 10 was subtracted from the high nibble.

DAS   Decimal Adjust after Subtraction

Use DAS after a subtraction of two pairs of packed BCD digits. The operation is the same as DAA, except that the carry flag is set if a borrow is needed.

AAA   ASCII Adjust after Addition

Use AAA after adding two unpacked BCD digits, as follows:

```
mov ax, 9            ; AH = 0, AL = 9
add al, 8            ; AL = 17 (11h)
aaa                  ; AH = 1, AL = 7
```

In this example, 9 and 8 are added. The proper result (17) is in the AL register, but is not in the proper unpacked BCD format. The AAA instruction checks the low nibble of AL to see if it is above 9, but the low nibble is only 1. This is where the auxiliary flag (AF) comes into use. During the add instruction, a bit was carried from the low nibble to the high nibble of the AL register. Either the auxiliary flag (AF) being set or the low nibble being greater than 9 will cause the AH register to be incremented, the carry flag to be set and the low nibble of AL to be adjusted. The bits in the high nibble of AL are always cleared.

AAS   ASCII ADJUST AFTER SUBTRACTION

Use AAS after subtracting two unpacked BCD digits. The operation is the same as AAA, except that the contents of AH is decremented and the carry flag (CF) is set if a borrow is needed.

AAM   ASCII ADJUST AFTER MULTIPLICATION

Use AAM after a multiplication of two unpacked BCD digits. The multiplication must be an 8-bit multiply, resulting in a 16-bit result, as follows:

```
mov  al, 3          ; AL = 3
mov  bl, 9          ; BL = 9
mul  bl            ; AX = 27 (1Bh)
aam               ; AH = 2, AL = 7
```

If you studied AAM long enough, you would discover that what it is really doing is a division. AAM divides AL by 10 and puts the result in AH and the remainder in AL. (Notice that the results are reversed from a normal division.)

AAD   ASCII ADJUST BEFORE DIVISION

Use AAD before dividing unpacked BCD digits. The AH and AL registers must contain one BCD digit each, the high digit in AH.

```
mov  ax, 0509h      ; AH = 5, AL = 9
mov  bl, 7          ; BL = 7
aad               ; adjust AX (AX = 003Bh)
div  bl; AL = 59/7 = 8, AH = remainder = 3
```

Again, if you studied what AAD is doing, you would find that it is converting the digits in the low nibbles of AH and AL from a decimal value to a binary (or hex) value. The value is stored in the AL register and the AH register is cleared.

A curious feature of the AAA and AAS instructions is that they work equally well on unpacked BCD data (i.e., each byte contains a value from 0 to 9) and on ASCII digits. (ASCII digits being the ASCII characters '0' to '9' or hex values 30h to 39h.) This is because the 3 value in the high nibble is "logically" ignored. When adding, the two threes become a six, which is cleared by the AAA. When subtracting, the two threes become a zero. This is not true for AAD and AAM. AAD requires two unpacked BCD digits (0 to 9) for proper operation. Other values tend to generate nonsense results with no errors. AAM is a division by 10 of a binary value. AAM can be used to divide AL by 10 for any purpose.

SHORTCUT
No shortcuts here. String instructions are important.

String Instructions

The basic string instructions operate on one byte or word (two bytes) at a time (also one dword on the 80386 and above). Strings can be up to 64K in length (65,536 bytes or 32,768 words). Strings need not be arrays of characters, as they usually are in high-level languages. In string instructions, the data can be of any data type that you wish to operate on a byte or word at a time. In fact, you can operate on any structure or block of memory. The only thing that defines a string is a pointer and a length. Some of the string instructions may be preceded by a repeat prefix (REP, REPE, REPZ, REPNE or REPNZ), allowing operations on an entire block of memory as a single string.

For all the string instructions, the source is always DS:SI and the destination is ES:DI. For the examples in this chapter, we will assume that the DS and ES segments registers are the same. When used, the count, or length, of the string is stored in CX.

One of the advantages of the string instructions is that they update the source register (SI) and/or the destination register (DI) automatically. The direction flag determines whether SI and/or DI are incremented or decremented after each operation. When operating on bytes, the increment or decrement amount is 1. For words it is 2. All of the string instructions have two assembler formats. First, you can follow the instruction opcode by a B or W to specify byte or word data types. Second, you can supply operands that are declared elsewhere and the assembler will use the appropriate data type. (I find the second method next to useless and so use only the first format.) Even when operands are supplied, SI and/or DI must be preloaded with the proper values. The operand(s) are used only for the data type information, although they may be helpful for documentation.

REPEAT PREFIXES

The repeat string prefixes allow a string instruction to be repeated a specified number of times. The count is placed in the CX register and then CX is decremented by 1 and tested after each operation. The decrementing of CX does not change any of the flags.

REP

The REP prefix can be thought of as repeat until CX = 0. The REP prefix may be used with the MOVS and STOS instructions.

REPE/REPZ

The REPE and REPZ prefixes are synonyms for the same op code. REPE can be thought of as "repeat while equal or until CX = 0" and REPZ can be thought of as "repeat while zero or until CX = 0." The REPE or REPZ prefixes may be used with the CMPS and SCAS instructions.

REPNE/REPNZ

The REPNE and REPNZ prefixes are synonyms for the same op code. REPNE can be thought of as "repeat while not equal or until CX = 0" and REPNZ can be thought of as "repeat while not zero or until CX = 0." The REPNE or REPNZ prefixes may be used with the CMPS and SCAS instructions.

MOVS/MOVSB/MOVSW (MOVE STRING)

These instructions (MOVS) move a byte or word from DS:SI to ES:DI and increments/decrements SI and DI by one (two for MOVSW).

REP MOVS

REP MOVS moves a block of bytes or words from DS:SI to ES:DI. The actual result of the operation that is performed depends on the state of the direction flag (DF) and whether the source and destination blocks overlap. If the DF is clear (i.e., forward direction) and the blocks do not overlap, a block of bytes or words is simply copied as would be expected. However, if the DF is set (reverse direction), the source (DS:SI) is actually pointing to the last byte (or word) to be copied in the block. Also, the addresses constituting overlapping blocks is different when the DF is set.

```
lea    si, string1      ; SI = offset of string1
lea    di, string2      ; DI = offset of string2
mov    cx, 10           ; CX = 10 (length of string)
```

```
rep movsb                    ; string2 = string1

; data
string1 DB 'abcdefghijk'
string2 DB 'lmnopqrstuv'
```

The data after the REP MOVSB:

```
string1 DB 'abcdefghijk'
string2 DB 'abcdefghijk'
```

Here is what happens when the string descriptions overlap:

```
lea    si, string1     ; SI = offset of string1
lea    di, [si+1]      ; DI = SI + 1
mov    cx, 10          ; CX = 10
rep movsb

; data
string1 DB 'abcdefghijk'
string2 DB 'lmnopqrstuv'
```

The data after one byte is moved:

```
string1 DB 'aacdefghijk'
string2 DB 'lmnopqrstuv'
```

The data after the completion of all 10 bytes:

```
string1 DB 'aaaaaaaaaaa'
string2 DB 'amnopqrstuv'
```

Note that when the move is completed, SI and DI will point to the next byte or word, not the last ones moved. In the case of a forward move, SI and DI will point to the byte or word after the final move. For a reverse move, SI and DI will point to the byte or word before the final move. In the preceding example, after the completion of the REP MOVSB, SI will point to the first byte in string2 ('a') and DI will point to the second byte in string2 ('m').

CMPS/CMPSB/CMPSW (COMPARE STRINGS)

CMPS compares the bytes or words at DS:SI and ES:DI and increments/decrements SI and DI by 1 (2 for CMPSW). The condition codes in the flags register are set based on the comparison the same as with the CMP instruction. The increment or decrement of SI and DI has no effect on the flags.

REPE CMPS/REPZ CMPS

The REPE CMPS instruction compares a block of bytes or words at DS:SI with another block at ES:DI. One byte or word is compared at a time until they are not equal or until the entire block is compared. Upon completion of the operation you must check to determine which condition caused termination. Testing the ZF with a conditional jump will do this.

```
        lea  si, string1
        lea  di, string2
        mov cx, 10
        repe cmpsb
        jne    no_match
match:
        ...
no_match:
        ...
string1db 'abcdefghij'
end1    db 0
string2db 'abcdefghij'
end2    db 0
```

After the completion of the REPE CMPSB instruction, if a complete match was found, CX will be 0 and SI and DI will point to the first byte after the string that was compared. In the preceding case, SI will point to the END1 byte and DI will point to the END2 byte. The comparison requires exact matches of bytes because the CPU really has no inherent concept of upper and lowercase. If the following data is used, SI and DI and CX will have the same values as on a complete match:

```
string1db 'abcdefghij'
end1    db 0
string2db 'abcdefghiJ'          ; (notice last J is uppercase)
end2    db 0
```

The only proper action after a REPx CMPSx instruction is a conditional jump instruction (although you could save the flags or perform other non–flag-changing instructions first).

When a match is not found, CX contains the number of bytes that were not compared. SI and DI will point to the bytes after the last ones compared.

REPNE CMPS/REPNZ CMPS

The REPNE CMPS instruction is the same as the REPE CMPS, except that the comparison continues until the end of the block or until a match is found.

```
        lea    si, string1
        lea    di, string2
        mov    cx, 10
        repne cmpsb
        jne    no_match
match:
        ...
no_match:
        ...
string1 db 'abcdefghij'
string2 db 'xxxxefghij'
```

In this case the comparison continues until the matching e's are found. The CX, DI and SI registers have the same outcome as REP CMPS.

SCAS/SCASB/SCASW (SCAN STRING)

SCAS compares the byte or word at ES:DI with AL or AX and increments/decrements DI by one (two for SCASW). The condition codes in the flags register are set based on the comparison the same as with the CMP instruction. The increment or decrement of SI and DI has no effect on the flags.

REPE SCAS/REPZ SCAS

REPE SCAS scans a string at ES:DI for a byte or word that matches the AL or AX register. The scan continues while the string matches the register or until the end of the block. Upon completion of the operation you must check to determine which condition caused termination. Testing the ZF with a conditional jump will do this.

```
        lea    di, string1
        mov    al, 20h; load ASCII space into al
        mov    cx, 10
        repe scasb
        jne    no_match
match:
        ...
no_match:
        ...
string1 db '     fghij'
```

Of course, usually the purpose of scanning a string is not just to determine if there is or isn't a match, but to obtain a pointer to the appropriate location in memory. Just as with the REPx CMPS instructions, CX ends with a count of bytes not compared. DI points to the byte *after* the last one compared. In this example, DI points to the letter g, because the f was the first compare that caused the REP loop to stop.

REPNE SCAS/REPNZ SCAS

The REPNE SCAS instruction is the same as the REPE SCAS, except that the comparison continues until the end of the block or until a match is found. This is a repeat scan while not equal.

```
      lea   di, string1
      mov   al, 20h        ; load ASCII space into al
      mov   cx, 10
      repne scasb
      jne   no_match
match:
      ...
no_match:
      ...
string1 db ' abcde   '
```

LODS/LODSB/LODSW (LOAD STRING)

LODS reads a byte or word from DS:SI, loads it into register AL or AX and increments/decrements SI by 1 (2 for LODSW). There is no use for a repeat prefix with LODS, because any repeated operation would continually load a new value in AL or AX, overwriting the previous value. The following example reads each byte of a string and converts all lowercase characters to uppercase:

```
      lea si, string1
      mov cx, 10
loop1:
      lodsb                ; read a byte
      cmp al, 'a'          ; skip if below lowercase a
      jb  next
      cmp al, 'z'          ; skip if above lowercase z
      ja  next
      sub al, 20h          ; convert to uppercase
      mov [si-1], al       ; overwrite back into memory
next:
      loop loop1
      ...
string1 db 'aBcdEfGhij'
```

STOS/STOSB/STOSW (STORE STRING)

STOS copies a byte or word from register AL or AX to ES:DI and increments/decrements DI by 1 (2 for STOSW).

```
      lea  si, string1
      lea  di, string2
loop1:
      lodsb                 ; read a byte
      stosb                 ; store a byte
      cmp  al, 0            ; check for end of string
      jne  loop1
      ...
string1 db 'abcdefghij',0   ; null terminated string
string2 db 11 dup(0)        ; space for copy of string1
```

REP STOS

The REP STOS, or repeat store string instruction, repeatedly stores the value in AL (or AX) to ES:DI and increments/decrements DI by 1 (2 for words) after each store. This instruction can be thought of as a block fill function. CX is the size of the block in bytes or words. This example overwrites a string with zeros.

```
      lea  di, string1
      mov  cx, 10
      cmp  al, 0
      rep  stosb
      ...

string1 db 'abcdefghij'
```

CAUTION FOR REPEAT PREFIXES

Repeated string operations may be interrupted. This is important, because operations on a large string can take more than a million cycles! For example, on the original IBM PC comparing two large strings could take a quarter of a second. But at the same time the timer interrupt must gain control about 18.2 times per second to update the internal time of day clock. When an interrupt takes control during a repeated string instruction, the state of the instruction is automatically preserved by the CPU. However, if a segment override is used, the segment override is forgotten after the interrupt. This bug was corrected by Intel on the 80186 and later CPUs. If you write any program that may still be run on a 8088 or 8086, do not use segment overrides with a repeat string instruction.

Interrupts

Imagine a phone with no bell. You wouldn't know when someone was calling. You could pick up the handset periodically and listen to see if anyone was there. However, it would not only be inefficient, it would get old very quickly. Adding a bell to the phone is a form of an interrupt. When the phone rings, you (theoretically) stop what you are doing, answer the phone, then return to your task. Interrupts work the same way on a computer, except the computer is fast and always single-minded. Before the computer responds to the interruption, it must save a pointer to where it was (like a bookmark), and it must save the flags. So, when an interrupt occurs, the CPU pushes the flags register, the code segment register (CS) and the instruction pointer (IP). Next, the CPU changes the state of some flags [clears the trap (TF) and interrupt-enable (IF) flags] to ensure proper CPU operation. This turns off single-stepping (in case a debugger was running and just gained control via an interrupt) and disables further interrupts until this one has been properly handled.

There are 256 possible interrupts on the 8088, numbered 0 to 255. For example, when you press a key on the keyboard a signal passes through various circuits to the CPU. The CPU must interrupt what it is doing and go find out what happened. Different devices (i.e., keyboards, printers, modems, etc.) send different signals and require different actions. Each device can be assigned its own interrupt number. The keyboard is interrupt 9, for example. There is an array of far pointers to the handler for every interrupt in a table called the Interrupt Vector Table (IVT). The IVT is located right at the beginning of the computer's memory at segment 0, offset 0 or 0000:0000. Since each far pointer requires four bytes, the handler for the keyboard is at address 0000:0024 (4 * 9 = 36 = 24h).

INT SOFTWARE INTERRUPT

The INT instruction generates a software interrupt. This is handled in the same way as a hardware interrupt, described earlier. A software interrupt is similar to a far CALL instruction, except that the flags are also pushed onto the stack before CS and IP are pushed (and the TF and IF flags are cleared).

The DOS and BIOS services are accessed via software interrupts. Each service has its own specifications as to what registers must be set to what. We'll learn more about this later, but here is an example:

```
mov ah, 9        ; 9 = display string function
lea dx, message  ; load pointer to message characters
int 21h          ; call the DOS services
```

The DOS services are invoked with int 21h. (21h was arbitrarily chosen as the DOS services interrupt number and has no inherent meaning.) Function 9 of the DOS services is a request to display a string on the monitor.

IRET

The IRET, or return from interrupt, instruction is the same as a return from a procedure, except that the flags are popped from the stack. You would only need to use this instruction if you are writing an interrupt service routine. IRET can be thought of as

```
pop ip              ; can't actually do this, but IRET does
pop cs              ; this combination
popf
```

CLI

The CLI instruction clears the interrupt enable flag. This causes interrupts to be disabled. Only external interrupts are disabled. Non-maskable interrupts (NMI) are not disabled (or masked out). After a CLI instruction is executed, only NMI interrupts are allowed. CLI would be used during the execution of a critical piece of code that cannot be interrupted. Use STI after the critical code to re-enable interrupts.

There are two types of hardware interrupts on the 8088. The first type are the polite, please perform some function, interrupts, such as the keyboard and timer interrupts. These can be disabled, or masked out by CLI. This is like turning the ringer on your phone off—you choose to ignore them. The second type is the NMI, interrupt number 2. You cannot shut this off. This is the pounding on your front door, get out of the house, there is a fire, interrupt. It's designed, for example, for network servers, so action can be taken when the power is being lost.

STI

The STI instruction sets the interrupt enable flag. This causes interrupts to be enabled. Use after a critical portion of code that started with CLI or in an interrupt handler when it is OK for further interrupts to occur.

Miscellaneous Instructions

XCHG

The XCHG instruction exchanges the contents of two registers or of a register and a memory location. For example:

```
xchg     ax, bx        ; temp = AX, AX = BX, BX = temp
```

XLAT

The XLAT instruction performs a translation of a byte in AL by looking up the translation in a table. The table's location starts at the address in the BX register. XLATB and XLAT are the same.

```
mov bx, OFFSET xlat_tbl
mov al, 5
xlat                   ; AL = [BX+AL]
```

LEA LOAD EFFECTIVE ADDRESS

The LEA instruction loads the effective address of the source operand into the destination operand. In other words, the offset of the source operand (rather than its value) is copied to the destination. The destination is always a register. The source can be any memory addressing expression. If the source contains only a displacement, then many assemblers can automatically use the more efficient format: MOV reg, OFFSET mem.

```
lea   bx, [si]         ; this is not useful because
mov   bx, si           ; it is the same as this
lea   bx, data_item    ; these are the same
mov   bx, OFFSET data_item
```

The next example of LEA is extremely powerful when optimizing programs. For example, LEA can add two registers and a constant.

```
lea   di, [si+bx+4]    ; DI = SI + BX + 4
mov   di, si           ; these next three instructions
add   di, bx           ; do the same thing as the LEA above
add   di, 4
```

LDS/LES   LOAD FAR POINTER USING DS/ES

The load far pointer instruction transfers a segment and offset from memory into a segment register and any 16-bit register (AX, BX, CX, DX, DI, SI, BP, SP). The far pointer must be stored in memory with the offset first, then the segment. For example:

```
les    di, str_ptr2          ; ES = segment containing str2
                             ; DI = offset of str2
lds    si str_ptr1           ; DS = SEG str1, SI = OFFSET str1

; this data declared elsewhere:

str_ptr1 dd str1
str_ptr2 dd str2
str1   db 'string1'
str2   db 10 dup(0)
```

CBW   CONVERT BYTE TO WORD

CBW converts a signed byte in AL to a word in AX maintaining the sign. This is done by copying the sign bit (bit 7) of AL into every bit of AH.

CWD

CWD converts a signed word in AX to a dword in DX:AX, maintaining the sign. This is done by copying the sign bit (bit 15) of AX into every bit of DX.

NOP   NO OPERATION

The NOP instruction performs no operation. This can be used to effectively erase instructions or to reserve space during debugging. NOPs may show up in your programs because assemblers tend to reserve the maximum space that might be required for instructions. When less space is determined to be needed then NOPs are inserted. NOPs are also put into code when aligning the start of loops on even word or dword boundaries.

Flag Summary

There is logical order to the seemingly random way in which the multitude of instructions affect the states of the various flags. In general, moving data does not affect any flags, but comparing data or changing data with an arithmetic operation does change the flags. Table 4.5 contains a summary of all flag changing operations.

Table 4.5 Instructions That Affect the Arithmetic Flags

	CF	PF	AF	ZF	SF	OF	
add/sub	M	M	M	M	M	M	CF = carry flag
adc/sbb	TM	M	M	M	M	M	PF = parity flag
cmp/cmps/scas	M	M	M	M	M	M	AF = auxiliary flag
inc/dec	M	M	M	M	M	M	ZF = zero flag
and/or/xor/test	0	M	—	M	M	0	SF = sign flag
shift	M	M	—	M	M	M	PF = overflow flag
rotate	M	M					
aaa/aas	M	—	M	—	—	—	
aad/aam	—	M	—	M	M	M	
daa/das	T			M	M	M	
mul/imul	M	—	—	—	—	M	
div/idiv	—	—	—	—	—	—	
stc	1						
clc	0						
cmc	TM						
popf/sahf	M	M	M	M	M	M	

Instructions that do not change the arithmetic flags: mov, lea, push, pushf, pop, not, xchg, call, ret, jmp, jcc, loop, loopxx, lods, stos, movs, hlt, in, out, cbw, cwd, lahf, lds, les, lock

Instructions that change flags other than the arithmetic flags:

cld, std, cli, sti, iret

Notes: M = modifies to 0 or 1; T = tests flag; 1 = sets to 1;
0 = resets to 0; – = undefined blank = not affected.

Writing Beginning Programs

5

> "Begin at the beginning . . . and go on till you
> come to the end: then stop.
>
> —Lewis Carroll from
> *Alice's Adventures in Wonderland*

I n the last chapter we reviewed all the basic instructions that the 8088 can execute. In this chapter we'll put those instructions together to form complete programs. This will involve learning about the structure of complete programs, the rules for creating labels and the memory organization of programs.

ASSEMBLER DIRECTIVES

The following example is about the smallest assembly program that can be written to do something you can see. You'll notice there is a mix of CPU instructions and assembler directives. We've covered the CPU instructions already, but the assembler directives are new. Assembler directives are not instructions to be executed by the CPU, but rather are directions or hints for the assembler to help it properly translate the CPU instructions, control listings and other housekeeping types of activities. Sometimes directives are referred to as pseudo-ops.

```
.model small
.stack
.code
main proc
mov ax,@data
mov ds,ax
lea dx,msg
mov cx,7
mov bx,1
mov ah,40h
int 21h
mov ah,4ch
int 21h
main endp
.data msg
db 'Yuck!',13,10
end main
```

Although it works, there are problems with this example. The code is not written in a
very readable format, and there are no comments to document the purpose of the program or the reasons for selecting the various instructions.

Figure 5.1 A Complete Example Program

```
A Complete Example Program
;----------------------------------------
; Hello.asm A friendly greeting
;
; Simple program to display a message
;----------------------------------------
.model small
.stack
.code
main proc
    mov    ax, @data          ; load the data segment
    mov    ds, ax
    lea    dx, msg            ; load address of msg
    mov    cx, 7              ; length of msg
    mov    bx, 1              ; stdout
    mov    ah, 40h            ; DOS function to write output
    int    21h                ; call DOS finish:
    mov    ah, 4ch            ; DOS function to terminate
    int    21h                ; call DOS
main endp
.data
msg db 'Hello',13,10
```

This version of the program is much better. Note all the comments (they are preceded by a semicolon). The details of formating and commenting your code are generally matters of personal style. You will see my style throughout this book and on the accompanying disk. You should choose a style you are comfortable with, and one appropriate for both your experience level and those that may have to maintain your code.

WHAT DO ALL THOSE STATEMENTS MEAN?

Most assemblers have many assembler directives available. Microsoft MASM 6.11, for example, has hundreds. You can use the reference manual that came with your assembler to learn them. In this book we are going to be concentrating on the optimum use of CPU instructions, so I'll only be reviewing the directives we'll need to write complete and useful programs.

The ".model" directive was new with MASM 5.0 (it's in all versions of TASM). This directive, along with .stack, .code and .data, can be collectively called the simplified segmentation directives. Prior to this, the code, data and stack segments had to be declared in a much more difficult and error-prone manner that I will not discuss until Chapter 18. There are still some advantages to using the older method, so you may eventually want to learn both methods. You can even combine the two methods in one file.

To use the simplified segmentation directives, you must use the .model directive before any other statement that generates any code or data. This declares a memory model (see Table 6.1 on page 82) for your program. Use the .code directive before writing your code and the .data directive before declaring any data. It is that simple.

At this point you may be wondering, "What are memory models and why do I need to know about them?" The answer is that the concept of memory models is due to the segmented nature of the 80x86 memory architecture. If there were no segments, there would be no memory models. Later on we'll discuss the various memory models in more detail.

LABELS AND IDENTIFIERS

Identifiers are names (or symbols) that you invent to define or attach to variables, constants, segments, procedures, code labels and elements of a program. Labels (or code labels) are identifiers that define addresses within a program. Labels can be defined in a number of ways, but most often they are specified by placing a colon after the label name. Labels can appear on a line by themselves or can be followed by a CPU instruction. In either case, the address is that of the first byte of the next instruction. Labels are used as the destination addresses for jumps and calls. The colon is placed after the label name only when the label is defined, not when the label is referenced. A label cannot be defined more than once, but it may be referenced any number of times.

In the HELLO example, the label FINISH is defined, but not referenced by any instruction. You can define and use labels any way you wish. In this example there are three labels:

```
    call   get_a_key      ; return ASCII code in AL
    cmp    al, 'A'         ; compare with uppercase A
    jb     done            ; if below, branch down
    cmp    al, 'Z'         ; compare with uppercase Z
    ja     not_upper       ; if above, branch down
    add    al, 32          ; convert to lowercase
    jmp    done
not_upper:
    cmp    al, 'a'         ; compare with lowercase a
    jb     done            ; if below, branch down
    cmp    al, 'z'         ; compare with lowercase z
    ja     done            ; if above, branch down
    sub    al, 32          ; convert to uppercase
done:
```

Two of the labels are defined and used (not_upper and done). The label "done" is used in four places. The label "get_a_key" is used, but not defined. In a complete program, the get_a_key label would need to be defined at some location in the program. A label may be defined at only one location.

There are several restrictions on the names that can be used for identifiers. Identifiers may start with any of the following characters:

A–Z
a–z
$ (dollar sign)
%   (percent)
.   (period)
?   (question mark)
@   (at sign)
_   (underscore)

The characters after the first character may contain any of the same characters (except the period) and may also contain the digits 0–9. My recommendation is to avoid the at sign (@) because it is used by many assembler internal symbols. Also, for clarity, the period has other uses and should be avoided.

You cannot use an identifier (or symbol) that has the same name as that of a directive or CPU instruction. Symbols are not case-sensitive. In general, all symbols are internally converted to uppercase by the assembler. (This behavior can be modified by assembler command line switches.) Symbols can be up to 31 characters in length. Some assemblers may allow longer symbols, but only the first 31 characters are significant.

PROCEDURES

The PROC directive is a way to define a label and to document it as the beginning of a procedure (or function). To end a procedure you must use the same identifier followed by ENDP.

@DATA

@data is a pre-defined symbol that returns the name of the data segment when the simplified segment naming scheme is used.

DEFINING DATA ITEMS

Data is defined and declared by using one or more of the data definition directives. The most frequently used ones are

DB define byte
DW define word
DD define dword

One or more data items of each type can follow the directive. Optionally, a name can be given to the first item on a line. Some examples:

```
db 1
db 2
db 'a'
db "don't"
dw 1,2,3
dd 4
name1 db 'a name'
```

USING DOS SYSTEM FUNCTIONS

The HELLO example program uses two DOS functions. The various DOS and BIOS system functions are accessed by using software interrupts. There are many system inter-

Figure 5.2

```
For function 40h:
  inputs:
    AH      40h
    BX      file handle (1 for screen)
    CX      length of block to write
    DS:DX ptr to block to write
  outputs:
    CF      set if error
    AX      error code if CF set or byte count written if success
For function 4Ch:
  inputs:
    AH      4Ch
    AL      program exit code (used by ERRORLEVEL in batch files)
  outputs:
    doesn't return
```

rupts, and coverage of even a reasonable subset of them is a topic that would fill a book. As a matter of fact just a list of them fills a book, and I highly recommend getting a copy of *PC Interrupts,* by Ralf Brown and Jim Kyle, Addison Wesley.

The two DOS functions used in HELLO are Int 21h, function 40h (write to file or device) and Int 21h, function 4Ch (exit program). The function number is placed in the AH register, then DOS is called by executing interrupt 21h. The specification for each function includes a description of the required input registers and their return values.

THE END DIRECTIVE

Every file must include an end directive, which must be at the end of the file. The end directive may also contain a label that is used as the starting address of the program. When linking multiple files, only one file should have an end directive with a starting address label. The linker will generate an error message if none of the linked files has a starting address specified in an end directive.

Figure 5.3 is a general template of a small memory model program.

MEMORY MODELS

Most of the examples in this book will use the small memory model. Memory models are conventions decided upon by Microsoft and the software industry. Assembly language programs can contain a mixture of the various memory models. In general, you

Figure 5.3

```
;---------------------------------------
; General ASM template
;---------------------------------------
.model small
.stack
.code
<name> proc
    mov   ax, @data            ; load the data segment
    mov   ds, ax
    ; < your code here >
    mov   ah, 4ch              ; DOS function to terminate
    int   21h                  ; call DOS
<name> endp
.data
; < your data here >
end <name>
```

should choose one model and stick to it, unless you are confident that you know exactly what you are doing.

When calling a procedure (or jumping to a label) it is possible for the new procedure to be in the same code segment or a different code segment from the segment making the call. A call to a different segment is called a FAR call. A call within a segment is a NEAR call. You can also perform an unconditional JMP to a NEAR of FAR address. One way to think of it is like a local telephone call or a long-distance one. And just as you get charged more for a long distance telephone call, you get charged more for a FAR call in terms of code size and CPU cycles.

If all the code for a program fits into one segment, then all the calls and jumps can be NEAR. However, when a program requires more than one segment, there is a problem. The simple solution is to convert every call and return to be FAR.

If calling distance was the only factor, we would have only two memory models to contend with. But the number of data segments is also an issue. When you pass one or more data pointers to a procedure, you need to be concerned about what segments the data is in.

All data pointers are far pointers (consisting of a segment and an offset). The only issues are how many pointers are assumed to share the same segment register and are any segment registers assumed to be the same. So with data segments is comes down to whether a program's data can fit into one segment (64K) or if two or more segments are required. (See Table 6.1 on page 82).

When programming in 32-bit protected mode, these same memory models could be used, but the size of a segment is now 4GB instead of 64K. Since 4GB is the limit of the

Table 6.1 Memory Models

Model	Code Segments	Data Segments	Notes & Assumptions
tiny	1	1	CS=DS=ES=SS
small	1	1	ES=DS
compact	1	>1	multiple data segments
medium	>1	1	ES=DS, multiple code segments
large	>1	>1	multiple code & data segments
huge	>1	>1	individual array >64K

address space, it makes little sense to write a program that has multiple code or data segments, although there are some valid reasons for doing so that I will not go into in this book.

So there is now a new memory model named FLAT. This is the 32-bit equivalent of the Tiny model. This makes programming for the 80386 (and above) the same as programming on any other 32-bit processor (such as a DEC VAX, Sun Sparc, or Motorola 680X0). The operating system just sets all segment registers to the same value, then your program never worries about them.

The only fault with the flat model is that you gain simplicity but are giving up some of the advantages of protected mode—namely, protection. In a 32-bit small model you would be protected (prevented) from modifying code and your stack segment could not be accidentally damaged by writing to the data segment, thus preventing crashes. The flat model does not provide this protection.

Now that we've reviewed what is necessary to write 8088 programs, we'll continue right along with the instruction sets for the 186, 286, 386, 486 and Pentium, so we can get to the business of optimizing for the Pentium.

Assembly Tools

6

*I wish to have no connection with
any ship that does not sail fast;
for I intend to go in harm's way.*
—John Paul Jones

Years ago I was a U.S. Navy submarine officer. On one cruise we were on our way from the Atlantic side of South America to the Pacific via the Straits of Magellan. The straits are a challenging passage because they are narrow and shallow, with strong tidal currents alternating east and west. Because of safety rules that do not allow submerged operation in shallow water, the trip must be made on the surface.

As we made our way west through the last outlet among the numerous small islands, the seas became violent. Modern submarines are designed and built to operate under the sea, so when on the surface in heavy seas they get battered around like a bobbing cork. (Unlike World War II–type diesel submarines, which were more like submersible surface vessels.)

In the several hours it took to reach deep water a large portion of the crew became sick, and most of the rest of us were in our bunks. We finally reached deep water, submerged and we recovered quite quickly.

So what's the point? Tools work best when they are used exactly as they are intended. You need to know what tools are designed for what jobs. You may have a very powerful tool, but using it for the wrong job may make you sick. On the other hand, sometimes you may get stuck doing a job with the only tools you have. I must admit I have been battered around many times by using the wrong tool. I usually have known I did not have the right tools; other times I just did not know what tools to use. To someone who only owns a hammer, everything looks like a nail.

EDITING

After the design work (not my subject here), you begin by writing your programs using a text editor (or word processor). Text editors are usually much better tools for writing programs (likewise, word processors are usually much better tools for general writing and document creation). Another choice is to use the editor included in one of the integrated development environments, Borland's IDE or Microsoft's PWB. Sometime soon (I don't know when) I think everyone will be using some type of integrated environment. Even if you use one of the integrated environments, you should still know all the individuals steps required to create an executable program.

Everyone seems to have their own favorite text editor, and it is extremely difficult to switch editors once you have some experience with one you like.

ASSEMBLING

Using your editor you create one or more assembly source files and possibly source files for other languages. The assembly files should be created with a **.ASM** file extension. These files are then assembled with an assembler (MASM or TASM) as shown below:

```
C:> masm sample;
  Microsoft (R) Macro Assembler Version 5.10
  Copyright (C) Microsoft Corp 1981, 1988. All rights reserved.
  49696 + 129629 Bytes symbol space free
    0 Warning Errors
    0 Severe Errors


C:> tasm sample;
  Turbo Assembler Version 2.02
  Copyright (c) 1988, 1990 Borland International
  Assembling file:    sample.ASM
  Error messages:     None
  Warning messages:   None
  Passes:             1
  Remaining memory:   167k
```

When the assembler finishes it creates an **.OBJ** file that is the machine code translation of your program. If you have any errors in your source file, the assembler will not generate the **.OBJ** file. Instead it will produce a list of errors for you to correct. Note that these are not design or logic errors, but statements that the assembler is unable to translate into machine code.

The examples in this book require MASM 5.0 (or above) or any version of TASM. The program name for MASM 5.0 and 5.1 is the same as the product name, MASM. However, for MASM 6.0 and above Microsoft changed the product significantly. The ML.EXE program that is used also invokes the linker, similar to their C compiler (CL.EXE). They also created a new MASM.EXE that accepts the same command line options as MASM 5.1, converts them to ML format and then invokes the ML program. See the MASM 6.0 or above manual for complete details. You can use whichever method you prefer or require for your programs, but I will use the term MASM, with no specified version, to refer to all versions of the Microsoft assembler.

LINKING

Once you have successfully corrected all assembly errors, a linker is used to combine (or link) one or more **.OBJ** files into an **.EXE** file. The linker (Microsoft's LINK or Borland's TLINK) is so named because labels referenced in one file must be linked to their definition in another file. The following examples show linking a single file with LINK and TLINK:

```
C:> link sample;
Microsoft (R) Segmented Executable Linker Version 5.30
Copyright (C) Microsoft Corp 1984-1992. All rights reserved.

C:> tlink sample
Turbo Link Version 3.01 Copyright (c) 1987, 1990 Borland International
```

DEBUGGING

After a program has been successfully linked, the **.EXE** file may be run and tested. For using a debugger, such as Microsoft's CodeView or Borland's Turbo Debbuger, it is beneficial to include debugging information in the **.EXE** file. This is done by providing options for the assembler to generate symbol and line number information in the **.OBJ** file(s). Then a linker option is used that collects this information and appends it to the end of the **.EXE** file. When DOS (or another operating system) loads an **.EXE** file, it ignores this debugging information. When a debugger loads an **.EXE** file, it reads the debugging information into tables and loads and runs the regular part of the **.EXE** file. For example, to use Microsoft's Codeview debugger, these are the required commands:

```
masm/zi sample;
link/co sample;
cv sample.exe
```

The MASM option **/zi** generates Codeview information and stores it in the **.OBJ** file. The **/co** (or **/codeview**) option puts the codeview information in the **.EXE** file. Codeview is then run from the command line with the **CV** command.

For Borland's Turbo Debugger the commands would be as follows:

```
tasm/zi sample;
tlink/v sample;
td sample.exe
```

DEBUG32

DEBUG32 is a 32-bit debugger included on the disk with this book. DEBUG32 is quite similar to DOS's DEBUG, but provides a number of minor improvements and many advanced features, such as

- 32-bit register and addressing support
- protected-mode debugging
- DPMI application support
- EMS memory support

DEBUG32 is a command line debugger, just as is DEBUG. (A commercial version of this program is available with full screen windows, source code displays and other features.) This program was created by Rob Larson of Larson Computing. I discovered that a special debugger was required after attempting to debug a program to run and test 32-bit code. To write true 32-bit code you must be running the code in protected mode in a segment that has been specified for 32-bit code. As we shall see in Chapter 18, protected-mode programs may have code that is in 16-bit segments (called **USE16**) and/or 32-bit segments (called **USE32**).

DPMI, DOS Protected Mode Interface, is a specification that allows DOS programs to access the advanced features of the 80386 (and above) in a coordinated fashion that does not compromise system protection. DPMI consists of a set of functions to manage system memory, switch modes, control interrupts and communicate with real-mode programs. Protected-mode multitasking environments, memory managers and operating systems that implement the DPMI functions are called DPMI hosts. Protected-mode applications that request services from a DPMI host are called DPMI clients. Some DPMI hosts are

- Windows 3.0 and above
- 386MAX from Qualitas
- QEMM from Quarterdeck.
- NETROOM and Cloaking Developers' Toolkit from Helix
- Novell DOS 7

In Chapter 18 we'll write a 32-bit protected-mode application that is a DPMI client and can be run from DOS. Debugging a DPMI client program requires the use of DEBUG32. Codeview and Turbo Debugger will crash when a DPMI function call is made to switch from real mode to protected mode.

Additional information and a complete command reference for DEBUG32 is provided in Appendix H.

Many different tools may be used when writing programs. The categories of tools I have presented are the bare-bones tools required for serious development. Libraries, code generators, version control systems, test case managers, etc., all have their place and should be used when required. The examples in this book are relatively simple in terms of total project size and do not require most of these. In Chapters 11 and 12 I will introduce you to two other tools provided on the disk with this book.

The Instruction Set Evolves

The 186 to the 386

7

In this chapter I'll discuss the details of the significant changes in the 80x86 instruction set and architecture as the 8086 evolved into the 80386. All the new chips were introduced at higher clock speeds and with new instructions. The changes can be summarized as follows:

- The 186 added a number of new instructions and new forms of instructions useful for application programming.
- The 286 added protected mode and the instructions required to control protected mode programs.
- The 386 added a number of new instructions, new forms and 32-bit code, more advanced addressing modes, 32-bit protected mode and paged virtual memory capabilities.

THE LOST BROTHER, THE *80186*

The 186 is the most widely unknown member of the 80x86 family. The chip was designed for embedded system use, so it has had little visibility in the PC marketplace. Most of the instruction set changes that are popularly described as new to the 286 were actually introduced on the 186.

Here are the new instructions:

BOUND   The **BOUND** instruction checks the range of a register to determine if it is within the lower and upper bounds of the limit for an array. If the condition is not met, then an interrupt 5 is generated. Because **BOUND** uses an interrupt, it is awkward and therefore rarely used. The memory operand is always two words, a lower limit followed by an upper limit.

```
bound reg16, mem32
```

ENTER *and* **LEAVE**.   The **ENTER** and **LEAVE** instructions can be used to set up a stack frame for passing parameters and storing local variables on the stack, as is common in most high-level languages. **ENTER** creates a stack frame at the start of a procedure, and **LEAVE** is the complementary instruction for exiting a procedure.

```
enter imm16, level
```

The **imm16** operand is a count of the number of bytes to reserve for local variables. The level is 0 for the calling conventions of most languages, including C, BASIC and Fortran. (In Pascal, the level operand allows a procedure access to the local variables of the calling procedures. We'll only be using a level of 0 in this book.) The following example shows the structure of setting up a stack frame:

```
enter 4, 0      ; create stack frame with 4 bytes
                ; of local storage
nop             ; do nothing
leave           ; terminate stack frame
ret             ; return
```

which is the same as

```
push  bp        ; preserve BP
mov   bp, sp    ; set BP for stack frame
```

```
sub    sp, 4      ; create local storage of 4 bytes
nop               ; do nothing
mov    sp, bp     ; terminate stack frame
pop    bp         ; restore BP
ret               ; return
```

INS and **OUTS**   **INS** and **OUTS** are repeated string instructions that perform input and output like the **IN** and **OUT** instructions. For **INS** the destination is specified by **ES:DI**, the port is in **DX** and the count is in **CX**. **INSB** receives byte data and **INSW** receives word data. **DI** is adjusted after each byte or word is received based on the direction flag. **OUTS** performs the opposite operation, with **DS:SI** pointing to the string of bytes or words to be sent; **DX** is the port and **CX** is the count. These are rarely used.

Signed Multiply: **IMUL**   Two new syntaxes of the **IMUL** instruction are available on the 186 and above. These are the two- and three-operand forms. In the two-operand form a 16-bit register is the destination and one of the factors. The other factor is given by an immediate constant. In the three-operand form the destination is given by the first operand, a 16-bit register, and the two factors are next, a 16-bit register or memory operand and an immediate constant. The overflow and carry flags (OF and CF) are set if the result is too large.

```
imul reg16, immed
imul reg16, reg16, immed
imul reg16, mem16, immed
```

PUSH imm   The **PUSH** instruction on the 186 accepts an operand that is an immediate value. This is used primarily when passing constant values as parameters to a procedure, such as

```
push 6
call print_num
```

PUSHA and **POPA**   **PUSHA** (push all) and **POPA** (pop all) push or pop a number of registers in a specific order. For **PUSHA** the order is: ax, cx, dx, bx, sp, bp, si, di. The value for SP is the value it had before the instruction started. For **POPA** the order is reversed: di, si, bp, sp, bx, dx, cx, ax. The actual SP value is discarded by **POPA**.

Rotates and Shifts   All the rotate and shift instructions on the 186 and above can accept an immediate value for the rotate or shift amount. Prior to this the only immediate shift/rotate amount was one. If the immediate value is larger than 31, it is truncated to a maximum value of 31. The instructions are: **RCL**, **RCR**, **ROL**, **ROR**, **SHL**, **SHR**, **SAL** and **SAR**.

The 80286

The changes in the 286 include protected-mode operation, new instructions and faster cycle times. Protected mode is a significant new feature, and all the new 286 instructions deal with writing protected-mode code. Although protected mode is significant, I am going to only touch on it briefly because for optimizing code, most protected-mode programming is the same as real-mode code. The protected-mode instructions are used primarily by the operating system.

The most important concept in protected-mode (PM) programming is that the segment registers do not contain addresses as they do in real mode. Recall that in real mode the starting address of a segment could be found by multiplying the value in the segment register by 16 (or 10 hex). In PM the value in the segment register is called a selector. The selector is a pointer into a table that contains the actual beginning address of the segment. This table (there can be many of them) is called a descriptor table. Descriptor tables contain other information, such as the segment size, protection level and whether the segment contains code or data.

The following is a list of the new protected-mode instructions on the 286. Complete descriptions are not given. (Chapter 18 contains protected-mode examples.)

arpl	adjust requested privilege
clts	clear task switched flag
lar	load access rights
lgdt	load global descriptor table
lidt	load interrupt descriptor table
lldt	load local descriptor table
lmsw	load machine status word
lsl	load segment limit
ltr	load task register
sgdt	store global descriptor table
sidt	store interrupt descriptor table
sldt	store local descriptor table
smsw	store machine status word
str	store task register
verr	verify read
verw	verify write

The 80386

The 386 chip has several significant changes. The first is that the 386 is a 32-bit computer with support for paged virtual memory. There are also a number of new instructions and new forms of old instructions. The cycle times of many instructions are improved.

Paged virtual memory is important because it allows programs to be written without (too much) regard for the amount of actual memory installed on the machine running the program. When more memory is required, a portion of memory that hasn't been recently used can be moved to a swap area on the disk if all of memory is in use. Pages of memory are 4K in length. The operating system must specifically implement this feature of the 386. Windows and OS/2 have this capability.

On the 386 the general-purpose registers are all 32 bits wide, as are the data and address buses. The 386SX has a 16-bit data bus. When the 386SX was announced, the 386 was renamed 386DX for clarity. Both the 386DX and the 386SX can run the same software.

The registers on the 386 are all 32-bits, except the segment registers which are still 16-bits. This provides compatibility with real-mode programs for the 8086/8088 and is still compatible with protected-mode programs. The data in the descriptor table is slightly different from the 286 to allow segments up to 4 gigabytes (GB) in length. There are two new segment registers, FS and GS.

Programs can use the 16-bit registers (i.e., AX, BX, etc.) or the new 32-bit registers (EAX, EBX, etc.). The 32-bit register names are the same as the 16-bit names, but with a prefix of "E." The code in each segment can use 16-bit segments or 32-bit segments as the default. An instruction prefix allows using 16-bit registers in a 32-bit segment and *vice-versa*. This can be a bit confusing and is a very important consideration when writing optimal code. The operation of 8-bit registers is not affected. Here are some examples:

```
mov    bx, cx            ; hex opcodes  89 CB
```

When the preceding instruction is assembled and loaded into a 16-bit segment, the hex opcodes are 89 CB. If those same opcodes show up in a 32-bit segment, then the instruction would be:

```
mov    ebx, ecx          ; hex opcodes  89 CB
```

How can this be? What happens is that the descriptor table for the current code segment (CS) loads (among other things) a bit that specifies whether operands are 16-bit or 32-bit. The following instructions are in a 16-bit segment:

Figure 7.1 32-bit Register Diagram

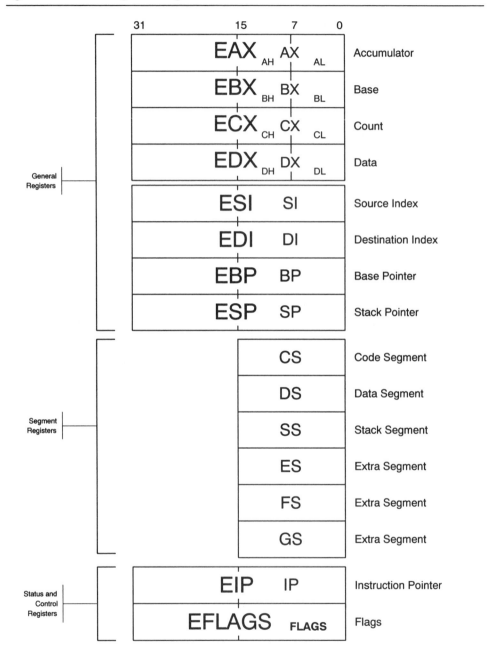

```
mov    bl, cl              ; hex opcodes   88 CB
mov    bx, cx              ; hex opcodes   89 CB
mov    ebx, ecx            ; hex opcodes   66 89 CB
```

The following instructions are in a 32-bit segment:

```
mov    bl, cl              ; hex opcodes   88 CB
mov    bx, cx              ; hex opcodes   66 89 CB
mov    ebx, ecx            ; hex opcodes   89 CB
```

The key point is that the operand-size prefix (66h) byte is required to override the default size of registers or memory operands. The assembler will automatically insert the prefix with no warning message. The assembler knows the type of segment based on the use of the USE16 or USE32 parameter in the SEGMENT directive. We will cover this with an example in a later chapter.

NEW 386 ADDRESSING MODES

Previous addressing modes consisted of any combination of base, index and displacement. The base register could be BX or BP and the index register could be SI or DI. In 32-bit addressing mode on the 386, addresses may be specified with any combination of a base register, a scaled index register and a displacement. The first change is that the index register can be scaled (multiplied) by 1, 2, 4 or 8. The second change is that the base and index registers can be any general-purpose register (EAX, EBX, ECX, EDX, EDI, ESI or EBP). And, of course, the final change is that the addresses are 32 bits.

NEW 386 INSTRUCTIONS

The following section describes each of the new or modified instructions on the 386.

Bit Scans: **BSF BSR** These instructions scan an operand to find the first set bit. **BSF** is bit scan forward and **BSR** is bit scan reverse. If a set bit is found, the zero flag (**ZF**) is cleared and the destination is returned with the bit index of the first bit found. The bit index is 0 for the least significant, etc. For example:

```
mov eax, 84h
bsf ebx, eax
jz  none
; ebx = 3
```

```
mov  eax, 84h
bsr  ebx, eax
jz   none
; ebx = 7
```

Bit Tests: **BT**, **BTC**, **BTR**, **BTS** The bit test instructions copy the value of a specified bit into the carry flag so that it can be tested with **JC** or **JNC**. **BT** (bit test) just copies the bit to the carry flag. **BTC** (bit test and complement) complements the specified bit, then copies it to the carry flag. **BTR** (bit test and reset) copies the bit to the carry flag and then resets the original bit. **BTS** (bit test and set) copies the bit to the carry flag and then sets the original bit. In all instructions the first operand (the destination) contains a register or memory operand to be tested. The second operand (the source) contains a register or immediate value that is the bit index of the bit to be copied. For example:

```
mov ax, 33h
...
bt  ax, 2   ; copy bit 2 to CF
jc  found
```

Converts: **CDQ**, **CWDE** **CDQ** (convert double to quad) is the 32-bit operand form of **CWD**. **CDQ** converts a signed dword in EAX to a signed quadword in EDX:EAX maintaining the sign. **CWDE** (convert word to extended double) is the 32-bit operand form of **CBW**. **CWDE** converts a signed word in AX to EAX, maintaining the sign.

Signed Multiply: **IMUL** There are two new forms of the **IMUL** instruction. The first allows multiplying two 16-bit (or two 32-bit) registers. The second allows the source to be a memory operand. Since the source and destination operands are both the same size, it is possible for the result to be too large to fit. In this case the carry and overflow flags are set. For example:

```
mov  ebx, 10
mov  ecx, 100000
imul ecx, ebx
```

Conditional Jumps Conditional jumps on the 386 can be near or short. Previously only short jumps were allowed (−128 to +127 bytes). Near jumps have a range of −32,768 to +32767 bytes.

LOOP The **LOOP** instruction decrements CX and jumps to the destination address if CX is not zero. In addition there are forms that allow testing the state of the zero flag (**ZF**). On the 386, in 32-bit mode the ECX register is used. By using the operand-size prefix there are several new **LOOP** forms, as follows:

Instruction	Alternate Instruction	Counter register 16-bit mode	Counter register 32-bit mode
loop	—	CX	ECX
loopw	—	CX	CX
loopd	—	ECX	ECX
loope	loopz	CX	ECX
loopew	loopzw	CX	CX
looped	loopzd	ECX	ECX
loopne	loopnz	CX	ECX
loopnew	loopnzw	CX	CX
loopned	loopnzd	ECX	ECX

MOV The 386 has several new special purpose registers. The **MOV** instruction now accepts moves into or out of these control, debug and test registers. They are CR0, CR2, CR3, DR0, DR1, DR2, DR3, DR6, DR7, TR6 and TR7. Consult the Intel manuals for use of these registers.

Extended moves: **MOVSX** (move with sign-extend) moves a signed 8- or 16-bit operand into
MOVSX, MOVZX a larger 16- or 32-bit register, copying the sign bit into the upper half of the destination. **MOVZX** (move with zero-extend) moves an 8 or 16-bit operand into a larger 16- or 32-bit register, filling zeros into the upper half of the destination.

PUSH/POP The various forms of the **PUSH** and **POP** instructions have been changed to accommodate 32-bit mode, as follows:

```
push    push 2 or 4 bytes based on 16 or 32-bit mode
pushw   push 2 bytes
pushd   push 4 bytes
pushf   push 16-bit flags
pushfd  push 32-bit eflags
pusha   push all 16-bit registers
pushad  push all 32-bit registers
pop     pop 2 or 4 bytes based on 16 or 32-bit mode
popw    pop 2 bytes
popd    pop 4 bytes
popf    pop 16-bit flags
popfd   pop 32-bit eflags
popa    pop all 16-bit registers
popad   pop all 32-bit registers
```

SETcc *Set conditionally* The **SETcc** instructions set the specified operand to 1 if the condition is true or to 0 if the condition is false. The **cc** condition codes are the same as conditional jumps, such as **Z**, **NZ** for zero and not zero.

Double Shifts: The double shift instructions allow two operands to be shifted as one en-
SHLD, **SHRD** tity. For example:

```
shld     ax, dx, 1   ; 16-bit double precision shift left
```

would be the same as

```
shl      ax, 1 ; shift left
rcl      dx, 1 ; rotate with carry left
```

The carry, if any, from the first shift (AX) is shifted into the low bit of DX. The high bit of DX is shifted into the carry flag. Shifting by a count of more than one is similar to a loop of these two instructions. For example, to double-shift right:

```
shrd     [ebx], eax, cl   ; 32-bit double precision shift
right
```

would be the same as

```
mov      ch, 0
lbl:
shr      [ebx], 1
rcr      eax, 1
loopw    lbl
```

PROTECTED MODE

Protected mode basically works like this: When the CPU starts, it is in real mode. The operating system or other control program sets up a descriptor table that consists of a list of code and data segments, their addresses and other attributes. The CPU is then put into protected mode. The operating system is supposed to control what memory a program can use so that one program cannot clobber the memory allocated to another program. When a program needs more memory, it is requested via the operating system. The operating system keeps track of what program owns what memory. Any communication between programs is controlled via the operating system.

Since protected mode is primarily an operating-system function, and the details of most protected mode operation are handled via operating-system calls, we will deal with it primarily in Chapter 18.

Introduction to Pentium and Tools

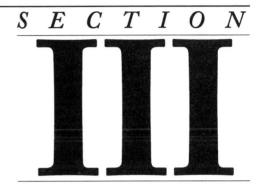

S E C T I O N

III

The 80486 and Pentium

8

> *You will see something new.*
> *Two things. And I call them*
> *Thing One and Thing Two.*
> —Theodore Seuss Geisel (Dr. Seuss)
> from *The Cat in the Hat*

In 1989 Intel announced the 80486 processor. There were no significant changes to the instruction set. The popularity of the Intel architecture had dictated the future for the 80x86 instruction set, and the rules were clear:

1. no major instruction set changes were needed;
2. even if changes were made, no one would use them for fear of being incompatible with the installed base;
3. performance gains would come mostly from hardware changes, not software.

However, the internal architecture of the 486 is vastly different from that of prior processors. RISC design techniques were employed, including the use of a five-stage instruction pipeline and on-chip cache memory. The floating-point processor (a separate chip on the 8088 through 80386) is now on the same chip, allowing for faster operation. The six new instructions are primarily for use in operating-system software, but I'll discuss the first three in detail because any application program can use them. The new instructions are:

bswap	byte swap
xadd	exchange and add
cmpxchg	compare and exchange
invd	invalidate data cache
wbinvd	write back and invalidate data cache
invlpg	invalidate TLB (translation lookaside buffer) entry

BSWAP   The byte swap instruction reverses the order of all bytes in a dword register. This could be used for a number of purposes, but was probably added to allow easier data conversion with machines using big-endian data format. (Recall that the 80x86 chips use the little-endian format.) An example:

```
bswap eax
```

XADD   The exchange and add instruction is a combination of the **XCHG** and **ADD** instructions. They are performed as one instruction that can be prefixed with the **LOCK** prefix. Presumably this is to aid operating systems in a multiprocessor environment. The destination operand ends up with the sum of the two operands, and the source operand ends up with the original value from the destination. The flags are changed the same as if an **ADD** instruction were executed. The operands can be 8, 16 or 32 bits. The destination operand can be a register or memory. The source operand must be a register. For example:

```
xadd    mem, eax
```

is about the same as

```
xchg    mem,  eax
add     mem,  eax
```

or

```
mov    tmp_reg,   eax
mov    eax,       mem
add    tmp_reg,   eax
mov    mem,       tmp_reg
```

There are three reasons to use **XADD**. The first is for the purpose for which it was intended, as a reliable multi-processor task table or intra-processor communication instruction. The second is for code size considerations. Finally, on the 486 it is faster than the equivalent other instructions, but on the Pentium **XADD** is slower than the equivalent instructions.

CMPXCHG The compare and exchange instruction is similar to the **XADD** in that its purpose is to aid multi-processor operating systems. Again, the **LOCK** prefix can be used to ensure system integrity during execution by locking the processor's bus. The operands are the same as for the **XADD** instruction. However, the accumulator (AL, AX or EAX) is always an additional implied operand for **CMPXCHG**. The operation is somewhat tricky, so here's an example:

```
cmpxchg   mem, ebx
```

In this example, this is what happens:

- eax is compared with **mem** (like **CMP eax**, **mem**)
- if they are equal **ebx** is copied to **mem** (like **MOV mem**, **ebx**)
- if they are not equal **mem** is copied to **eax** (like **MOV**, **eax**, **mem**)

So here is the equivalent code for the general form (**cmpxchg dest, src**):

```
        cmp       eax, dest
        jne       not_equal
        mov       dest, src
        jmp       done
not_equal:
        mov       eax, dest
done:
```

Pentium

In 1993 Intel announced the Pentium processor. There are several major changes that make the Pentium significantly faster than the 486. The primary change is that there are two integer pipelines that can be used to simultaneously execute two instructions. Many instructions have improved timings, especially floating-point instructions. A new branch prediction feature allows the processor to predict the destination of a branch instruction to eliminate branch delays. Most of the other changes just help alleviate the inevitable bottlenecks that occur when executing more instructions at a faster rate. Here is a brief list of the changes:

1. 64-bit bus
2. 8K code cache and 8K data cache (vs. 8K combined cache on 486)
3. fewer clock cycles for some instructions (especially floating point)

4. branch prediction logic
5. dual integer pipelines
6. higher clock speeds

The Pentium has what is known as a "superscalar pipelined architecture." Superscalar means that the CPU can execute two (or more) instructions per cycle. (To be more precise: The Pentium can generate the results of two instructions in a single clock cycle.) A pipelined architecture refers to a CPU that executes each portion of an instruction in different stages. When a stage is completed, another instruction begins executing in the first stage while the previous instruction moves to the second stage. The 80486 and Pentium have five-stage pipelines. The Pentium has two pipelines, named the U pipe and the V pipe.

At some points in the pipeline some instructions may prevent other instructions from advancing in the pipeline because of conflicts in register usage or address generation. We'll discuss this in more detail in Chapter 10.

BIGGER CACHE

The Pentium cache is now 8K for code and 8K for data vs. 8K combined on the 486. (Note: some newer 486s now have a 16K combined cache.) There are advantages in having the code and data caches separated. Instruction fetches come from the code cache, and data read and writes take place in the data cache. This separation generates fewer internal bus conflicts that could cause delays. But more importantly, this allows the code cache to contain additional information about each byte in the cache. It appears that the Pentium retains instruction pairing information with each instruction. More about this in later chapters.

NEW PENTIUM INSTRUCTIONS

There are six new instructions on the Pentium and some new forms of the **MOV** instruction:

CMPXCHG8B   *Compare and Exchange 8 Bytes.* The **CMPXCHG8B** is unique in that it sets a new record for the length of a mnemonic. It is similar to **CMPXCHG** (new for the 486) except that it compares 8 bytes and only one operand is specified. EDX:EAX and ECX:EBX are implied operands. EDX:EAX is compared with the memory operand. If they are equal, the value in ECX:EBX is stored in memory; otherwise, the memory value is copied into EDX:EAX.

CPUID   *CPU Identification.* The **CPUID** instruction returns information about the CPU so that a program can determine what features are available on the chip. I could go on for pages about how long-overdue this is, but you still must determine if your program is running on an 8088 through 80486 first. However, Intel did help in detecting whether this instruction is available. There is a new bit in the EFLAGS register. Bit 21 is the new ID flag. If a program can set and clear this bit, then the CPUID instruction is supported. (It's possible that new 386s or 486s could support this.) Here's how this instruction works:

```
mov     eax, 0
cpuid
```

Upon return, EAX contains the maximum input EAX value. The current maximum value is one. The EBX, ECX and EDX registers return the vendor identification string ("GenuineIntel") as follows:

```
EBX = 'Genu'     ('G' in register BL)
EDX = 'ineI'     ('i' in register DL)
ECX = 'ntel'     ('n' in register CL)
```

When an EAX value of 1 is used, the following information is returned:

```
EAX bits 0–3     stepping ID   (0Bh or higher)
EAX bits 4–7     model number (1 or higher)
EAX bits 8–11    family number (5 for Pentium)
EAX bits 12–31   reserved
EBX              reserved (0)
ECX              reserved (0)
```

EDX feature flags as follows:

```
EDX bit 0        1 = FPU on chip
EDX bits 1–6     undocumented
EDX bit 7        1 = machine check exception
EDX bit 8        1 = CMPXCHG8B instruction
EDX bits 9–31    reserved
```

RDTSC   *Read Time Stamp Counter.* This is a curious instruction because it is potentially very useful, but Intel does not document it. They do list it in the Pentium Processor User's Manual in the opcode map and in a list of new instructions. However, they do not specify how to use it. But here is how it works. Every CPU cycle a 64-bit counter is incremented. **RDTSC** returns this count in EDX:EAX. The instruction opcode for **RDTSC** is **0F 31**.

RDMSR *Read from Model Specific Register.* The **RDMSR** instruction returns Pentium-specific information in the EDX and EAX registers. The ECX register is loaded with a value specifying what information is to be returned. Intel documents the following two items:

```
ECX  internal register name    description
0    Machine check address     address of cycle causing
                               exception
1    Machine check type        cycle type of cycle causing
                               exception
```

WRMSR *Write to Model Specific Register.* The **WRMSR** instruction is the inverse of **RDMSR**. The Intel documented values for ECX are the same as for **RDMSR**.

RSM *Resume from System Management Mode.* The **RSM** instruction returns from System Management Mode (SMM). SMM allows software to perform power management and/or security functions in a manner that is transparent to application programs and operating systems. SMM is entered via a hardware signal and causes code in a separate address space to be executed. SMM is like real mode, but with 4GB of address space.

Summary

Well, that's it—you've completed the instruction description triathlon. Although we've covered many new things in this chapter, there are two things of paramount importance. Thing One is the U pipe and Thing Two is the V pipe.

Now it's time to relax and take a well-deserved break. When you've recovered, we will begin training to run two races simultaneously, one in each of the Pentium's pipelines.

Superscalar Programming

9

This chapter and the next one describe the details of the Pentium that make it such a powerful microprocessor. Until this point most of the material should have been a review of (at least vaguely) familiar concepts. If you are not comfortable with writing and debugging assembly programs, at this point you may want to spend more time reviewing these concepts.

There are three features of the Pentium that make programming it significantly different from the 386 and the 486:

- Superscalar pipelined architecture
- branch prediction
- optimized cycle times

In this chapter, I'll describe each of these, starting with the superscalar architecture.

Dual Integer Pipelines

The Pentium processor has two integer pipelines: the U pipe and the V pipe. The U pipe is fully capable of executing any (integer) instruction. The V pipe can only execute simple instructions. When two simple instructions are next in the prefetch queue and the conditions of several rules are met, then the CPU "pairs" them and begins execution of both at the same time. When a processor has two or more parallel pipelines it is called a superscalar architecture.

One of the key points in optimizing for the Pentium is knowing and following the instruction pairing rules as closely as possible.

Whether two instructions pair or not is determined by the Pentium in the second stage of the pipeline. There are two parallel decoders that attempt to decode and issue the next two instructions. This determination is based on a set of pairing rules, described in Figure 9.1.

SIMPLE INSTRUCTIONS

Previously I mentioned that the V pipe can only execute simple instructions. Simple instructions are a specific subset of the 80x86 instruction set. Basically, simple instructions are MOV's, **alu** operations (i.e., **ADD, SUB, CMP, AND, OR,** etc.), **INC, DEC, PUSH, POP, LEA, NOP,** shifts, **CALL, JMP** and conditional jumps. Table 9.1 has a complete list of each simple instruction and all their formats.

There are a number of instructions that are not in this list that one might consider to be rather simple instructions, such as the flags register operations (**STC, CLC, CMC,** etc.), the **XCHG** instructions, type conversions (**CBW**), **NOT** and **NEG.** Intel's choice of instructions to be in this list was probably based on frequency of use as well as the difficulty of implementation (i.e., the number of transistors required on the chip).

Besides the requirement that both instructions must be simple, there are some other requirements. Some have to do with preventing conflicts between the actions of the two instructions being paired. For example, two instructions can pair if they both read the same register, but not if they both write to the same register. Other pairing requirements have to do with various limitations of the Pentium design. Figure 9.1 is a complete list.

You can do well just by using rules 1–4 and 8 of Figure 9.1. However, there are a lot of rules to keep track of while you are coding. That is why I've developed a program to do this. It is called PENTOPT and is described in Chapter 11; it is on the disk included with this book.

Table 9.1 Simple Instructions

MOV	reg, reg	
MOV	reg, mem	
MOV	reg, imm	
MOV	mem, reg	
MOV	mem, imm	
alu	reg, reg	
alu	reg, mem	
alu	reg, imm	
alu	mem, reg	
alu	mem, imm	

where **alu = add, adc, and, or, xor, sub, sbb, cmp, test**

INC	reg	
INC	mem	
DEC	reg	
DEC	mem	
PUSH	reg	
POP	reg	
LEA	reg, mem	
JMP	near	
CALL	near	
Jcc	near	(jump on condition code)
NOP		
shift	reg,	where shift = **sal, sar, shl, shr,**
shift	mem,1	**rcl, rcr, rol, ror**
shift	reg, imm	
shift	mem, imm	

Notes:
- **rcl** and **rcr** are not pairable with immediate counts other than 1
- all memory-immediate (**mem, imm**) instructions are not pairable with a displacement in the memory operand
- instructions with segment registers are not pairable

NOTES ON THE PAIRING RULES

In this section I'll explain the rules in more detail. The first four rules are fairly self-explanatory. So I'll only cover rules 5 through 10.

Figure 9.1 Instruction Pairing Rules

1. Both instructions must be simple.
2. Shift/rotate can only execute in U pipe.
3. **ADC** and **SBB** can only execute in U pipe.
4. **JMP/CALL/Jcc** can only execute in V pipe (**Jcc** = jump on condition code).
5. Neither instruction can contain *both* a displacement and an immediate operand.
6. Prefixed instructions can only execute in the U pipe (except for **OF** in **Jcc**).
7. The U pipe instruction must be only 1 byte in length or it will not pair until the second time it executes from the cache.
8. There can be no read-after-write or write-after-write register dependencies between the instructions except for special cases for the flags register and the stack pointer (rules 9 and 10).
9. The flags register exception allows a **CMP** or **TEST** instruction to be paired with a **Jcc** even though **CMP/TEST** writes the flags and Jcc reads the flags.
10. The stack pointer exception allows two **PUSH**es or two **POP**s to be paired even though they both read and write to the SP (or ESP) register.

The displacement-immediate rule (rule 5) is a limitation that must be based on the number of instruction components and/or operand bytes that the Pentium decoders can process in order to determine if two instructions are pairable. It's a rule that we must live with. Memory operands can be made up of several components (a base register, a scaled index register and a displacement). The displacement is a constant offset value that is added to the other two registers. Each component is optional, but there must be at least one of the three components. An immediate operand is a constant that is the source portion of an instruction.

For example:

```
mov   [bx], 1          ; base only      OK
mov   [ebx+esi], 2     ; base + index   OK
mov   [ebx+2], 2       ; base + disp    no pairing
mov   var1, 4          ; disp only      no pairing
```

The prefix byte rule (rule 6) is important for two primary cases. The first is when using segment overrides. Remember that **MASM** and **TASM** automatically insert segment overrides based on the **ASSUME** directive parameters. The second case is when you are writing mixed 16-bit and 32-bit code. The **REP, REPE** and **REPNE** prefixes cannot be used on any simple instructions. The **LOCK** prefix can be used with some **alu** instructions.

Because of the one-byte rule (rule 7), the only instructions that will pair on the first execution are **INC/DEC reg**, **PUSH/POP reg** and **NOP**. This should never be a consideration in real applications because worrying about optimizing code that only executes one time (per cache fill) is of little value. The only time that this might be of interest is when you are performing timing tests of code that is repeated in-line. But it also means that instructions may pair differently on the first execution as compared to subsequent executions. For example:

	First	Subsequent	
mov ax, 1	1	1	(numbers are CPU cycle numbers)
inc bx	2	1	
mov cx, 1	2	2	
call xyz	3	2	

The logic that determines read/write dependencies (rules 8, 9 and 10) is based on each register as a single 32-bit entity. Therefore, a read or write to one part of a register is the same as using the entire register. So writing to **AL**, **AH** or **AX** is the same as writing to **EAX**. And although Intel is vague in the description about pairing instructions that change the flags, I determined that all the simple alu/inc/dec instructions can be paired with conditional jumps. This brings up an interesting optimization in that you should always use **CMP** or **TEST** to set the flags (when possible) since they only write to the flags register. For example, the following three instructions could be used to test if **AX** is 0:

```
cmp     ax, 0
or      ax, ax
test    ax, ax
```

The **CMP** instruction is three bytes long, the others are two. The **OR** instruction writes to **AX**, reducing pairing opportunities.

Here are some other read/write dependencies examples:

read-after-write (do not pair)

```
mov al, 1
add bh, ah
mov ax, 1
add bx, ax
```

write-after-write (do not pair)	`mov eax, 1`
	`add eax, ebx`
	`mov ax, 1`
	`mov ax, 2`
write-after-read (pairs)	`mov ax, bx`
	`inc bx`
read-after-read (pairs)	`mov eax, ebx`
	`add ecx, ebx`

Branch Prediction Logic

Branch prediction is a new feature on the Pentium. When a jump or call instruction is encountered, the address of the instruction is used to access the BTB (Branch Target Buffer) to predict the outcome of the instruction. There is not much more that you can do to take advantage of the branch prediction logic since it is automatic. Most every jump or call in a loop will execute in one cycle if the prediction logic is correct.

But just in case you have an oddball procedure and you're worried about the effect of the branch prediction logic, here is how it works. The Pentium keeps track of the last 256 branches in the BTB and tries to predict the destination for each call/jump. It does this by keeping a history of whether a jump was taken or not. If the prediction is correct, then a conditional jump, for example, takes only one cycle.

There are now two prefetch queues, both 32 bytes long. The branch prediction takes place in the D1 pipeline stage (second stage) and predicts whether a branch will be taken or not and its destination. When it predicts a branch, the other prefetch queue begins fetching instructions. If the prediction turns out to be incorrect, then both queues are flushed and prefetching is restarted. For the 486 and previous CPUs, the best optimization in regard to conditional branching was to not do the branch. The best optimization for the Pentium is to just be consistent; i.e., always take the conditional jump or always don't. On the 486 and early processors the code is always fastest when a conditional jump is not taken. In general, this is also true on the Pentium. However, once a loop is determined to usually take the jump, then it runs at the fastest rate and a failure to jump will cause a delay. The delay is substantial; see Table 9.2.

Table 9.2 Branch Misprediction Delays

Instruction	U pipe	V pipe
conditional jumps	4	5
jmp	3	3
call	3	3

When will you exceed the 256 branch limit? First, during a hardware interrupt while in a tight loop it would be possible to exceed 256 branches before control is returned. Also, during a task switch in a multi-tasking environment, each task switch will impose a restart penalty on each task while it refills the branch target buffer. There is not anything you can do in an application program to prevent these delays.

Here is an example of a case where you might unknowingly cause the branch table buffer to overflow:

```
                           ; with without branch prediction
                           ; (cycles are for a case of non-space character)
        loop1:
          mov  al, [si]    ;        1          1
          inc  si          ;        0          0 (0 due to pairing)
          cmp  al, ' '     ;        1          1
          jne  foo         ;        0          3
          call space       ;
          jmp  bar         ;
        foo:
          inc  dx          ;        1          1
        bar:
          dec  cx          ;        0          0
          jnz  loop1       ;        1          3
          ;                 total   4          10
```

The preceding code scans a string of known length for spaces. When a space is found a function is called, else a counter is incremented. When a space character is found, if the space function is small, then the next iteration of the **loop1** code will run in four cycles; otherwise, it will run in 10 cycles. This is a dramatic change and could be worse. However, the space function would need to be at least several hundred instructions in length to completely modify the BTB. The additional six cycles for the next iteration of **loop1** would be insignificant.

But here is why an understanding of this is important. Let's say that you are timing the **loop1** code but not the space function using a hardware timing device or by some other method. Let's say you modify the space function and remove several jumps. Your timing will now show the **loop1** code as being faster.

Optimized Cycle Times

As with each member of the 80x86 family after the 8086/8088 chips, the Pentium was delivered with a number of instructions that operate in fewer cycles than before. Of course, what this means is that programs will automatically run faster on the Pentium than on the older members of the 80x86 family. Well, yes and no. You do have to know what these instructions are and how to arrange them. Instruction combinations that were the fastest in the past may not be as fast as other combinations on the Pentium. Later chapters have some specific examples. (Also see Appendix B.)

The most significant advance on the Pentium (in terms of CPU cycles) is the floating-point performance. Multiplies and additions are now completed in one to three cycles. Previously, when precision would allow, it was advantageous to multiply by the inverse of a number instead of performing a division—for example, multiplying by 0.1 vs. dividing by 10. On the 486 a multiply is 11–16 cycles and a divide 73–89. So multiply could be six or seven times faster. On the Pentium, a multiply is 1–3 cycles and a divide is 39. Multiply is now 13 to 39 times faster. Clearly, these types of code rewrites can dramatically improve the speed of floating-point operations.

Possibly a more significant performance change in the FPU is the fact that the **FXCH** instruction can be paired with some common FPU instructions. See Chapter 16 for an example.

Table 9.3 contains a list of the most significant changes in Pentium cycle times from the 386 and 486.

Table 9.3 Significant Cycle Time Changes

	386	486	Pentium
add reg, reg	2	1	1 (other alu same as **add**)
add mem, reg	2	1	1
inc reg	2	1	1 (**dec** and **inc** the same)
inc mem	2	1	1
mov reg, reg	2	1	1
mov mem, reg	2	1	1
mul	9–41	13–42	10–11
nop	3	3	1
pop reg	4	1	1
push reg	2	1	1

Table 9.3 Significant Cycle Time Changes (Continued)

	386	486	Pentium
popa	24	9	5
pusha	18	11	5
ret	11	5	2
jcc	3/7	1/3	1* (jcc = jump on condition code)
jmp near	8/9	3/5	1*
call near	8	3	1*
(* = assumes correct branch prediction)			
loop	13	6/9	7/8
lods	5	5	2
rep movs	4	3	1
rep stos	5	4	1
repe/ne cmps	9	7	4
repe/ne scas	8	5	4
fadd	23–72	8–32	1–3
fmul	29–82	11–16	1–3
fcos, fsin	123–772	257–354	16–126
fdiv	88–128	73–89	39

Integer and Floating-Point Pipeline Operation

> *Delay is preferable to error.*
> —Thomas Jefferson

This chapter covers the operation of the integer and floating-point pipelines on the Pentium. A good understanding of pipeline operation is helpful in understanding why certain instructions or combinations of instructions are more efficient than others. We'll begin by exploring the reasons for using a pipeline and then describing the simpler 486 pipeline. Finally we'll take a look at the Pentium's floating-point pipeline.

INSTRUCTION FETCHING

Every instruction must be fetched (or read) from memory. This process can be one of the biggest bottlenecks in a system. It is possible for a CPU to be able to execute instructions faster than new instructions can be read. To relieve this bottleneck the 80x86 processors have always had a "prefetch queue." A fetch is an operation that the CPU performs automatically and is the process of reading the byte or bytes that make up the next instruction to be executed from memory. The prefetch queue is a small FIFO (first-in, first-out) buffer contained inside the CPU. See Table 10.1.

Table 10.1 Prefetch Queue Sizes

Processor	Prefetch Queue Size	Notes
8088	4	
8086	6	
80188	4	
80186	6	
286	8	
386	16	Many systems have an external cache
486	32	8K (or 16K) code/data internal cache
Pentium	2×32	8K code cache & 8K data cache

THE MEMORY CACHE

By the time the 486 was designed, the CPU was so quick that an on-chip memory cache had to be included so that instructions could be fetched fast enough. A memory cache is a small block of high-speed memory designed to hold the most active parts of the larger, slower main system memory. The logic in a cache circuit is designed so that when the CPU reads one byte from an area of memory, an entire block of (for example) 32 or 64 bytes is read into the cache. The idea is that the next thing the CPU will want to do is to read the next sequential byte from memory. In the case of fetching instructions to be executed, this will be true until the program performs a CALL, JMP or other branching instruction. But the cache is designed to handle this because it can store many independent blocks of memory. The usage of each cache line is tracked based on a most recently used algorithm. When the cache is full the least recently used block can be discarded and reused.

The 486 has an 8K on-chip cache that is shared between data and code. A newer 486DX4 chip has a 16K cache. The Pentium has a 16K cache, but there are separate blocks for code and data, of 8K each.

PIPELINES

Several independent steps must be performed by the CPU to complete even the simplest of instructions. Let's take a look at the internal operations of the CPU for a few instructions.

To load data from memory, i.e.,

```
mov    ax, [bx]
```

the processor must perform the following actions:

- fetch the instruction
- decode what actions must be taken
- calculate the effective address by combining: **(DS * 16) + BX**
- read the data from memory
- store the data in the AX register

Let's look at another instruction.

```
add    ax, bx
```

For this instruction, the processor must:

- fetch the instruction
- decode what actions must be taken
- add the two registers
- store the data in the AX register

And, finally one more instruction:

```
inc byte ptr [bx+2]
```

For this instruction the processor must:

- fetch the instruction
- decode what actions must be taken
- calculate the effective address by combining: **(DS * 16) + BX + 2**
- read the byte from memory
- add 1
- store the data in memory

Not every instruction needs to perform all the same steps, but they certainly are very similar. What if a computer were designed like a factory assembly line? Each instruction would move from station to station as if it were on a conveyor belt. At each station a specialist would perform its job. This is how a pipeline works. It was first used by Intel's 80x86 processors on the 486. The stations, or stages are as follows:

PF prefetch
D1 instruction decode
D2 address generation
EX execute and cache access
WB write back

Here is a brief description of what happens during each pipeline stage:

PF: *Prefetch.*   Instructions are fetched from the cache or memory are stored in the prefetch queue.

D1: *Instruction decode or* **Decode1**.   The instruction is decoded and broken into component parts, opcode and operands. An extra cycle is required for instructions that contain a prefix.

D2: **Decode2** *or Address Generation.*   The effective address of the memory operand, if present, is calculated. On the 486 an extra cycle is required if an address contains both a base and an index component or both a displacement and an immediate data value.

EX: *Execute and Cache Access.*   The processor performs the action(s) required by the instruction, including reading data from memory and storing the results in registers.

WB: *Write Back.*   Instructions complete and data to be written to memory is sent to a write buffer. Instructions are enabled to modify the CPU state.

Instructions proceed from one stage to the next stage in one cycle, (usually). So even the fastest instruction on the 486 takes five cycles to complete. But wait! If you've looked at any of the CPU cycle tables you've seen that many instructions take only one cycle on the 486. How can this be?

The published cycle times are actually the fewest number of cycles that an instruction would take when added to a stream of other instructions. Think of it as the effective throughput, not the actual time an instruction is in the pipeline. Cars may drive off an assembly line every two minutes, but each one takes many hours to assemble. Here's an example (see Table 10.2).

Most of the time instructions complete each of the pipeline stages in one cycle, except possibly the execute (EX) stage. When one of the more "complex" instructions is encountered, it may take two or more cycles in the EX stage. In this case all the instructions in the previous stages are suspended (i.e., the conveyor belt is stopped) until the instruction in the EX stage is completed. Note, however that the CPU is smart enough

Table 10.2 Normal Pipeline Operation

			Stages			
Cycles	PF	D1	D2	EX	WB	
1	I1					I1 starts
2	I2	I1				I2 starts
3	I3	I2	I1			I3 starts
4	I4	I3	I2	I1		
5	I5	I4	I3	I2	I1	I1 completes
6	I6	I5	I4	I3	I2	I2 completes
7		I6	I5	I4	I3	I3 completes

(I1 = instruction #1, I2 = instruction #2, etc.)

Note: The Intel documentation normally shows the pipeline execution diagram with the stages shown on the left and the cycles across the top. I have shown the pipeline with cycles increasing from top to bottom. This allows analysis of longer sequences of instructions.

to keep instructions started before the stalled instruction moving (i.e., there are two conveyor belts, one up to the EX stage and one from EX to WB). Table 10.3 shows an example of a case where an instruction stalls, taking four cycles in the EX stage.

So we know that if an instruction can't complete a stage in one cycle, then the pipeline is said to be "stalled." Here is some code that could cause the stall shown in Table 10.3:

```
                     ;    cycles
        lea    bx, tbl1  ;    I1        1
lbl:    mov    al, [si]  ;    I2        1
        xlat             ;    I3        4
        inc    si        ;    I4        1
        cmp    al, dl    ;    I5        1
        je     lbl       ;    I6        1
```

ADDRESS GENERATION INTERLOCK (AGI)

We've seen what happens when an instruction is too complex to complete the EX stage in one cycle. Are there any conditions that could cause an instruction to take more than one cycle for any other stages? You bet there are. And sometimes these cases are more

Table 10.3 Pipeline Operation with a Stall

| | Stages | | | | | |
Cycles	PF	D1	D2	EX	WB	
1	I1					I1 starts
2	I2	I1				I2 starts
3	I3	I2	I1			I3 starts
4	I4	I3	I2	I1		I4 starts
5	I5	I4	I3	I2	I1	I5 starts
6	I6	I5	I4	I3	I2	I3 starts
7	I6	I5	I4	I3	–	I3 stalls pipeline
8	I6	I5	I4	I3	–	
9	I6	I5	I4	I3	–	
10	I7	I6	I5	I4	I3	I3 completes

difficult to account for, because the published cycle times are really an indication of the number of cycles spent in the EX stage. Other pipeline stalls are usually a result of the order of a particular combination of instructions.

What happens to the pipeline in the following example?

```
mov    ax, 1          ; I1
lea    bx, table_1    ; I2
mov    cx, [bx]       ; I3
add    cx, ax         ; I4
```

From previous chapters, we've learned about AGIs (address generation interlocks). A look at Table 10.4 shows why it happens.

Instruction I2 executed the LEA at cycle #5. At the same time I3 attempted to generate the address that it would need. The address would be **(DS * 16) + BX.** If this operation were allowed to occur, the address would be incorrect because the BX register is being simultaneously updated by the previous instruction, I1. The 486 and the Pentium detect this condition and generate what is called an AGI (address generation interlock). An AGI is generated when a register is used as a component of an effective address and is also the destination register of an instruction in the previous cycle.

Table 10.4 Pipeline Operation with AGI

| Cycles | Stages | | | | | |
	PF	D1	D2	EX	WB	
1	I1					I1 starts
2	I2	I1				I2 starts
3	I3	I2	I1			I3 starts
4	I4	I3	I2	I1		I4 starts
5		I4	I3	I2	I1	I2 executes, AGI
6			I3	–	I2	I3 generates address
7			I4	I3	–	

PAIRED PIPELINES

When working on the Pentium we must take into account the fact that there are now two pipelines (the U pipe and the V pipe)—like a factory with two assembly lines or two conveyor belts. However, unlike building cars or some other product, the outputs from the two pipelines must be kept in order. Each instruction in each pipeline can modify data in memory, data in registers and the state of the CPU. Because of this it is sometimes necessary for activities in one pipeline to be known by the other pipeline. This is done so that the end result is exactly the same as if instructions were executed sequentially in the exact same order in which they were fetched.

While progressing through the pipeline, instructions may stall for various reasons. To ensure proper sequencing of instruction results, instructions in the U pipe and V pipe enter and leave the D1 and D2 pipeline stages in unison. When an instruction in one pipe causes a stall, then both pipelines stall. When an instruction in the U pipe stalls in the EX stage, the instruction in the V pipe also stalls. However, if the V pipe instruction stalls, the U pipe instruction is allowed to continue to the WB stage. The next instruction (or instruction pair) is not allowed to enter the EX stage until both previous instructions enter the WB stage. This prevents the possibility of a V pipe instruction stalling in the EX stage and being passed by instructions in the U pipe.

Although instructions in each pipeline execute independently, it also means that pipeline stalls can be caused by more than just the previous instruction. For example:

Table 10.5 Pentium Pipeline Operation

Cycles	Pipe	PF	D1	D2	EX	WB	
1	U	I1					I1 starts
	V	I2					I2 starts
2	U	I3	I1				I3 starts
	V	I4	I2				I4 starts
3	U	I5	I3	·I1			I5 starts
	V	I6	I4	I2			I6 starts
4	U	I7	I5	I3	I1		I7 starts
	V	I8	I6	I4	I2		I8 starts
5	U	I9	I7	I5	I3	I1	I1 completes
	V	I10	I8	I6	I4	I2	I2 completes
6	U	I11	I9	I7	I5	I3	I3 completes
	V	I12	I10	I8	I6	I4	I4 completes

```
mov    bx, offset mem    ; I1
mov    ax, 1             ; I2
mov    cx, 1000          ; I3
add    dx, [bx]          ; I4
```

In this code for Table 10.4 (see next page), the move into BX causes an AGI for the **ADD** instruction that is three instructions later.

486 PIPELINE DELAYS

On the 486 there are two pipeline delays:

- address generation delay (486 only)
- address generation interlock (AGI)

On the 486 the D2 pipeline stage takes an extra cycle when an effective address calculation uses a base register and an index register. An extra cycle is also required when an instruction has a displacement and an immediate data value.

Table 10.6 Pentium Pipeline Operation with AGI

Cycles	Pipe	Stages					
		PF	**D1**	**D2**	**EX**	**WB**	
1	U	I1					I1 starts
	V	I2					I2 starts
2	U	I3	I1				I3 starts
	V	I4	I2				I4 starts
3	U	I5	I3	I1			
	V	I6	I4	I2			
4	U		I5	I3	I1		I3 stalls w/I4
	V		I6	I4	I2		I4 AGI
5	U		I5	I3	—	I1	I1 completes
	V		I6	I4	—	I2	I2 completes
6	U			I5	I3	—	
	V			I6	I4	—	
7	U				I5	I3	I3 completes
	V				I6	I4	I4 completes

An AGI occurs on the 486 when an instruction writes to a register that is used in an effective address calculation in the next instruction.

PENTIUM PIPELINE DELAYS

There are four pipeline delays that can occur in the Pentium that do not (directly) affect instruction pairing, but do add extra cycles and should be considered when re-ordering instructions. They are:

- data-cache memory bank conflict
- address generation interlock (AGI)
- prefix byte delay
- sequencing delay

Data-Cache Memory Bank Conflict

First, if two paired instructions access the same data-cache memory bank, then there is a one-cycle delay in the second instruction. A data-cache memory bank conflict occurs when bits 2–4 are the same in the two physical addresses. Sometimes this is a difficult delay to try to program around, especially in low-level subroutines that only receive pointers to data items. The best overall strategy is to try and not pair instructions that might access the same data-cache memory bank.

The bank conflict is an extremely important concept, so it is vital that it is properly understood. Take a look at the layout of the cache in Figure 2.1. Each cache line (i.e., 0, 1, 2, 3 in Figure 2.1) consists of a 32-bit address (16 bits shown) that can be broken down into three parts:

```
bits: 0-1  byte within the dword
bits: 2-4  cache bank
bits: 5-31 cache line address tag
```

Cache lines are always filled on even 32-byte boundaries, so it is easy to determine when a bank conflict will occur. This happens when the bank number is the same (i.e., when bits 2–4 in the addresses are the same). Here is an example:

Figure 2.1 Sample Cache Layout

Bank:		0	1	2	3	4	5	6	7
Bytes:		0–3	4–7	8–B	C–F	10–13	14–17	18–1B	1C–1F
Cache Line Address (Bits 5–15 Shown)									
0.	0000 0000 000	This	is s	ampl	e da	ta.	Ther	e ar	e fo
1.	0000 0000 001	ur l	ines	in	this	sam	ple.	But	note
2.	0000 0000 011	ed i	n se	quen	tial	ord	er.		
3.	0000 0000 010	tha	t th	ey d	o no	t ne	ed t	o be	stor
...									
127.									

Notes: Each line contains 32 bytes from an even 32-byte boundary from main memory. The main memory address of a cache line is a 32-bit physical address with the 5 lower bits equal to zero. There are 128 cache lines that can be arranged within the cache in any order. Sequential lines of the cache do not need to contain sequential blocks of memory. (Notice that lines 2 and 3 of the cache contain out-of-order memory addresses.)

```
lbl:
mov   al, [si]
mov   bl, [si+1]
...
add   si, 2
loop  lbl
```

This loop will have a bank conflict on every loop if SI is started with an even number. The loop will have a bank conflict 50% of the time if SI starts as an odd number. So sometimes misaligned data can cause a program to run faster! We'll examine this phenomenon more in Chapter 13.

Address Generation Interlock (AGI)

We've already covered the second delay, the AGI, earlier in the pipeline section. The general rule is that an AGI will occur when any instruction in a given cycle writes to a register that is used in an effective address calculation in any instruction during the next cycle. This can occur in two basic ways: when an instruction in one cycle changes a register that is the base or index portion of an effective address calculation for the next cycle, or when an instruction in one cycle changes SP (or ESP) and the next instruction relies on SP (or ESP). However, there is an exception to the AGI rule. When the instructions both use SP (or ESP) implicitly, such as PUSH or POP, there is no AGI. Here are some AGI examples:

```
inc   bx          ; two INCs pair
inc   ax
mov   cx, [si]    ; two MOVs pair
mov   dx, [bx]    ; AGI delay because BX changed in previous cycle
pop   bx          ; two POPs pair
pop   ax
ret               ; no AGI delay
pop   bx          ; two POPs pair
pop   ax          ;
add   sp, 10
ret               ; AGI delay
```

Prefix Byte Delay

The third delay is the prefix byte delay. On the 486 prefix bytes did not add any cycles. On the Pentium a prefix, such as a segment override, will take one extra cycle to process. Also, beware of rule 6 (see Table 9.2) because a prefixed instruction cannot be paired in the V pipe. Although it may not actually work like this, I like to think of prefix bytes as separate one-byte, non-pairable instructions. This conceptual model works well in predicting the number of cycles required for a block of instructions. (See Appendix F for a list of prefixes.) Here is an example of a prefix causing two otherwise pairable instructions to not be paired:

```
lbl:
    mov    al, [si]        ; 1 cycle
    mov    bl, ES:[di]     ; 2 cycles (1 for prefix, 1 for MOV)
    ...
    loop   lbl
```

When the instructions can be rearranged, place the instruction with the prefix (ES segment override in this case) so it will pair in the U pipe, as follows:

```
lbl:
    mov    bl, ES:[di]     ; 2 cycles
    mov    al, [si]        ; 0 cycles
    ...
    loop   lbl
```

Sequencing Delay

The fourth delay is a sequencing delay. Most of the simple instructions execute in one cycle because they are hardwired (i.e., no microcode). There are some forms of ALU (arithmetic logic unit) instructions that execute in two or three cycles. For example:

```
add    mem, reg   ; 3 cycles (read-modify-write)
add    reg, mem   ; 2 cycles (read-modify-register)
```

Sequencing hardware allows them to function as simple instructions. Both the two- and three-cycle forms are pairable. However, when two read-modify-write instructions (three-cycle forms) are paired together, there is a two-cycle sequencing delay. For example:

```
add    ax, [bx]   ; 2 (two-cycle forms completely overlap)
add    cx, [si]   ; 0

add    [bx], 2    ; 3
add    [si], 2    ; 2 (first cycle overlaps with previous)
```

These last two instructions take three cycles each. When paired they take a total of five cycles because there is a two-cycle sequencing delay.

Eliminating the Sequencing Delay

Our first real coding challenge will be to eliminate this two-cycle delay. By using a spare register, we can rewrite the code to this:

```
mov    ax, [bx]    ; 1
add    ax, 2       ; 1
mov    [bx], ax    ; 1
mov    ax, [si]    ; 0
add    ax, 2       ; 1
mov    [si], ax    ; 1
```

But this still takes five cycles (the third and fourth instructions should pair). This leads one to believe that this is exactly how the CPU sequences the operation using an internal scratch register. So now that we've discovered this "extra register" it should be taken into account when you write your code. You could rewrite the preceding code as follows:

```
mov    ax, [bx]    ; 1
add    ax, 2       ; 1
mov    [bx], ax    ; 1
add    [si], 2     ; 2 (first cycle overlaps with previous)
```

This still takes five cycles, but is smaller. The problem is that in writing the code this way we are blocking ourselves from finding other pairing opportunities. Another way to write the code with two spare registers is

```
mov    ax, [bx]    ; 1
add    ax, 2       ; 1
mov    [bx], ax    ; 1
mov    cx, [si]    ; 0
add    cx, 2       ; 1
mov    [si], cx    ; 1
```

Again, this still takes five cycles, but it can be reordered to

```
mov    ax, [bx]    ; 1
mov    cx, [si]    ; 0
add    ax, 2       ; 1
add    cx, 2       ; 0
mov    [bx], ax    ; 1
mov    [si], cx    ; 0
```

This sequence only takes three cycles and is written in classic load, operate, store fashion. This is why one of the basic concepts of RISC machines, the load/store architecture, is so important. When code is written in this manner it can easily be re-ordered for more efficient execution.

If you need to save and restore the two registers used to change this sequence of code, this will take back the two cycles you saved. But if the pushes and pops are outside of a loop, then this portion of the loop code has gone from five to three cycles, a 40% improvement.

Pentium Floating-Point Pipeline

We'll finish this chapter by describing the FPU pipeline and instruction issue on the Pentium. It is not necessary to understand FPU programming to follow most topics in the rest of this book. Only Chapter 16 has an FPU programming example. Most readers will find it advantageous to have previous experience programming the 8087, or other FPU, to fully understand the floating point material in this book.

The FPU pipeline has eight stages, the first five of which are shared with the integer unit. Here is a brief description of what happens during each pipeline stage:

PF: *Prefetch.* Instructions are fetched from the cache or memory are stored in the prefetch queue.

D1:   *Instruction decode or Decode1.* The instruction is decoded and broken into component parts, opcode and operands. An extra cycle is required for instruction that contain a prefix.

D2:   *Decode2 or Address Generation.* The effective address of the memory operand, if present, is calculated. On the 486 an extra cycle is required if an address contains both a base and an index component or both a displacement and an immediate data value.

EX: *Cache Access and register read.* Conversion of FP data.

X1:   *FP Execute stage one.* Conversion of FP data to internal data format.

X2:   *FP Execute stage two.*

WF: *Perform rounding and write FP results to a register file.*

ER: *Error reporting.* Status word update.

Floating-point (FP) instructions cannot be paired with integer instructions; however some FP instructions can be paired together. Integer instructions and FP instructions can execute simultaneously (see later discussion). The pairing rules for the FPU are fairly strict; see Table 10.7.

Table 10.7 Floating-Point Pairing Rules

FPU pairing rules:

1. The U pipe instruction must be a simple FPU instruction.

2. The V pipe instruction must be **FXCH**.

Simple FPU instructions:

FABS	absolute value
FADD	add
FADDP	add and pop
FCHS	change sign
FCOM	compare real
FCOMP	compare real and pop
FDIV	divide
FDIVP	divide and pop
FDIVR	reverse divide
FDIVRP	reverse divide and pop
FLD	load real, single or double or st(i)
FMUL	multiply
FMULP	multiply and pop
FSUB	subtract
FSUBP	subtract and pop
FSUBR	reverse subtract
FSUBRP	reverse subtract and pop
FTST	test
FUCOM	unordered compare real
FUCOMP	unordered compare real and pop
FUCOMPP	unordered compare real and pop twice

The 8087 family of math processors have a stack architecture, similar in operation to the Hewlett Packard scientific calculators. The stack consists of eight 80-bit registers and a stack pointer. Normally, which register a variable is in is not of concern; only its position relative to the stack pointer is significant. The FPU registers are always specified relative to the top of the stack as follows:

```
st        top of stack (last item loaded or pushed)
st(0)     same as st
st(1)     second to last item loaded
st(2)     third to last item loaded
...
st(7)     bottom of stack
```

Operands can be loaded (pushed) onto the stack with **FLD**, for example. Results can be copied into memory from the stack, or stored, with **FST** and its variants. Results can also be discarded, or popped, from the stack at the conclusion of many instructions. The instruction mnemonic ends with the letter **P** for these instructions. Here is a brief example:

```
                 ;                          st(0)   st(1) st(2) ...
    fld    n0    ; load n0                  n0      -     -
    fld    n1    ; load n1                  n1      n0    -
    fadd         ; st(0) = st(0)+st(1)      n1+n0   n0    -
    fstp   ans_1 ; ans_1 = st(0), pop       n0      -     -
    fld    n2    ; load n2                  n2      n0
    fld    n3    ; load n3                  n3      n2    n0
    fmul         ; st(0) = st(0)*st(1)      n3*n1   n1    n0
    fst    ans_2 ; ans_2 = st(0)           n3*n1   n1    n0
```

All two-operand instructions require one source operand to be on the top of the stack, i.e., **st(0)**. Many common instruction forms also have a destination that is also the top of the stack. This results in a "bottleneck" at the top of the stack. You can see from the preceding example that every instruction uses the top of the stack, **st(0)**. This bottleneck can be relieved by using the **FXCH** instruction to quickly exchange the **st(0)** register with one of the other registers. On the Pentium, the **FXCH** instruction takes zero cycles when it pairs with one of the instructions in Table 10.7.

FPU Pipeline Delays

There are several FPU pipeline delays that can degrade performance. Sometimes the performance penalty may be hard to detect, but sometimes it can cause an instruction to take three times as many cycles. These delays are:

- write-back latency
- **FST** delay
- repeated **FMUL** delay
- **FXCH**-Integer delay

FPU instructions, such as **FADD** and **FMUL**, have been optimized on the Pentium so that they take only one cycle to execute. However, because of the complexity of the FPU pipeline, a stall occurs if the results of one operation are required as an input for the next operation. This write-back latency can be as much as four extra cycles. The only way around it is to interleave other non-conflicting FPU instructions. Table 10.8 lists the affected instructions. Chapter 16 contains examples showing how to eliminate these delays.

The **FST** delay is an additional one-cycle delay added on to the write-back latency when an **FST** (floating-point store) instruction uses the result of the previous floating point operation.

When the **FMUL** instruction is followed immediately by another **FMUL** instruction, the maximum throughput is two cycles rather than one because of contention for the execution stage hardware.

For maximum performance, the **FXCH** instruction must be followed by another FPU instruction, not an integer instruction. If an integer instruction follows an **FXCH**, then there is a delay. The delay is one cycle for a "safe" pair of instructions and four cycles for an unsafe pair. You may be wondering, what is a safe instruction?

Table 10.8 FPU Instruction Cycles with Write-back Latencies

Instructions	Throughput	With Latency Delay
FADD, FADDP	1	3
FMUL, FMULP	1	3
FSUB, FSUBP, FSUBR, FSUBRP	1	3
FCOM, FTST	1	4
FUCOM, FUCOMP, FUCOMPP	1	4
FSTSW AX	2	6
FSTSW	2	5
FICOM	4	8
FIADD, FISUB, FILD	4	7

Safe Instruction Recognition

When I think of safe instructions I remember taking calculus and differential equations in school. At some point we began deriving equations to do things such as determine the stress loading of beams in bridges at varying temperatures. I was proficient at using these equations from my engineering classes, but the derivation of the equations was beyond me. I think I passed the class because I knew the answers and could eventually stumble upon them. This is what I would call unsafe mathematics.

Not surprisingly, the FPU has a different definition of unsafe. On a blackboard every mathematical operation is safe, in that a symbol has been defined for every situation. There are mathematical symbols for infinity (both positive and negative); any number can, theoretically, be written on the board; etc. But on the computer there are many limits—for example, a single-precision floating point number must fall in the range of 1.18×10^{-38} and 3.4×10^{38} or negative values in the same range (or zero). An operation that results in a number outside of this range would possibly cause a program error.

A floating-point exception is a numeric error such as a divide by zero, underflow or overflow. Only certain instructions can generate one of these errors (i.e., only divide can generate a divide by zero). In addition, each of the various exceptions can be disabled by programmer control, directing the FPU to use a default fix-up for that operation. For example, if a divide results in a very small number, too small to represent in the range of values supported by the FPU, an underflow would normally occur. If underflows are masked out, then the FPU would substitute a "special" result of 0.0 and not generate an exception. The generation of special results when an exception condition is masked out is done through the use of microcode in the FPU.

An instruction is considered safe if it cannot generate a floating-point exception and it does not use microcode in the FPU to generate special results. The range of possible exceptions is great, but here is how it works for **FADD**, **FSUB**, **FMUL** and **FDIV**. The instructions both have exponents that are in the range

```
-8,190 <= exp <= 8,190
```

Note that this is a much greater range than single- or double-precision numbers because the FPU converts all operands to an internal 80-bit format.

If an instruction is declared safe, then the next instruction is allowed to complete the EX pipeline stage. If an instruction is declared unsafe, the next FPU instruction stalls in the EX stage until the unsafe instruction finishes with no exception. From looking at the FPU pipeline description, we can see that this stall will be at least four cycles. Note that this stall will occur even if the FPU operation does not generate an exception. An instruction declared as unsafe means an exception is a possibility; therefore, the FPU must wait for the instruction to finish to see if an exception occurs before allowing the next instruction to proceed.

CONCURRENT INTEGER AND FPU PROCESSING

Because the integer unit (IU) and the FPU are separate, it is possible for FPU instructions to be executing in parallel with integer instructions. This was possible from the very first 8086 and 8087. Because FPU operations, generally, take longer to execute, the IU can often execute several instructions while the FPU is completing one instruction. For example, this code calculates the square roots of an array of single-precision numbers:

```
lbl:
        fld     dword ptr [esi] ; load 4-byte real
        fsqrt                   ; calculate square root
        fst     dword ptr [edi] ; store result
        add     esi, 4          ; advance source pointer
        add     edi, 4          ; advance destination pointer
        dec     ecx             ; decrement loop count
        jnz     lbl             ; continue loop if ecx not 0
```

This next loop does the same thing, but takes advantage of the long execution time of the **FSQRT** instruction to perform some of the integer instructions required for the loop management:

```
lbl:
        fld     dword ptr [esi] ; load 4-byte real
        fsqrt                   ; calculate square root
        add     esi, 4          ;; advance pointers while
        add     edi, 4          ;; the square root is executing
        dec     ecx             ;; decrement loop count
        fwait                   ; wait for square root to finish
        fst     dword ptr [edi-4]; store result
        jnz     lbl             ; continue loop if ecx not 0
```

When this code is run the time for the three instructions after the **FSQRT** can be observed as taking zero cycles.

Because the Pentium executes many FPU instructions in as little as a single cycle, concurrent processing is a less meaningful strategy for the Pentium. However, trigonometric functions, logarithms, etc., can still take more than 100 cycles and division takes 39 cycles, so there is still opportunity for concurrent processing.

Managing the parallel execution of the IU and FPU can be difficult, especially when a program must account for numerical exceptions. High-level languages tend to do this in a reliable, but slow, manner, primarily because the floating-point operations are usually contained in a library that is isolated from the loop control code generated by the compiler. In Chapter 16 we'll see how integer instruction pairing, concurrent integer and floating-point execution and floating point instruction pairing can all be combined to increase FPU performance more than 10-fold.

Using the Pentium Optimizer Program

11

*"Intelligence . . . is the faculty of making
artificial objects, especially tools
to make tools."*
—Henri Bergson

This chapter and Chapter 12 describe the use and operations of two tools provided on the disk supplied with this book. This chapter describes PENTOPT, an optimization analyzer for the Pentium. The next chapter describes a library of procedures for timing critical sections of code.

The PENTOPT version enclosed is a fully functional program based on my company's commercial Pentium Optimizer (PentOpt Professional) product. Both programs were derived from another product, ASMFLOW Professional, a general-purpose assembly-language flow charter and source-code analysis program.

In simple terms, what PENTOPT does is to flow-chart assembly-language source code and produce an analysis of each instruction's optimized use on the Pentium. The commercial version of PENTOPT has additional features for handling large projects with multiple files as described on the disk. For all the examples in this book and similar code you may write, the version of PENTOPT included on the disk is adequate. The PENTOPT version included with the book will be maintained, and upgrades may be ordered with the enclosed coupon.

Figure 11.1 is an example of the output provided by PENTOPT.

Figure 11.1 Sample Output from PENTOPT

```
12              main proc                   ;Pentium cycles
13              push  bx                    ;   1 cy              UV  1
14              push  cx                    ;   1 cy              UV  *
15              push  dx                    ;   1 cy              UV  *
17              mov   bx, offset tbl1       ;   1 cy              UV  *
18              mov   cx, [bx]              ;   1 cy              UV  4 AGI-1
19              shl   cx, 1                 ;   1 cy              U   2
20              mov   bx, offset array      ;   1 cy              UV  *
22              cmp   cx, 0                 ;   1 cy              UV  *
23              je    main_3                ;   1 cy              V   *
24   main_1:
25              mov   ax, [si]              ;   1 cy              UV  2
26              mov   bx, [si+2]            ;   1 cy              UV  *
27              mul   bx                    ;  10 cy  / 11 cy NP
29              cmp   ax, 1                 ;   1 cy              UV  1
30              je    main_2                ;   1 cy              V   *
32              add   si, 4                 ;   1 cy              UV  2
33              cmp   si, x_end             ;   2 cy              UV  4
34              jae   main_3                ;   1 cy              V   *
35              dec   cx                    ;   1 cy              UV  2
36              jnz   main_1                ;   1 cy              V   *
37   main_2:
38              inc   si                    ;   1 cy              UV  2
39              inc   si                    ;   1 cy              UV  3
40   main_3:
41              pop   dx                    ;   1 cy              UV  *
42              pop   cx                    ;   1 cy              UV  *
43              pop   bx                    ;   1 cy              UV  *
44              ret                         ;   2 cy              NP
46              main endp

48              proc2 proc near             ;Pentium cycles
50              push  bx                    ;   1 cy              UV  1
51              push  cx                    ;   1 cy              UV  *
52              push  dx                    ;   1 cy              UV  *
54   p0:
55              inc   di                    ;   1 cy              UV  *
56   p1:
57              inc   dx                    ;   1 cy              UV  *
58   p2:
59              add   si, 2                 ;   1 cy              UV  *
60              mov   ax, [si]              ;   1 cy              UV  4 AGI-1
61              mul   ax                    ;  10 cy /  11 cy NP
62              div   bx                    ;  17 cy /  41 cy NP
64              dec   cx                    ;   1 cy              UV  1
65              jnz   p2                    ;   1 cy              V   *
67              mul   ax                    ;  10 cy /  11 cy NP
68              div   bx                    ;  17 cy /  41 cy NP
69              dec   bx                    ;   1 cy              UV  1
70              jnz   p1                    ;   1 cy              V   *
72              add   ax, bx                ;   1 cy              UV  2
73              jnc   p0                    ;   1 cy              V   *
75              pop   dx                    ;   1 cy              UV  2
```

```
76              pop   cx                    ;   1 cy        UV   *
77              pop   bx                    ;   1 cy        UV   *
78              ret                         ;   2 cy        NP
80              proc2 endp
```

Notes: * = pairable with previous instruction
1 = previous instruction is NP (Not pairable)
2 = U and V pipe mismatch (previous not U or this one not V)
3 = repeated register destination (write after write)
4 = register conflict (read after write)
5 = stack pointer or flags register conflict (read after write)
6 = memory operand conflict (read or write after write)
AGI n = Address Generation Interlock on instruction -n

Running PENTOPT is simple; it requires only the name of the assembly language source file as a command line argument:

```
C:> pentopt sample.asm
```

The output is automatically sent to the screen in this case. To send the output to a file or a printer you must use DOS output redirection, as follows:

```
C:> pentopt sample.asm > output.txt
```

How It Works

The inner workings of PENTOPT are fairly complex; however, the basic functionality of the most interesting part works like this. PENTOPT examines each assembly source code statement and determines if the statement is a CPU instruction or not. If the statement is an instruction, then PENTOPT places the instruction in one of the following categories:

NP   not pairable
UV   pairable in U or V pipes
U   pairable in the U pipe only
V   pairable in the V pipe only

This category is printed in the notes column on the right of display. When an instruction is pairable in the V pipe, PENTOPT attempts to determine if the instruction could pair with the previous instruction. When pairing is possible, an asterisk is printed to the right of the category. The asterisk does NOT mean the instruction will pair in the V pipe, only that it is possible. The lack of an asterisk means pairing is not possible. If there is no asterisk and the instruction can sometimes be paired in the V pipe, then the reason for lack of pairing is given by a numerical code. These codes are shown at the bottom of Figure 11.1 on page 140.

The following is a list of situations where two instructions might not pair when pairing is possible (i.e., an asterisk is shown):

- the previous instruction is also pairable in the V pipe and paired in the V pipe
- the instruction may be the first instruction after a jump or call

ADDRESS GENERATION INTERLOCKS

In addition to the pairing information, AGIs are detected and shown to the right of the pairing information. (See Chapter 10 for a description of AGIs.) The AGI information includes the relative line number of the instruction that generates the address causing the conflict with the current instruction. Based on the actual run-time pairing that occurs, it is possible for an AGI to not occur when one is shown for an instruction two or three before the marked instruction.

On the 486, AGIs can also occur. However, they only occur for the case of the address being generated on the previous instruction. Therefore, when writing code that is only targeted at the 486, only AGI-1 is of interest.

Timing with a Software Timer

12

Since the measuring device has been constructed by the observer . . .
we have to remember that what we observe is not nature in itself
but nature exposed to our method of questioning.
—Werner Karl Heisenberg

Up until now the discussions about CPU cycle counts and pairing of instructions have been assumptions. You must check your assumptions by timing actual code. The Pentium has 8K of cache for code, so virtually every loop will run out of the cache and can be highly optimized. But you still need to time your code to see if it operates as expected.

There are at least three different methods to time Pentium code:

- Use a hardware device, such as an ICE
- Use the built-in Pentium timer
- Use software to control the PC's timer chips

ICE

Most programmers do not have access to an ICE (in-circuit emulator), so I'll just discuss this method in general terms. An ICE can trace and record every machine cycle in a high-speed circular RAM buffer. The size of the buffer determines the number of cycles that can be viewed when a breakpoint is reached. The great advantage is that you get to see exactly what happened during each cycle and, assuming the trace buffer is large enough, you can account for every cycle in a typical loop. The disadvantage is that an ICE is expensive, usually costing several times the price of a typical system. Also, new hardware is required for every CPU type.

BUILT-IN PENTIUM TIMER

Every Pentium has its own built-in timer. There is a new instruction (**RDTSC**—Read Time Stamp Counter) that is not fully documented by Intel. *The Intel Pentium Processor User's Manual, Volume 3: Architecture and Programming Manual,* does not list it anywhere except in Appendix A (in the opcode map) and in chapter 10 (in a description of the TSD bit, the Time Stamp Disable bit). There is no description of what the instruction is or what it does in the otherwise complete 291-page chapter that describes the instruction set.

Here is how the Pentium timer works. There is an internal 64-bit counter on the Pentium that is incremented on every cycle. This means that the timer accurate to 1 machine cycle with a range of up to 8,800 years (at 66 MHz). MASM 6.11 can assemble the **RDTSC** instruction, but on other assemblers you may need to use data bytes to insert the hex opcodes:

```
rdtsc              ; read time stamp counter
db 0Fh, 31h        ; equivalent hex opcodes for rdtsc
```

What **RDTSC** does is simple—it returns the value of the internal cycle counter in EDX:EAX. (EDX contains the high 32 bits, EAX contains the low 32 bits).

Here is a routine that uses this new instruction:

```
rdtsc
mov    start_low, eax
mov    start_hi, edx
call   test_proc
rdtsc
sub    eax, start_low
sbb    edx, start_hi
```

You can use **RDTSC** in any 16-bit real mode program. However, in protected mode the instruction may (optionally) be protected by the operating system. In this case **RDTSC** requires a protection level of ring 0. This means that a normal application (ring 3) can generate a protection violation. Protected mode programs can test a bit to determine if **RDTSC** is a privileged instruction. When bit 2 of CR4 is set to a one, it makes **RDTSC** a privileged instruction. A full discussion of the special registers is beyond the scope of this book. Simply put, however, there are several control registers (CRx), debug registers (DRx) and test registers (TRx) on the 386 and above. Writing to the control registers is a privileged operation but any application can read them. To see if **RDTSC** is privileged:

```
mov    eax, CR4
test   eax, 4
jz     ok
priv:
                        ; RDTSC privileged
ok:
                        ; RDTSC available
```

Even if **RDTSC** is privileged, this does not mean that it cannot be safely executed from a protected mode application. When the operating system gains control from the general protection fault it can choose to execute the instruction and return the results to the application as if it were not a privileged instruction. Because of this it is wise to use **RDTSC** in a manner that automatically subtracts out the overhead of reading the value twice by actually measuring the overhead on the fly.

SOFTWARE TIMER

The disadvantage of using the **RDTSC** instruction is that it makes your code Pentium-specific. I began using timing software when developing test code for the Pentium before there the chip was widely available. After learning of the **RDTSC** instruction I intended to abandon this timing method. However, I soon learned that it was sometimes a disadvantage to have code that was Pentium-specific. You may not have a Pentium machine yet, or may only have limited access to one. With a software timer you can run the same code on other machines, such as a 486. The choice of timing methods is yours to make depending on your situation.

I used the timer (included on the accompanying disk) to check the results of the examples in this book. Using this timer has several advantages. First, you can write and test programs that use the timer on any machine. Second, you can run the same code on several machines to compare performance from 386 to 486 to Pentium.

You must be more careful when timing Pentium code than timing other 80x86 code because the interaction of the code cache with instruction pairing is critical. Most instructions that are pairable will do so only on the second and subsequent executions from the cache. This means that the following test is NOT representative of true execution speed:

```
call   timer_on
rept   1000
```

```
mov   bx, 1              ; 1 cycle
mov   ax, 1              ; 1 cycle, 0 when paired
endm
call  timer_off
```

This test will give a result of 2,000 cycles. A better test would be:

```
call test1              ; preload cache with code and data
call timer_on           ; start timer
call test1              ; perform the test
call timer_off          ; stop timer
...
test1 proc
 rept 1000
 mov bx, 1              ; 1 cycle
 mov ax, 1              ; 1 cycle, 0 when paired
 endm
 ret
test1 endp
```

This test will give a result of about 1,006 cycles. You could try to remove the overhead due to the **CALL** and **RET** instructions, but it is not necessary for most calculations. In this case we learned that the two **MOV** instructions pair, taking only one cycle and not two cycles. Using repeat macros (**REPT nn ... ENDM**) is a handy way of duplicating code to test its speed. However, on the Pentium, be sure you understand precisely what it is you are actually measuring.

There are some things that can cause inaccuracies when using this method:

• The timer code and data affect the contents of the code and data caches. This may slow the timed procedure slightly.
• Do not attempt to time any code near the code cache size (8K) and expect to get meaningful results.
• Interrupts, cache load time, secondary cache size and type will all affect results.
• Preloading data, if any, into the cache will make your tested code appear to be faster than it may actually run.

The intent of this timing method is to show the best performance of a block of code, with the maximum instruction pairing occurring. This helps you determine if you have properly arranged instructions to pair and accounted for various delays, etc.

Depending on the purpose of a test, you can use different data each time a procedure is called, as follows:

```
lea  si, string1
lea  di, string1a
```

```
        mov    cx, 10000
        call   test2            ; preload cache with code and data
        lea    si, string2
        lea    di, string2a
        mov    cx, 10000
        call   timer_on         ; start timer
        call   test2            ; perform the test
        call   timer_off        ; stop timer
        ...
test2 proc
        mov    al, [si]         ; copy string test
        inc    si
        mov    [di], al
        inc    di
        test   al, al
        loopne test2
        ret
test2   endp
```

In this case, with a large string and a small loop, it is unnecessary to call the test procedure before timing it because the difference in the number of instruction pairings would be very small relative to the number of iterations in the loop.

Depending on what you are trying to measure, here are some general rules for ensuring you are testing the fastest, repeatable execution speed:

- Code and data must be aligned on dword boundaries
- Strings should be small enough to fit entirely in the data cache
- All code and data should be preloaded into the cache
- Use code that represents your application (i.e., are you moving data between segments; do you have misaligned data?)

TIMER SOFTWARE FUNCTION REFERENCE

The following is a list of each function in the timer library on the disk. There are six versions of the library on the disk, as follows:

TTIMER.lib	Tiny model
STIMER.lib	Small model
CTIMER.lib	Compact model
MTIMER.lib	Medium model
LTIMER.lib	Large model
TIMER32.LIB	32-bit protected mode

For example, to use the timer in a small model DOS program you would link as follows:

```
C:> link sample,,,stimer;
```

To use the timer in a 32-bit protected mode program (see Chapter 18) you would link as follows:

```
C:> link sample32,,,timer32;
```

Timer_init   The **timer_init** function initializes timer variables for performing multiple tests of the same code. See **timer_show_average**. This is not required for the simple case of timing a section of code and immediately printing the results.

Timer_on   Starts the timer. In real mode, interrupts should be disabled (by using **CLI**) before this call for is made. In protected mode **CLI** cannot be used because it may cause a general protection (GP) fault.

Timer_off   Stops the timer and records the elapsed time for later use. This function returns one of the following values in the AL register:
0   success
1   error, timer overflow (event too long, maximum is about 0.0549 seconds)
2   error, timer underflow (event too short, minimum is about 0.0000025 seconds or 2.5 microseconds)
3   error, overhead too large (similar to underflow, the internal routine to determine overhead is greater than the timed event. Normally this is less than 2.5 microseconds.)

Timer_show   Display the results of the last single timed event to the screen (STDOUT). The results are displayed in the default format, which is in microseconds. This can be changed with **timer_set_format.**

Timer_show_ticks   Display the results of the last single timed event to the screen (STDOUT). The results are displayed in number of clock ticks. Each clock tick is approximately 0.8381 microseconds.

Timer_show_microseconds   Display the results of the last single timed event to the screen (STDOUT). The results are displayed in microseconds.

Timer_show_average   Display the average of the last group of timed events to the screen (STDOUT). The results are displayed in the default format, which is in microseconds. This can be changed with **timer_set_format**. See **timer_init**.

Timer_set_format   Sets the default output format for **timer_show** and **timer_show_average**. The AL register must contain a 0 for the clock tick format and a 1 for the microsecond format.

Timer_write   Converts a value of timer clock ticks to an ASCII string then writes the resulting string to the specified file or the screen. The inputs are:

```
AX    ticks
BX    file handle for output (i.e. 1 = stdout)
```

Timer_ticks_to_ascii   Converts the specified timer clock ticks to an ASCII string. The inputs are:

```
AX       timer ticks
DS:SI    pointer to 5 byte buffer for ASCII string
```

Timer_ticks_to_microsec   Converts the specified timer clock ticks to microseconds. The inputs are:

```
AX    timer ticks
```

Outputs:

```
AX    microseconds
```

Percent Speed Changes

In this book I will show percent changes in speed based on the following formula:

$$\%\text{change} = \left(\frac{T1 - T2}{T1} - 1 \right) \times 100 \ , \hspace{2cm} \text{(Formula 1)}$$

where: $T1$ = first time, $T2$ = second time.

The times can be in any units as long as they are both the same, i.e. cycles, seconds or microseconds. For example, a change from 20 seconds to 10 seconds would be stated as a 100% improvement. One could argue that only half the time was eliminated, thus it should be expressed as a 50% improvement, using this formula:

$$\% \text{ change} = \left(\frac{T1 - T2}{T1} \right) \times 100 \qquad \text{(Formula 2)}$$

However, when subsequent comparisons are made to code taking fewer cycles, these improvements would tend to seem minor. See the table following for an example.

	$T1$	$T2$	Formula 1	Formula 2	Formula 2 ($T1$ = previous $T2$)
1.	20	10	100%	50%	—
2.	20	8	150%	60%	20%
3.	20	6	233%	70%	25%
4.	20	4	400%	80%	33%
5.	20	2	900%	90%	50%

As each two seconds are eliminated from the original code it appears that each second has the same effect with formula 2. Using formula 2 with the previous $T2$ as the basis ($T1$) does show an increasing importance of each second eliminated as the time diminishes. However, when discussing the performance improvement of one portion of code over another it is fairly clear that two seconds is 10 times as fast 20 seconds, which is a 900% improvement.

Superscalar Pentium Programming

Optimization Warm-ups

13

The difference between the almost-right word and the right word is really a large matter—it's the difference between the lightning bug and the lightning.
—Mark Twain

With all the groundwork set in the previous chapters, we're now ready for some real optimizing.

The "optimization" process starts early in the development cycle. It should really start even before choosing an algorithm. The requirements of the project should clearly define the performance criteria. But that rarely happens. The design includes, among other details, your choice of data structures and algorithms. Your data structures and algorithms will have the most drastic impact on performance in all but the most extreme cases.

There are many sources of information on good algorithms, including your colleagues, on-line information services and books. My favorite book for algorithms is *Algorithms* by Robert Sedgewick, Addison Wesley. I don't know how long I would have studied Quicksort before understanding it without this book. A few hours spent working with the correct algorithms will almost always pay off more than days of code twiddling—"an ounce of design is worth a pound of debugging."

For the most part, the optimizations in this book are focused on replacing almost-right instructions with the right instructions.

In this chapter and the next we'll attempt various techniques for optimizing code that operates on strings. Keep in mind, although many routines operate on ASCII string data, this is not a requirement. In most cases, with few modifications, the string could just as easily be structures of numbers or graphics data.

You'll also notice we're going to be primarily interested in working with small loops. We'll be doing this for several reasons. First, small loops of code are ideal for learning superscalar programming techniques. Second, these loops are of great practical use for everyday programming. And third, optimizing the innermost loops in any routine usually provides the best first level of optimization for the Pentium. Optimizing code that does not run in a loop on the Pentium may not speed up the code at all.

STRING INSTRUCTION OPTIMIZATIONS

Consider the following code I wrote in the early 1980s for the 8086. This code copies an ASCIIZ string (a string of ASCII characters terminated with a null byte).

```
lbl:                                                    (Listing 13.1)
   lodsb                ; load a byte
   stosb                ; store a byte
   or     al, al        ; check for a null
   jne    lbl           ; loop if not a null
```

An alternative to writing the code with the string instructions is to use the combination of the corresponding **MOV** and **INC** for the **LODSB** and **STOSB** (see Figure 13.1b). This does not duplicate the original function exactly, since **STOSB** uses the ES segment by default. Adding a segment override to the second **MOV** in Figure 13.1b would do this and change the cycle counts by 1 or 2 on some CPUs. Throughout all the examples, unless stated otherwise, I will assume the code has been rearranged to eliminate segment overrides, or some initialization code has made this unnecessary. When required to perform intra-segment operations, such as a copy from one segment to another, the code will be slower. I will defer discussing this until the end of this section.

As each new CPU was introduced over the last decade, I reviewed code such as the string copy to see if it would benefit from being changed. On the 8088 through the 386, string instructions are generally better or equal in performance to simple load and store instructions. On the 486 (being more RISC-like), simple load and store instructions tend to perform better. Although string operations on the 486 do not continue to measure up in speed, they are still more compact (in this case, 6 bytes vs. 11). With the Pentium, the speed up is dramatic—from 6 cycles to 3, a (theoretical) 100% speed-up, while on the 486 the speed-up is 75% (14 to 8 cycles). Notice that in the figures I have indicated the number of cycles for each Pentium instruction assuming no pairing

Figure 13.1 ASCIIZ String Copy with Max String Length

(a)   (Listing 13.2)

		8088	286	386	486	Pent.	w/pair	bytes
loop1:								
lodsb		16	5	5	5	2	2	1
stosb		15	3	4	5	3	3	1
or	al, al	3	2	2	1	1	1	2
jne	loop1	16	8	8	3	1	1	2
		50	18	19	14	7	7	6

(b)   (Listing 13.3)

		8088	286	386	486	Pent.	w/pair	bytes
loop2:								
mov	al, [si]	17	5	4	1	1	1	2
inc	si	3	2	2	1	1	0	1
mov	[di], al	18	4	2	1	1	1	2
inc	di	3	2	2	1	1	0	1
cmp	al, 0	4	3	2	1	1	1	2
jne	loop2	16	9	8	3	1	0	2
		61	25	20	8	6	3	11

Notes: w/pair = cycles with pairing   bytes = instruction length in bytes

occurs. In the next column (titled "w/pair") the cycles are given assuming pairing occurs according to the pairing rules. An instruction that executes in the V pipe will show the number of cycles beyond those required for the U pipe instruction (usually 0).

We've seen that some 80x86 string instructions are slower than executing the simple move and increment instructions, since the simple instructions can be paired and execute in a single cycle. In addition the **CMP/Jcc** (or **TEST/Jcc**) combination can be paired so this is also executed in a single cycle. See Table 13.1. (We'll cover the repeat string instructions later.)

As an exercise: Further optimize the Figure 13.1b code from 3 cycles per byte to 2 cycles per byte.

The next example (see Figure 13.2) is an ASCIIZ string copy with a limitation on the maximum string length. This example shows that **LOOPNE** (also **LOOPE**) is much slower than the equivalent **Jcc/DEC/Jcc**. Again, the **LODSB** and **STOSB** are replaced with **MOV/INC** pairings. This reduces the Pentium cycle count from 13 to 4 cycles, a 225% speed-up.

Table 13.1 CPU Cycles for String and Related Instructions

	486	Pentium	Pairing
`MOV reg, mem`	1	1	UV
`MOV mem, reg`	1	1	UV
`INC/DEC reg`	1	1	UV
`TEST/CMP reg, reg/imm`	1	1	UV
`Jcc`	1/3*	1**	PV
`LODS`	5	2	NP
`STOS`	5	3	NP
`REP` `MOVS` repeat move string	3	1	NP
`REP` `STOS` repeat store string	4	1	NP
`REPE/NE` `CMPS` repeat while (not) equal compare	7	4	NP
`REPE/NE` `SCAS` repeat while (not) equal scan	5	4	NP

Notes: UV = pairable in U or V pipes
         PV = pairable in V pipe
         NP = not pairable
         Jcc = jump on condition code
         * = 1 for no jump, 3 for jump
         ** = assumes correct branch prediction
         string cycles are per repeated element

In our next example, we'll copy a string of known length from one location to another. You've seen the detailed cycle counts for each CPU in the first examples, so I won't show them in future examples. Instead, only the Pentium cycles will be shown, since this provides the most relevant information. Here is a good way to copy a fixed length string:

```
rep    movsb          ; 1 cycle per byte
```

Here is a way to do the same thing using only simple instructions:

```
lbl:                  ; cycles                    (Listing 13.5)
    mov al, [si]      ; 1    read a byte
    inc si            ; 0    advance ptr
    mov di], al       ; 1    store a byte
    inc di            ; 0    advance ptr
    dec cx            ; 1    dec loop count
    jnz lbl           ; 0    loop while CX not 0
                      ; ---
                      ; 3 cycles per byte
```

Figure 13.2 ASCIIZ String Copy with Max String Length

(a) (Listing 13.3)

		8088	286	386	486	Pent.	w/pair
loop3:							
lodsb		16	5	5	5	2	2
stosb		15	3	4	5	3	3
or	al, al	3	2	2	1	1	1
loopne	loop3	19	10	13	9	7	7
		53	20	24	20	13	13

(b) (Listing 13.4)

		8088	286	386	486	Pent.	w/pair
loop4:							
mov	al, [si]	17	12	4	1	1	1
inc	si	3	2	2	1	1	0
mov	[di], al	18	9	2	1	1	1
inc	di	3	2	2	1	1	0
cmp	al, 0	4	3	2	1	1	1
je	exit4	4	3	3	1	1	0
dec	cx	3	2	2	1	1	1
jnz	loop4	16	9	8	3	1	0
exit 4:							
		68	42	25	10	8	4

Notes: w/pair = cycles with pairing   bytes = instruction length in bytes

This shows that not every complex string operation can take advantage of the two Pentium pipelines and be faster. On the other hand, maybe the **REP MOVSB** instruction *is* using both pipes on the Pentium. (Intel doesn't document how various instructions are implemented, but they have said the Pentium uses both pipes for some non-pairable instructions.) There are faster ways to copy strings than the **REP MOVSB** instruction. If we knew that there was an even number of bytes, we could just use half the number of words.

```
shr  cx, 1      ; divide byte count by 2 (remainder to CF) (Listing 13.6)
rep  movsw      ; move words
rcl  cx, 1      ; restore CF to CX
rep  movsb      ; move 0 or 1 byte
```

or

```
shr  cx, 1          ; divide byte count by 2 (remainder to CF)
rep  movsw          ; move words
jnc  exit           ; check CF, exit if not set
movsb               ; move 1 byte
exit:
```

We could also move four bytes at a time:

```
mov  ax, cx         ; save copy of byte count                  (Listing 13.7)
shr  cx, 2          ; divide by 4 to get dword count
rep  movsd          ; move dwords
mov  cx, ax         ; restore byte count
and  cx, 3          ; get low 2 bits (div by 4 remainder)
rep  movsb          ; move 0 to 3 bytes
```

The code in Figure 13.1b could be rewritten several ways to handle words or dwords instead of only bytes. Each method has its own design trade-offs. For example, we could rewrite the code like this:

```
lbl:                ; cycles                                   (Listing 13.8)
  mov  ax, [si]     ; 1    read a word
  add  si, 2        ; 0    advance ptr
  mov  [di], ax     ; 1    store a word
  add  di, 2        ; 0    advance ptr
  cmp  al, 0        ; 1    check for null in 1st byte
  je   exit         ; 0    exit if end of string
  cmp  ah, 0        ; 1    check for null in 2nd byte
  jnz  lbl          ; 0    continue loop if not end of string
exit:               ; ---
                    ; 4 cycles -- 2 cycles per byte
```

This code copies a byte every two cycles, compared with three cycles in the previous code. The design trade-off is that there is a 50% chance that this loop will copy an extra byte past the null. This may or may not be a problem in your code. This example does not have this side effect:

```
lbl:                ; cycles                                   (Listing 13.9)
  mov  ax, [si]     ; 1    read a word
  add  si, 2        ; 0    advance ptr
  mov  [di], al     ; 1    store 1st byte
  add  di, 2        ; 0    advance ptr
  cmp  al, 0        ; 1    check for null in 1st byte
  je   exit         ; 0    exit if end of string
  mov  [di-1], ah   ; 1    store 2nd byte
```

```
        cmp  ah, 0            ; 0  check for null in 2nd byte
        jne  lbl             ; 1  continue loop if not end of string
    exit:                    ; ---
                             ; 5 cycles -- 2.5 cycles per byte
```

The trade-off for ensuring that an extra byte past the null is not copied appears to be 0.5 extra cycle per byte (2.5 cycles vs. 2.0 cycles). However, here is a way to code the string copy with no extra byte being copied:

```
    lbl:                     ; cycles                               (Listing 13.10)
        mov  ax, [si]        ; 1  read a word
        add  si, 2           ; 0  advance ptr
        cmp  al, 0           ; 1  check for null in 1st byte
        je   exit2           ; 0  exit if end of string
        mov  [di], ax        ; 1  store two bytes
        add  di, 2           ; 0  advance ptr
        cmp  ah, 0           ; 1  check for null in 2nd byte
        jne  lbl             ; 0  continue loop if not end of string
    exit:                    ; ---
        jmp  exit3           ; 4 cycles -- 2 cycles per byte
    exit2:
        mov  [di], al
    exit3:
```

On the Pentium, it is especially wise to work for these types of optimizations. Saving one or two cycles per loop on the 8088, or even the 386, may not noticeably increase performance. Saving one or two cycles is a lot when loops take only 3 to 10 cycles per iteration on the Pentium.

Here is the same code as before, but I have now included the segment override required for copying data from one segment to another:

```
    lbl:                     ; cycles                               (Listing 13.11)
        mov  ax, [si]        ; 1  read a word
        add  si, 2           ; 0  advance ptr
        cmp  al, 0           ; 1  check for null in 1st byte
        je   exit2           ; 0  exit if end of string
        mov  ES:[di], ax     ; 2  store two bytes
        add  di, 2           ; 0  advance ptr
        cmp  ah, 0           ; 1  check for null in 2nd byte
        jne  lbl             ; 0  continue loop if not end of string
    exit:                    ; ---
        jmp  exit3           ; 5 cycles -- 2.5 cycles per byte
    exit2:
        mov  ES:[di], al
    exit3:
```

Because the segment override (**ES:**) is on the instruction that executes in the U pipe, there is a one-cycle penalty. If we had added the segment override to an instruction that would have executed in the V pipe, pairing would not occur. This would, effectively, be a two-cycle penalty.

When an example is shown with 32-bit code, it is intended to be run as 32-bit code in a USE32 segment. Generally this code must be run from Windows NT, OS/2 2.x or from a 32-bit DOS extender (also see Chapter 18 for a 32-bit DPMI example). Although 32-bit instructions can be mixed with 16-bit instructions, only the native instruction size performs at full speed. The non-native instruction size incurs a one-cycle delay and can pair only in the U pipe. Even with this restriction it may be advantageous to mix 16- and 32-bit code.

Here is a 32-bit example of a string copy:

```
lbl:                                          (Listing 13.12)
    mov    eax, [esi]    ; 1
    add    esi, 4        ; 0
    mov    [edi], eax    ; 1
    add    edi, 4        ; 0
    cmp    al, 0         ; 1
    jz     exit          ; 0
    cmp    ah, 0         ; 1
    jz     exit          ; 0
    bswap  eax           ; 1
    cmp    al, 0         ; 1
    jz     exit          ; 0
    cmp    ah, 0         ; 1
    jne    lbl           ; 0
exit:                    ; ---
                         ; 7 cycles -- 1.75 cycles per byte
```

This code writes up to three extra bytes and takes only 1.75 cycles per byte. This is about as close to the speed of the **REP MOVSB** instruction as we can get. But remember, this string copy example checks each byte for the end of the string. How could we possibly make it any faster?

The only way I have come up with is to require our strings to have extra nulls at the end. For example, to handle two bytes at a time we could require an extra two nulls, and for four-byte copies, six extra nulls. The fastest (maybe) code would then be:

```
lbl:                                          (Listing 13.13)
    mov eax, [esi]    ; 1
    add esi, 4        ; 0
    mov [edi], eax    ; 1
    add edi, 4        ; 0
    test eax, eax     ; 1
    jne lbl           ; 0
exit:                 ; ---
                      ; 3 cycles -- 0.75 cycles per byte
```

This shows that for applications where you can control the data specification, you can more than double the speed.

Some readers may feel the problems and solutions presented so far have been arranged in less than an ideal order. This is intentional. I want to encourage you to try various solutions to problems, then code and test them. You've seen that there is not a single solution to a simple string copy, much less a more complex problem.

These string copy examples are just the beginning of what can be done on the Pentium. Also recall that these operations are not limited in use to text strings. We have taken an apparently simple operation, usable in most every major application, and shown how it can be changed to produce speed improvements of up to 900%. We started with a 50-cycle loop on the 8088 (7 on the Pentium) and have seen how to improve it to 1.75 cycles and as little as 0.75 cycles with a minor data format requirement.

String Search and Translate

14

*I don't like work—no man does—
but I like what is in work: The
chance to find yourself.*
—Joseph Conrad

It's the middle of the night and the phone rings. I let the answering machine answer —who would be calling at this time? A man has been lost in the mountains at a state park for two days. Meet at the park's entrance in one hour.

I'm a member of my county's search and rescue (SAR) team and this was my first search in this area. I've hiked and climbed in this park more than a hundred times in the past 12 years, so I was very familiar with the area, or so I thought. At sunrise I began searching a trail with a dog team. The only thing we found was that the maps and the trails did not match very well. I'd been all over the park, but not in this particular area.

Another dog had picked up a scent trail on the opposite side of the park. So, in the afternoon I was sent with another searcher to this area which is closer to the areas that I frequent. From the topo map it looked as if the two of us could easily cover the area before dark. We searched for four hours in the dense vegetation off the trails. We did find that we were easily disoriented because the steep angle and dense vegetation blocked our view of any landmarks. We became so wrapped up in finding our way back up to the trail that we really didn't know half of where we had been. We may have covered 20% of the area.

I remember thinking how well I know this area, but when forced to go to places I'd only looked at, I was not much better at navigation than someone new to the area. I discovered what I really knew was a few major landmarks and several miles of trails. I have also found this to be true for the 80x86 instruction set. Until you actually have experience with all the various instructions, used them and been bitten by various bugs in your software, the descriptions might as well be a trail map with half the trails missing.

STRING SEARCH

Appropriately enough, our next topic for optimization is string searching.

Much work has been done on algorithms for efficient string searching. The problem can be generally stated as finding the occurrence of a given string pattern within a given text string. (If a large file is being searched, it is read into a buffer in blocks.) Complicated techniques such as the Boyer–Moore algorithm and the Knuth–Morris–Pratt algorithm have been shown to be more efficient on a theoretical basis, but the brute force method has been highly optimized by the 80x86 architecture. The brute force method involves scanning the text string for a match of the first character of the string pattern. If a match is found, then the rest of the pattern is checked. Scanning then continues on the character after the initial match. This algorithm works well when there are relatively low number of scan matches and a small pattern. It is fast because the inner loop for this type of routine that has only one instruction:

```
                         ;          8088 286 386 486 Pentium
      repne scasb        ; cycles: 15    8   8   5    4
```

As you can see, **REPxx SCASB** has always been quite fast for the work it can accomplish. However, the Pentium changes things a little. The branch prediction logic and instruction pairing of the Pentium allow the **REPNE SCASB** instruction to be recoded and replaced by the following code, which is one cycle faster:

```
                   ; (note: DL holds byte to match)      (Listing 14.1)
lbl:               ; cycles
    mov al, [di]   ; 1   read a char
    inc di         ; 0   advance mem ptr
    cmp al, dl     ; 1   compare with scan char
    je  exit       ; 0   exit (not shown) if a match
    dec cx         ; 1
    jnz lbl        ; 0
                   ; ---
                   ; 3 cycles per byte
```

This loop runs at three cycles per byte, and we've just begun optimizing. There are six execution slots (two per cycle), and two of them are for loop control. We can make this faster by processing two bytes per loop and adding some other code (not shown) to handle an odd byte:

```
lbl:                    ; cycles                              (Listing 14.2)
   mov  ax, [di]        ; 1   read two char's
   add  di, 2           ; 0   advance mem ptr
   cmp  al, dl          ; 1   compare 1st with scan char
   je   exit1           ; 0   exit (not shown) if a match
   cmp  ah, dl          ; 1   compare 2nd with scan char
   je   exit2           ; 0   exit (not shown) if a match
   dec  cx              ; 1
   jnz  lbl             ; 0
                        ; ---
                        ; 4 cycles, 2 cycles per byte
```

Following this same trend, we can process four bytes per loop. This creates more auxiliary code to handle the odd 0 to 3 bytes and saves only 0.25 cycles per byte (about 12%):

```
lbl:                    ; cycles                              (Listing 14.3)
   mov  ax, [di]        ; 1   read two char's
   mov  bx, [di+2]      ; 0   read two more char's
   cmp  al, dl          ; 1   compare 1st with scan char
   je   exit1           ; 0   exit (not shown) if a match
   cmp  ah, dl          ; 1   compare 2nd with scan char
   je   exit2           ; 0   exit (not shown) if a match
   cmp  bl, dl          ; 1   compare 3rd with scan char
   je   exit3           ; 0   exit (not shown) if a match
   cmp  bh, dl          ; 1   compare 4th with scan char
   je   exit4           ; 0   exit (not shown) if a match
   add  di, 4           ; 1   advance ptr
   dec  cx              ; 0
   jnz  lbl             ; 1
                        ; ---
                        ; 7 cycles, 1.75 cycles per byte
```

For most purposes, this brute-force method, using **REPNE SCASB** provides excellent performance on the 8088–486. On the Pentium, the brute-force method has come full circle to using discrete instructions. This last implementation is more than twice the speed of the **REPNE SCASB**.

There is one problem with the preceding code. Recall from Chapter 10 the one-cycle delay that can be caused by a data-cache memory bank conflict. The only way this won't happen in the preceding code is if the starting address is on an even word boundary but not an even dword boundary. Randomly, this would occur only 25% of the time. The following code takes care of this problem:

```
lbl:                    ; cycles                          (Listing 14.4)
  mov ax, [di]          ; 1   read two char's
  add di, 4             ; 0   advance ptr
  cmp al, dl            ; 1   compare 1st with scan char
  je  exit1             ; 0   exit (not shown) if a match
  mov bx, [di-2]        ; 1   read two more char's
  cmp ah, dl            ; 0   compare 2nd with scan char
  je  exit2             ; 1   exit (not shown) if a match
  cmp bl, dl            ; 1   compare 3rd with scan char
  je  exit3             ; 0   exit (not shown) if a match
  cmp bh, dl            ; 1   compare 4th with scan char
  je  exit4             ; 0   exit (not shown) if a match
  dec cx                ; 1
  jnz lbl               ; 0
                        ; ---
                        ; 7 cycles, 1.75 cycles per byte
```

There are a number of algorithm optimizations that can be applied to this method. A popular one, when searching ASCII text files, is to search for a character other than the first character in the string to be matched. The idea is to search for a character that is least likely to appear in the text being searched. When searching for the word "easy," for example, the scan would look for the letter "y" since it probably occurs at a lower frequency than any of the other letters in the word. Of course, it would be wise to know the frequency distribution for your specific data before applying this optimization.

String Translations

In this example, we'll start with a loop that converts a string to lowercase. The same loop could be used to perform any translation on a string depending on the translation table that is used. Let's take a look:

```
      lea si, string      ; load ptr to string            (Listing 14.5)
      mov cx, max_str_len ; get maximum length of string
      lea bx, tbl         ; load ptr to translation table
                          ; tbl is a 256-byte table of translations
                          ; for any purpose, such as converting
                          ; to lowercase.
lbl:                      ; cycles
      lodsb               ; 2   read a byte
      xlatb               ; 3   translate in table
      mov [si-1], al      ; 1   store translation
      test al, al         ; 1   check for end of string
```

```
loopnz lbl          ; 7  loop if not done
                    ; ---
                    ; 14 cycles
```

This loop is pretty simple. It reads characters from a string one at a time, translates them via a table, stores the new value and then checks for the end of the string (a null). In addition, there is a maximum number of characters specified in CX as an alternate means of terminating the loop. If the string length were known, we could write the code as follows:

```
lbl:                ; cycles                    (Listing 14.6)
  lodsb             ; 2  read a byte
  xlatb             ; 3  translate in table
  mov [si-1], al    ; 1  store translation
  loop lbl          ; 5  loop if not done
                    ; ---
                    ; 11 cycles
```

To optimize for the Pentium, the first thing that we need to do is to convert everything to use the simple instructions. Here are two slightly different ways of doing that:

```
lbl:                ; cycles                              (Listing 14.7)
  mov bl, [si]      ; 1
  mov al, tbl[bx]   ; 2 <-- AGI delay
  mov [si], al      ; 1 <-- register conflict, no pairing
  inc si            ; 0
  test al, al       ; 1
  jz  done          ; 0
  dec cx            ; 1
  jnz lbl           ; 0
done:               ; ---
                    ; 6 cycles
```

```
lbl:                ; cycles                              (Listing 14.8)
  mov bl, [si]      ; 1
  inc si            ; 0
  mov al, tbl[bx]   ; 2 <-- AGI delay
  mov [si-1], al    ; 1 <-- register conflict, no pairing
  test al, al       ; 0
  jz  done          ; 1
  dec cx            ; 0
  jnz lbl           ; 1
done:               ;---
                    ; 6 cycles
```

Although both attempts produce code that is more than twice as fast as the original (6 vs. 14 cycles) they could both be improved. (Eliminating the test for the end of string could save one cycle, if the string length were known.) Both loops have an address generation interlock (AGI) and a lack of pairing because of a register conflict. The register conflict and the AGI can be removed by reading ahead. That is, we preload the loop with the first character, then the first time through the loop we read the second character, while we are manipulating the first character, and so on:

```
        mov  bl, [si]          ;      read first byte        (Listing 14.9)
        inc  si
lbl:                           ; cycles
        mov  al, tbl[bx]       ; 1   translate in table
        mov  bl, [si]          ; 0   read second byte
        mov  [si-1], al        ; 1   store translation of first byte
        inc  si               ; 0   advance ptr
        test al, al            ; 1   check for null
        jz   done              ; 0   exit if end of string
        dec  cx                ; 1
        jnz  lbl               ; 0   loop if not done
done:                          ; ---
                               ; 4
```

This cleans up the problems, so we might think we are done. We have full pairing and we're using eight out of eight execution slots. But we can still do more.

Atomic Programming

By knowing the best performance we could achieve, we gain a better understanding of when to stop trying to improve performance. Here is the method I have used to gauge what is the best performance. The first step is to think in what I call "atomic" operations. Atomic operations are single CPU functions that cannot be made more simple (along the lines of RISC processor actions). Properly selected and arranged atomic operations can be executed two at a time, or one per pipeline. There are four atomic steps required to translate a string:

- read a char
- read the translation
- store the result
- advance the pointer to the next position

When these four operations are properly arranged in the two pipelines, they will take only two cycles. Managing a loop takes two atomic operations, a decrement and a conditional jump. Checking for a null byte terminating a string requires an additional two atomic operations. Thus, it is theoretically possible to write a string translation loop that takes four cycles per byte. And we've already done that.

Do not be seduced by the simplicity of this method into blindly believing you have achieved an optimum result. We are assuming that we have chosen the best algorithm and correctly identified the atomic operations. In this case it is possible to do better than four cycles per byte because only three cycles are required—the loop overhead can be eliminated by duplicating the code inline, or unrolling the loop.

CAUTION
While the use of unrolling is very useful on the 8088–486, on the Pentium it can backfire, making the code slower.

Instruction pairing requires the U pipe instruction to be only one byte in length or to have already been executed from the cache. Instructions that are pairable and only one byte in length are rare (see Appendix F). The first time through a loop, there may be no pairing, possibly doubling the execution time. This extreme optimization effort should only be made for loops that will execute many times.

Here is a loop that processes two bytes per iteration:

```
      mov  bl, [si]                              (Listing 14.10)
      inc  si
lbl:                    ; cycles
      mov  al, tbl[bx]  ; 1   translate first byte
      mov  dx, [si]     ; 0   read second and third bytes
      mov  [si-1], al   ; 1   store translation of first byte
      mov  bl, dl       ; 0   move second byte
      test al, al       ; 1   check for null
      jz   done         ; 0   exit if end of string
      mov  al, tbl[bx]  ; 1   translate second byte
      mov  bl, dh       ; 0   move third byte for next loop
      mov  [si], al     ; 1   store translation of second byte
      test al, al       ; 0   check for null
      jz   done         ; 1   exit if end of string
      add  si, 2        ; 0   advance ptr
      dec  cx           ; 1
      jnz  lbl          ; 0   loop if not done
done:                   ; ---
                        ; 7 total    3.5 per byte
```

Adding code to process four bytes per iteration would be 13 cycles or 3.25 cycles per byte. Keep in mind, the more complex that a loop is made (i.e., the handling of more bytes), the more complex it becomes to write the code outside of the loop to handle the odd bytes. Sometimes loops can be arranged so that the odd bytes can be handled by jumping into the middle of the loop, as follows:

```
       mov  bl, [si]          ; read ahead first byte            (Listing 14.11)
       inc  si
       shr  cx, 1             ; divide byte count by 2 to get word count
       jnc  lbl              ; check for no odd byte
       inc  cx               ; handle odd byte by increasing count,
       inc  si               ;   moving ptr ahead
       jmp  lbl2             ;   then jumping into middle of loop

   lbl:                       ; cycles
       mov  al, tbl[bx]       ; 1   translate first byte
       mov  bl, [si]          ; 0   read second byte
       mov  [si-1], al        ; 1   store translation of first byte
       add  si, 2             ; 0   advance ptr
       test al, al            ; 1   check for null
       jz   done              ; 1   exit if end of string
   lbl2:
       mov  al, tbl[bx]       ; 0   translate second byte
       mov  bl, [si-1]        ; 1   read first byte for next loop
       mov  [si-2], al        ; 0   store translation of second byte
       test al, al            ; 1   check for null
       jz   done              ; 0   exit if end of string
       dec  cx               ; 1
       jnz  lbl              ; 0   loop if not done
   done:                      ; ---
                              ; 7 total    3.5 per byte
```

The loop needed to be more than just rearranged to be able to entered in the middle. I presented the last two examples this way for a purpose. These were my first attempts at writing this routine, and they show some awkwardness and imperfections (not that any code is ever perfect). But you should not get the idea you will start writing dual pipeline code and instantly be proficient. There will be a period of stumbling and restarting while you learn the rules and test your code.

The first string translation with two bytes per loop is slightly more conventional because it advances the pointer at the end of the loop. Initially, I thought that it might be best to read two bytes at a time. Once I began this way it was difficult to see another way to write the code, until I forced myself into thinking about it from a different angle. This angle was the ability to enter the loop in the middle to handle the odd byte.

By removing the end-of-string tests we have this code:

```
       mov  bl, [si]                                            (Listing 14.12)
       inc  si
   lbl:                       ; cycles
       mov  al, tbl[bx]       ; 1   translate first byte
       mov  bl, [si]          ; 0   read second byte
       mov  [si-1], al        ; 1   store translation of first byte
       mov  al, tbl[bx]       ; 0   translate second byte
       mov  bl, [si+1]        ; 1   read first byte for next loop
```

```
        mov  [si], al        ; 0*  store translation of second byte
        add  si, 2           ; 1   advance ptr
        dec  cx              ; 0
        jnz  lbl             ; 1
                             ; ---
                             ; 5 total   2.5 per byte
```

The operation of this loop should be studied in detail. This could be a model of properly interleaved instructions on two data streams from one string. The problem is that the fifth and sixth instructions both access memory in adjacent bytes. This may cause a one-cycle delay because of a data-cache memory bank conflict. The delay will be 100% of the time if the data is aligned on an even word boundary and 50% of the time if the data is aligned on an odd byte.

One way to fix this might be to make the second byte processed in each loop be offset five bytes ahead of the first byte instead of one. But this wouldn't completely eliminate the delays, because the memory bank conflict occurs when reading the first byte to be processed in the next loop (ahead two bytes from the first byte in the current loop). If we start seven bytes ahead, we will not have any conflicts. This will require us to have special code to handle bytes two, four and six in advance:

(Listing 14.13)

```
      mov  bl, [si]
      inc  si
lbl:                         ; cycles
      mov  al, tbl[bx]       ; 1   translate first byte
      mov  bl, [si+6]        ; 0   read second byte (+7 from first byte)
      mov  [si-1], al        ; 1   store translation of first byte
      mov  al, tbl[bx]       ; 0   translate second byte
      mov  bl, [si+1]        ; 1   read first byte for next loop
      mov  [si+6], al        ; 0   store translation of second byte
      add  si, 2             ; 1   advance ptr
      dec  cx               ; 0
      jnz  lbl              ; 1
                            ; ---
                            ; 5 total   2.5 per byte
```

Besides the preceding example, I tried about six other ways to modify this code, before I discovered that I could add a NOP to speed it up:

(Listing 14.14)

```
lbl:                         ; cycles
      mov  al, tbl[bx]       ; 1   translate first byte
      mov  bl, [si]         ; 0   read second byte
      mov  [si-1], al        ; 1   store translation of first byte
      mov  al, tbl[bx]       ; 0   translate second byte
      mov  bl, [si+1]        ; 1   read first byte for next loop
      nop                   ; 0   NOP to prevent bank conflict
```

```
mov [si], al         ; 1   store translation of second byte
add si, 2            ; 0   advance ptr
dec cx              ; 1
jnz lbl             ; 0
                    ; ---
                    ; 5 total   2.5 per byte
```

CODING CHALLENGE

You may be thinking, "If we used 32-bit code, then we could get twice the performance." Probably not, and here's why. Look back at the atomic operations. What would be different for 32-bit code? I can't think of anything. However, one method that might speed up the code would be to use a 64K lookup table, therefore translating two bytes at the same time. The main disadvantage of this method is that the 64K table would be accessed randomly, constantly refilling the data cache, and probably slowing the loop. A data cache miss incurs a three-cycle delay. So even if a loop could process four bytes in the same (theoretical) five cycles, there would usually be a six-cycle delay.

Here's the challenge. Rewrite the translation code to be *less* than two cycles per byte on a Pentium and take no more than 1K of code.

REALITY CHECK

Just to be sure that we haven't made a major blunder, it would be a good idea to check another popular method for converting strings to lowercase. This method is not as versatile, but is much smaller since it just performs two compares instead of using a table. Here it is, before speed optimizing:

```
lbl:                    ; cycles                        (Listing 14.15)
  lodsb                 ; 2   read a byte
  cmp al, 'A'           ; 1
  jb  lbl3              ; 0   skip down if below 'A'
  cmp al, 'Z'           ; 1
  ja  lbl2              ; 0   continue loop if above 'Z'
  or  al, 20h           ; 1   convert to lower case
  mov [si-1], al        ; 1   store translation
lbl2:
  loop lbl              ; 5
  ...                   ; ---
lbl3:                   ; 11 cycles per byte converted
  test al, al           ;     check for null
  jnz lbl2              ;     jump back up if not end of string
```

That's a surprise. Compare this code to the code at the start of this section. This compare and jump method of writing the code is actually faster on the Pentium than the unoptimized translation table method. This is because the **CMP/Jcc** instruction pair takes only one cycle. Not so quick. If you take the time to measure the speed of this code and the optimized version shown below, you'll find that the time is very data-dependent. A **CMP/Jcc** or a **DEC/Jcc** takes only one cycle when the branch prediction on the Pentium is able to predict correctly. Here's a version of the code using simple instructions:

```
lbl:                    ; cycles                          (Listing 14.16)
    mov  al, [si]       ; 1   read a byte
    inc  si             ; 0
    cmp  al, 'A'        ; 1
    jb   lbl3           ; 0   skip down if below 'A'
    cmp  al, 'Z'        ; 1
    ja   lbl2           ; 0   continue loop if above 'Z'
    or   al, 20h        ; 1   convert to lower case
    mov  [si-1], al     ; 1   store translation
lbl2:
    dec  cx             ; 1
    jnz  lbl            ; 0
    ...                 ; ---
lbl3:                   ; 6 cycles per byte converted
    test al, al         ;     check for null
    jnz  lbl2           ;     jump back up if not end of string
```

This is still not a very elegant block of code. But it does get the job done and is a reasonable trade-off from the table method since it eliminates the 256-byte table. The two internal jumps in this loop can be arranged several different ways, the best case yielding three cycles per byte, the worst case being 16. One cycle per byte can be eliminated by processing two bytes per loop.

Case-Independent String Searching

The final problem for this chapter is to combine the string search and the case conversion routines to perform a string search that is case-independent. The basic algorithm is to scan a string, converting each character to a decided-upon case and comparing it. When a match is found, the full string is compared, converting each character before the compare. We'll start by merging simple forms of our scan routines and case-conversion routines. We'll assume we are searching a string with a known length.

```
                            ; inputs:  DI ptr to text string      (Listing 14.17)
                            ;          CX length of string
                            ;          SI ptr to pattern to find
                            ;              (in lowercase)
    xor bx, bx
    mov dl, [si]            ;     load char to scan for
    inc si                  ;     advance ptr for compare
lbl:                        ; cycles
    mov bl, [di]            ; 1   read a char
    inc di                  ; 0   advance mem ptr
    mov al, tbl[bx]         ; 2   translate to lowercase (AGI)
    cmp al, dl             ; 1   compare with scan char
    je  compare            ; 0
lbl2:
    dec cx                 ; 1
    jnz lbl                ; 0
    jmp no_match           ; ---
                            ; 5 cycles per byte
compare:
    push si
    push di
ml:
    mov al, [si]           ; 1   read next char in pattern
    inc si                 ; 0   advance ptr
    test al, al            ; 1   check for null
    jz  exit               ; 0   done if end of string
    mov bl, [di]           ; 1   read string char to convert
    inc di                 ; 0   advance ptr
    mov ah, tbl[bx]        ; 2   read lowercase conversion (AGI)
    cmp al, ah             ; 1   check for match
    je  ml                 ; 0   continue while matching
exit:                      ; ---
    pop di                 ; 6 cycles per pattern char
    pop si
    jne lbl2               ;     return to scan if not a match
```

CASE-INDEPENDENT STRING SCAN

We'll consider the optimization of the scanning and matching parts of this code separately. The scanning portion is plagued by the same two problems as our original translation code—an AGI and a register conflict that prevents pairing. We'll fix these the same way as before and process two bytes per loop. For simplicity, we'll assume an even byte count in CX, as follows:

```
    xor bx, bx                                               (Listing 14.18)
    mov dl, [si]           ;     load char to scan for
    mov bl, [di]           ;     read first char
    inc di                 ;     advance ptr
```

```
        shr cx, 1               ;       adjust loop counter
        inc si                  ;       advance ptr for compare
    lbl:                        ; cycles
        mov al, tbl[bx]         ; 1     translate first to lowercase
        mov bl, [di]            ; 0     read second char
        cmp al, dl              ; 1     compare with scan char
        je  compare             ; 0
        mov al, tbl[bx]         ; 1     translate second byte
        mov bl, [di+1]          ; 0     read first byte for next loop
        cmp al, dl              ; 1     compare with scan char
        je  compare             ; 0
    lbl2:
        add di, 2               ; 1     advance ptr
        dec cx                  ; 0
        jnz lbl                 ; 1
                                ; ---
                                ; 6 cycles, 3 per byte
```

From looking at this code it is easy to see the atomic operations:

- read a character from memory
- translate to lowercase
- compare with the scan character
- jump if a match

The optimum coding of these operations is two cycles per byte plus loop management, which is what we have. We could easily add the processing of more bytes per loop and reduce the cycle count to 2.67 (three bytes) or 2.5 (four bytes).

When I initially considered this example, I thought one solution worth exploring would be scanning the string for an exact match twice, once for lowercase and once for uppercase. (The maximum text string would be required to be smaller than the data cache for this to have any chance of good performance.) But doing the case conversion requires only one additional operation, averaging only 0.5 cycles per byte.

CASE-INDEPENDENT STRING COMPARE

The second part of this example is the loop that compares the string for a match after the scan finds a match on the first character. Normally the speed of the compare will have a small effect on overall search performance. However, data that contains many similar strings may have the performance skewed more toward the efficiency of the compare routine. The interface to the compare routine has changed slightly because of the changes to the scanning routine. The BX register now needs to be preserved, and the DI register may have different values than assumed previously. To get the absolute best speed, two different, but equivalent compare routines could be written, one for a scan match on the first byte and one for a match on the second byte. To simplify the explanation, I'll just use one routine:

```
compare:                                              (Listing 14.19)
  push   di
  push   si
  ; inc di                   ;      (insert for 2nd-byte version)
  push   bx
m1:
  mov    ax, [si]            ; 1  read next char in pattern
  add    i, 2               ; 0  advance ptr
  mov    bl, [di]            ; 1  read string char to convert
  add    di, 2               ; 0  advance ptr
  test   al, al             ; 1  check for null
  jz     exit                ; 0  done if end of string
  mov    dh, tbl[bx]         ; 1  read lowercase conversion
  mov    bl, [di-1]          ; 0  read second string char to convert
  cmp    al, dh             ; 1  check for match on first char (reg conflict)
  jne    exit                ; 0  continue while matching
  test   ah, ah             ; 1  check for null
  jz     exit                ; 0  done if end of string
  mov    dh, tbl[bx]         ; 1  read lowercase conversion
  cmp    ah, dh             ; 1  check for match on first char
  je     m1                  ; 0  continue while matching
exit:                        ; ---
  pop    bx                  ; 8 cycles, 4 per pattern char
  pop    si
  pop    di
  jne    lbl2               ;      return to scan if not a match
```

This code has a register conflict which is of no real consequence because there is a an extra half-cycle slot not being used. But we can reduce the number of cycles per loop by cleverly observing that two compares and jumps per character is redundant. If we are at the end of the string pattern (a null), it will not match the translated character from the text string. The text string can be specified to contain no nulls, and a null at the end of the text string can be translated to some other sentinel value, such as a control-Z (end of file) or a −1, etc. If an application cannot have a restriction such as this, the length of the string pattern can be compared with the remaining bytes in the text string. If the remaining byte count is less than the string pattern length, there cannot be a match.

```
compare:                                              (Listing 14.20)
                             ;      (remaining byte check here)
  push   di
  push   si
  ; inc di                   ;      (insert for 2nd byte version)
  push   bx
```

```
      mov   bl, [di]       ;     read string char to convert
m1:
      mov   ax, [si]       ; 1   read next char in pattern
      add   si, 2          ; 0   advance ptr
      mov   dh, tbl[bx]    ; 1   read lowercase conversion
      mov   bl, [di+1]     ; 0   read second string char to convert
      cmp   al, dh         ; 1   check for match on first char
      jne   exit           ; 0   exit if no match
      mov   dh, tbl[bx]    ; 1   read lowercase conversion
      mov   bl, [di+2]     ; 0   read string char to convert
      add   di, 2          ; 1   advance ptr
      cmp   ah, dh         ; 0   check for match on second char
      je    m1             ; 1   continue while matching
exit:                      ; ---
      pop   bx             ; 6 cycles, 3 per pattern char
      pop   si
      pop   di
      test  al, al
      jz    done
      test  ah, ah
      jne   lbl2
done:
```

The atomic operations for one character in the preceding compare loop are:

- read a character from the text string
- advance text ptr
- read a character from the search pattern
- advance pattern ptr
- translate text string character to lowercase
- compare the characters
- jump if a match

There are seven operations here, and we've doubled up three of them by processing two bytes per loop. And we have 11 of 12 execution slots filled in the loop. But there is one more optimization we can make. This loop may be run often, but a high percentage of the time will terminate after only one or two characters are compared. Here are some changes with a look at the cycles for a termination after only one byte compared:

```
compare:          ; 1 byte   2 bytes        (Listing 14.21)
    push bx       ; 1         1
    mov  bl, [di] ; 0         0
    push di       ; 1         1
    push si       ; 0         0
m1:
    mov  ax, [si] ; 1         1
    add  si, 2    ; 0         0
```

```
        mov  dh, tbl[bx]    ; 1            1
        mov  bl, [di+1]     ; 0            0
        cmp  al, dh         ; 1            1
        jne  exit1          ; 0            0
        mov  dh, tbl[bx]    ;              1
        mov  bl, [di+2]     ;              0
        add  di, 2          ;              1
        cmp  ah, dh         ;              0
        je   m1             ;              1
     exit:                  ;
        pop  si             ;              1
        pop  di             ;              0
        pop  bx             ;              1
        test ah, ah         ;              0
        jne  lbl2           ;              1
        jmp  found          ;              0
     exit1:                 ;            ---
        pop  si             ; 1     11 cycles for 2 bytes to exit
        pop  di             ; 0
        pop  bx             ; 1
        test al, al         ; 0
        jne  lbl2           ; 1
     found:                 ;---
                            ; 8 cycles for 1 byte to exit
```

CONCLUSIONS

There are several other optimizations that could be implemented that have more to do with algorithm selection. First, we could scan the text string for an infrequently occurring character, rather than the first character. An extension of this idea, for the case-independent search, is to modify the frequency information in favor of choosing a character that is not alphabetic. When a non-alphabetic character is used for the scan, it is not necessary to use the case-independent version, which would be faster.

We've now explored the operation, optimization and pairing of a number of instructions. However, our knowledge and experience is concentrated on a few well-beaten paths. Now that we have some experience, it is time to draw a good map that includes landmarks to provide orientation during unexplored direct routes in the future.

Checksums and Extended Precision Addition

15

*The brain is like a muscle. When it
is in use we feel very good.*
—Carl Sagan

I n this chapter we'll continue with more Pentium loop optimizations; however, these examples will involve integer arithmetic. A good understanding of the last two chapters is a requirement for this chapter. In addition to presenting and optimizing more example code, we'll develop a methodology for superscalar optimization that can be used for many optimization efforts.

We'll start with a code fragment I first used when I started 8086 programming. I was working on a space shuttle computer that was used to control and monitor scientific experiments. The project required memory tests to be run on power-up, continuously in the background or by manual command. The paranoia was due to possible damage by the high levels of solar radiation in space. As it turned out, there were no memory errors during the 10-day flight, but the checksum routines detected several unintentional errors during development and testing. On the prototype we had inserted chips with broken or bent pins and put boards in the wrong slots, etc. Almost every time the alarm light lit up on the prototype system, my first thought was there was a software error.

This code reads each byte in a block of memory and sums it into a 16-bit value. So, here is the basic loop:

```
    xor bx, bx                                      (Listing 15.1)
    mov ah, 0
lbl:                    ; cycles
  lodsb                 ; 2
  add bx, ax            ; 1
  loop lbl             ; 5
                        ; ---
                        ; 8 cycles per byte
```

This is a very simple loop, and it would be difficult to write it in a more compact manner. The challenge is to make it run faster. We're also interested in discovering the process of how to find the best-performing Pentium version of this code, if there is such a process. You can watch how I did it, or if you're interested in a challenge, get out some paper and see what your brain cells can do with these three instructions before you read on.

STEP 1

As we've seen in the previous chapters, the first step is to change all instructions to simple, pairable instructions if possible. If you need help, refer to Chapter 9 (Table 9.1). These instructions usually have the fewest official cycle counts, which is important. More importantly, these instructions can be paired with other instructions. When arranged properly, the cycle counts can effectively be cut in half. Here's a rewrite with simple instructions:

```
    xor bx, bx                                      (Listing 15.2)
    mov ah, 0
lbl:                    ; cycles
  mov al, [si]          ; 1
  inc si                ; 0
  add bx, ax            ; 1
  dec cx                ; 0
  jnz lbl              ; 1
                        ; ---
                        ; 3 cycles
```

We've expanded the code by adding more instructions, but we've also decreased the cycle counts from eight to three. Every instruction pairs with another one, except the last one. This isn't too bad. As a matter of fact, that was downright easy. We could quit right here. Wrong.

STEP 2

The code runs faster, but look at what is happening. In the three cycles there are six possible execution slots. One is not used at all, and two are for the loop overhead. That's only a 50% utilization. Let's try two adds per loop:

```
        xor  bx, bx                                          (Listing 15.3)
        mov  ah, 0
        mov  dh, 0
        shr  cx, 1           ; (divide count by 2)
        jc   lbl_2           ; (skip down if odd count)

lbl:                         ; cycles
        mov  al, [si]        ; 1
        inc  si              ; 0
        add  bx, ax          ; 1
lbl_2:
        mov  dl, [si]        ; 0 + 1 (AGI)
        inc  si              ; 1
        add  bx, dx          ; 0
        dec  cx              ; 1
        jnz  lbl             ; 0
                             ; ---
                             ; 5 cycles, 2.5 per byte
```

We've added two cycles, but increased the performance to 2.5 cycles per byte. We've also introduced an AGI, which should be removed. Note the method used to handle the case of an odd number of bytes to be processed. For clarity, I'll drop the details of handling this in subsequent examples. Also note that the cycles are shown for the loop execution from the top of the loop, not for the one-time jump into the middle of the loop.

STEP 3

We've doubled the amount of work performed per loop, but we're still not done. You probably noticed SI is incremented twice in the loop (causing an AGI in one case). We can get rid of these problems easily enough:

```
lbl:                         ; cycles                        (Listing 15.4)
        mov  al, [si]        ; 1
        add  bx, ax          ; 1 <-- register conflict, no pairing
```

```
lbl_2:
  mov  dl, [si+1]        ; 0 <-- bug
  add  si, 2             ; 1
  add  bx, dx            ; 0
  dec  cx               ; 1
  jnz  lbl              ; 0
```

Whoops. It isn't quite that easy. By removing the first **INC SI** we created a register conflict. And by adjusting the second memory read we created a bug. (The bug has to do with processing an odd byte count.) This could be fixed by an extra jump in the code before the loop starts by decrementing SI. Let's back up and try another method:

```
lbl:                     ; cycles              (Listing 15.5)
  mov  dl, [si+1]        ; 1
  add  bx, dx            ; 0
lbl_2:
  mov  al, [si]          ; 1
  add  bx, ax            ; 1
  add  si, 2             ; 0 <-- bug
  dec  cx               ; 1
  jnz  lbl              ; 0
```

Maybe you noticed, but this also messed up the code and didn't gain us anything. The SI register should have one added on the first loop if there is an odd byte.

Here's another attempt, but with the odd byte summed completely outside of the loop we're trying to optimize. If you are programming for speed, there is no reason to force a loop to handle odd bytes and such. If it can be done with no performance penalty, then great. Otherwise, handle these cases outside the loop, as follows:

```
  xor  bx, bx                                 (Listing 15.6)
  mov  ah, 0
  mov  dh, 0
  shr  cx, 1           ; divide count by 2
  jnc  lbl            ; skip down if even count
  lodsb
  add  bx, ax
lbl:                     ; cycles
  mov  al, [si]          ; 1
  mov  dl, [si+1]        ; 0 + 1 bank conflict
  add  bx, ax            ; 1
  add  si, 2             ; 0
  add  bx, dx            ; 1
  dec  cx               ; 0
  jnz  lbl              ; 1
                         ; ---
                         ; 5 cycles, 2.5 per byte
```

This code still takes five cycles per loop, no matter how we seem to arrange it. There is only one empty execution slot. This code runs at 2.5 cycles per byte compared to eight in the original code. At this point it must be time to give up.

STEP 4

Not a chance. We have fewer loop instructions (compared to step 2), but the same speed, and we're wasting one execution slot. We could process a third byte in each loop, but we'd still be wasting one slot because two more instructions would be added. If you look at each instruction, there seems to be no way to actually eliminate any of then. Each one is required. The only credible options are to add more bytes per loop or go to 32-bit code.

Now it's time to end the warm-up phase. Let's get rid of CX. It serves no real purpose except to count the number of loops. What if SI could do that? How would that work?

Let's say SI were to start at 2000h and CX is 3000h. We'll just change it to start at some larger number minus an offset. The idea is to start SI at negative CX so it will count to up to 0. SI is then adjusted by a displacement to get it to the proper value when addressing memory. The table shows an example with these numbers.

	Original	**Adjusted**
SI	2000h	D000h
CX	3000h	—
Displacement	0	+5000h

What happens is this: SI counts from D000h up to zero. The loop stops when SI gets to zero (or more). The address used to read from memory is the combination of SI and 5000h. The first address will be D000h plus 5000h or 12000h, but since we are working with 16-bit registers the 1 is ignored, leaving 2000h. The same principles can be applied to 32-bit code and 32-bit registers.

For clarity, we'll use the symbol "disp" for the adjusted displacement. We'll assume the odd byte is taken care of outside the loop.

```
lbl:                  ; cycles                              (Listing 15.7)
  mov  al, [si+disp]  ; 1+1 <--- AGI delay
  mov  dl, [si+disp+1] ; 0+1 <--- bank conflict delay
  add  bx, ax         ; 1
  add  bx, dx         ; 1  <--- no pairing, register conflict
  add  si, 2          ; 0  <--- address generation
```

```
        jnc lbl              ; 1
                             ; ---
                             ; 6
```

Now we've really created problems. We have a register conflict, an AGI delay and a bank conflict. The last two instructions in the loop cannot be easily changed, although an instruction that does not change the flags could be placed right before the conditional jump. However, the only candidates for moved instructions depend on SI. The first four instructions cannot be rearranged without causing another register conflict— that is, unless we perform the additions before the moves. Introducing a new register will also eliminate the register conflict of the two adds. We'll just add the two sums when the loop ends.

```
        mov al, [si+disp]                       (Listing 15.8)
        mov dl, [si+disp+1]
    lbl:                     ; cycles
        add bx, ax           ; 1
        add cx, dx           ; 0
        mov al, [si+disp+2]  ; 1
        mov dl, [si+disp+3]  ; 0+1 <--- bank conflict
        add si, 2            ; 1
        jnc lbl              ; 0
                             ; ---
                             ; 4 cycles, 2 cycles per byte
```

Don't worry about the bank conflict—we'll deal with that later. We have a loop that sums bytes in two cycles. How much better can it get? Recall the concept of atomic operations. For this loop the operations are:

- read a byte
- add the byte to a word
- advance pointer

However, we've eliminated the pointer operation on a per-byte basis by combining it into the loop management code. So the theoretical limit is one cycle per byte, and we're not there yet.

STEP 5

We still have not used two registers. So we should be able to sum three bytes per loop. The limitation in many algorithms is the sparse number of registers that are available on the Pentium. Here's a way to process three bytes per loop:

```
        mov  al, [si+disp]                              (Listing 15.9)
        mov  bl, [si+disp+1]
        mov  cl, [si+disp+2]
      lbl:                    ; cycles
        add  di, ax           ; 1
        add  bp, bx           ; 0
        mov  al, [si+disp+3]  ; 1
        mov  bl, [si+disp+4]  ; 0+1 <-- bank conflict
        add  di, cx           ; 1
        mov  cl, [si+disp+5]  ; 0
        add  si, 3            ; 1
        jnc  lbl              ; 0
                              ; ---
                              ; 5 cycles, 1.67 cycles per byte
```

We are now calculating checksums at five cycles per loop or 1.67 cycles per byte. For clarity, I have not shown the details of handling the extra bytes when the memory block is not an even multiple of three. This would be messy, probably involving a divide. So we're going to skip right to four bytes per loop:

```
        mov  al, [si+disp]                              (Listing 15.10)
        mov  dl, [si+disp+1]
      lbl:   ; cycles
        add  cx, ax           ; 1
        add  di, dx           ; 0
        mov  al, [si+disp+2]  ; 1
        mov  dl, [si+disp+3]  ; 0+1 <-- bank conflict
        add  cx, ax           ; 1
        add  di, dx           ; 0
        mov  al, [si+disp+4]  ; 1
        mov  dl, [si+disp+5]  ; 0+1 <-- bank conflict
        add  si, 4            ; 1
        jnc  lbl              ; 0
                              ; ---
                              ; 7 cycles, 1.75 cycles per byte
```

We've gone backwards slightly, but the code has a nice organized look about it. We still need to get rid of those bank conflicts.

Step 6

Bank conflicts are the last delays to be handled. Each case can be different, so I'll show two methods for eliminating bank conflicts. The preferred method is to reorder the instructions, if possible. Many times instruction reordering looks obvious after you've seen it done. It's a little bit like watching someone else do a crossword puzzle. It doesn't look too difficult until you try it yourself. In this case it is not too hard:

```
        mov  al, [si+disp]                              (Listing 15.11)
        mov  dl, [si+disp+1]
lbl:                          ; cycles
        add  cx, ax           ; 1
        mov  al, [si+disp+2]  ; 0
        add  di, dx           ; 1
        mov  dl, [si+disp+3]  ; 0
        add  cx, ax           ; 1
        mov  al, [si+disp+4]  ; 0
        add  di, dx           ; 1
        mov  dl, [si+disp+5]  ; 0
        add  si, 4            ; 1
        jnc  lbl              ; 0
                              ; ---
                              ; 5 cycles, 1.25 cycles per byte
```

If you tried it yourself, you may have discovered one of the most important techniques in code reordering:

> *A register that must be written in every loop can usually be written to in the paired instruction right after it has been read.*

A second method for eliminating bank conflicts is to have the second data stream read ahead by one bank. In this case we have to add code to handle the second and fourth bytes (in addition to any odd bytes because of the count, zero to three for a four-byte loop).

```
        mov  al, [si+disp]                              (Listing 15.12)
        mov  dl, [si+disp+1]
lbl:                          ; cycles
        add  cx, ax           ; 1
        add  di, dx           ; 0
        mov  al, [si+disp+2]  ; 1
        mov  dl, [si+disp+7]  ; 0
        add  cx, ax           ; 1
        add  di, dx           ; 0
        mov  al, [si+disp+4]  ; 1
        mov  dl, [si+disp+9]  ; 0
        add  si, 4            ; 1
        jnc  lbl              ; 0
                              ; ---
                              ; 5 cycles, 1.25 cycles per byte
```

This is it. We have two spare registers and a theoretical speed of 1.25 cycles per byte. I think you can see how to go to six, eight or any number of bytes per loop. If there is a faster way to do this problem, then it will need to be done in a completely different way. Send me E-mail if you have a faster method.

You probably noticed that the use of the displacement "disp" was introduced in step 4 without noting the use of a constant, such as this limits the functionality of the code. This loop will only work for the specific values of SI and the block size that "disp" was calculated for. To fix this, we can replace "disp" with the BX register, calculating it when needed:

```
                        ; handle odd bytes first        (Listing 15.13)
    mov bx, si          ;
    add bx, cx          ; BX = SI + CX
    mov si, cx          ;
    neg si              ; SI = - CX
    mov al, [si+bx]
    mov dl, [si+bx+1]
lbl:                    ; cycles
    add cx, ax          ; 1
    mov al, [si+bx+2]   ; 0
    add di, dx          ; 1
    mov dl, [si+bx+3]   ; 0
    add cx, ax          ; 1
    mov al, [si+bx+4]   ; 0
    add di, dx          ; 1
    mov dl, [si+bx+5]   ; 0
    add si, 4           ; 1
    jnc lbl             ; 0
```

Coming Completely Undone

Of course, it is possible to unroll this loop completely. And this would provide the best possible performance of 1.0 cycles per byte. First, this isn't true and second, it would not be practical, except for relatively small blocks to be checksummed. It's not true because for the Pentium to pair instructions together, they need to have already been executed from the cache (or be one of the few instructions that are one byte in length).

Summary

I tried many techniques while developing this example. At times it may have seemed like a random walk through an optimization maze. But puzzles like mazes have less than optimum methods for insuring success. When walking through a maze if you always turn right (or left) you will head down some dead ends, but you will always find the exit. I believe that this same principle can work for hand-optimized superscalar programming (assuming that there is an exit point). Table 15.1 summarizes the techniques shown in the preceding steps.

Table 15.1   The Six-Step Superscalar Optimization Process

1.   Re-code with simple instructions.
2.   Use the two pipelines for independent streams of data.
3.   Eliminate redundant pointer operations.
4.   Eliminate the loop counter, if advantageous.
5.   Unroll the loop, as required.
6.   Re-order to eliminate bank conflicts, register conflicts.

You may find other methods that work well. Work a problem until you come to a dead end, back up and try another approach. You'll run into a dead end somewhere. The question that you must ask yourself is, "Is this dead end close enough to where I want to be?"

FALSE STEPS

If you try a technique that doesn't pay off, do not make the mistake of giving up too soon. Remember in step 4 earlier, we initially lost some speed. Here is another common mistake.

Let's go back to the step 1 code and try to eliminate the loop counter.

```
    xor bx, bx                           (Listing 15.14)
    mov ah, 0
lbl:                ; cycles
    mov al, [si+disp] ; 1+1 <--- AGI
    add bx, ax        ; 1  <--- register conflict, no pairing
    inc si            ; 0  <--- address generation
    jnz lbl           ; 1
```

This gets us nowhere and actually slows down the loop! The use of fewer registers creates a greater chance for register conflicts and AGIs. Of course, a loop with more operations on each data item may not have this problem.

Extended Precision Addition

I've always thought it interesting the way the 80x86 is able to add (or subtract) binary values of any number of bytes, words or dwords, such as:

```
        clc                 ; clear carry for first addition    (Listing 15.15)
lbl:
  mov al, [si]              ; read a byte
  adc [di], al              ; add byte with carry from previous addition
  inc si                    ; advance to next source byte
  inc di                    ; advance to next destination byte
  loop lbl                  ; loop till done
```

After studying this loop, you will discover several interesting facts. This works properly because the **INC** and **LOOP** instructions do not modify the carry flag. It can be changed to use words (or dwords) with no problems. It can also be changed to use string instructions. This exact type of loop was probably a design criterion for the 8086/8088. Here's a word-sized version:

```
        clc                                  (Listing 15.16)
lbl:                        ; cycles
  lodsw                     ; 2   read a word
  adc [di], ax             ; 3   add word with carry
  inc di                    ; 1
  inc di                    ; 1   advance to next destination word
  loop lbl                  ; 5   loop till done
                            ; ---
                            ; 12 cycles per word
```

Problems can arise when this loop is converted to using simple instructions. Changing two **INC**s to an **ADD** causes the carry flag to be modified. Although changing the **LOOP** to **DEC/JNZ** does not affect the carry flag, we'll assume other instructions might need to be inserted that do change the carry flag.

```
        clc                                  (Listing 15.17)
lbl:                        ; cycles
  mov ax, [si]             ; 1
  lea si, [si+2]           ; 0  (LEA does an add without changing the flags)
  mov bx, [di]             ; 1
  lea di, [di+2]           ; 0
  adc ax, bx              ; 1
  mov [di-2], ax          ; 1
  loop lbl                  ; 5
                            ; ---
                            ; 9 cycles per word
```

This is faster (9 cycles vs. 12), but still not very good because only 11 out of 18 execution slots are being used. We need to try some other method of saving the flags in the loop, such as **PUSHF** and **POPF**:

```
        clc                                                     (Listing 15.18)
        pushf                   ; push flags before loop
lbl:                            ; cycles
        mov   ax, [si]          ; 1
        add   si, 2             ; 0
        mov   bx, [di]          ; 1
        add   di, 2             ; 0
        popf                    ; 6, PM = 4
        adc   ax, bx            ; 1
        mov   [di-2], ax        ; 1
        pushf                   ; 9, PM = 3
        dec   cx               ; 1
        jnz   lbl              ; 0
        popf                    ; (restore flags after the loop)
                                ; ---
                                ; 20 cycles
```

By pushing and popping the flags, we slow down the code. So we need to try some other method. The **LAHF** and **SAHF** instructions (quirks from the 8080) are much faster than the **PUSHF/POPF**:

```
        clc                                                     (Listing 15.19)
        lahf                    ; save flags before loop
lbl:                            ; cycles
        mov dx, [si]            ; 1
        add si, 2               ; 0
        mov bx, [di]            ; 1
        add di, 2               ; 0
        sahf                    ; 2
        adc dx, bx              ; 1
        mov [di-2], dx          ; 1
        lahf                    ; 2
        dec cx                 ; 1
        jnz lbl                ; 0
                                ; ---
                                ; 9 cycles
```

Using **SAHF** and **LAHF** just gets us back to the same place as using **LOOP**. Originally, I gave up finding an elegant solution to this problem; then I realized there is a *simple* instruction that will save the carry flag. Take a look and see if you can find it in Appendix D before you look at the next section of code.

```
        xor  dx, dx                              (Listing 15.20)
    lbl:                  ; cycles
        mov  ax, [si]     ; 1
        add  si, 2        ; 0
        mov  bx, [di]     ; 1
        add  di, 2        ; 0
        rcr  dx, 1        ; 1
        adc  ax, bx       ; 1
        rcl  dx, 1        ; 1
        mov  [di-2], ax   ; 0
        dec  cx           ; 1
        jnz  lbl          ; 0
                          ; ---
                          ; 6 cycles
```

You probably cheated. I know I would have. So now you know that **RCR** and **RCL** can save and restore the carry flag. (As a matter of fact, they each do both, simultaneously.) This code suffers only because the rotates and **ADC** instructions can only pair in the U pipe. But they would have a flags register conflict even if this were not the case.

Since you may have cheated on the last question, here's a chance to redeem yourself. Re-order and/or re-code the preceding instructions so each instruction pairs properly and there are no register conflicts.

```
        xor  dx, dx                              (Listing 15.21)
        mov  bx, [di]
    lbl:                  ; cycles
        add  di, 2        ; 1
        mov  ax, [si]     ; 0
        rcr  dx, 1        ; 1
        lea  si, [si+2]   ; 0
        adc  ax, bx       ; 1
        mov  bx, [di]     ; 0
        rcl  dx, 1        ; 1
        mov  [di-2], ax   ; 0
        dec  cx           ; 1
        jnz  lbl          ; 0
                          ; ---
                          ; 5 cycles
```

This loop runs at five cycles per word. (It could also be changed to five cycles per byte or five cycles per dword.) This is probably the most difficult optimization problem in this book. I doubt any compiler (other than a human one) could generate this code. And that is the advantage of hand-optimizing especially time-critical sections of code in assembly for the Pentium. However, this code is (almost) completely useless.

That's right, useless. What application would use this? Most of the other examples in this book could be used fairly often. I chose this example because it clearly shows how to preserve the carry flag throughout a loop when this would not have been required using the complex 80x86 instructions. In other words, the techniques may be useful, while the specific example is not. How many times have you needed variable-precision integer addition? Instead, if you want, for example, six words of precision, start with this:

```
              ; cycles                              (Listing 15.22)
mov  ax, [si]    ; 1
add  [di], ax    ; 3
mov  ax, [si+2]  ; 1
adc  [di+2], ax  ; 3
mov  ax, [si+4]  ; 1
adc  [di+4], ax  ; 3
```

This code starts at four cycles per word. It can be optimized several ways. First, just use more registers and re-order the instructions:

```
              ; cycles                              (Listing 15.23)
mov  ax, [si]    ; 1
mov  bx, [si+2]  ; 0
add  [di], ax    ; 3
mov  ax, [si+4]  ; 0
adc  [di+2], bx  ; 3
adc  [di+4], ax  ; 3
```

The second way is to eliminate the three-cycle instructions:

```
              ; cycles                              (Listing 15.24)
mov  ax, [si]    ; 1
mov  bx, [di]    ; 0
add  ax, bx      ; 1
mov  cx, [si+2]  ; 0
mov  [di], ax    ; 1
mov  dx, [di+2]  ; 0
adc  cx, dx      ; 1
mov  ax, [si+4]  ; 0
mov  [di+2], cx  ; 1
mov  bx, [di+4]  ; 0
adc  ax, bx      ; 1
mov  [di+4], ax  ; 1
```

Something to consider before getting carried away is the number of times a loop will execute. In this extended addition problem, the final code has no loop. This means the pairing assumptions we have made may not be correct. Again, recall that the U pipe instruction must be one byte in length or previously executed from the cache to allow pairing. If this code is part of a frequently called procedure, then it would stay in the cache and run at seven cycles per 48-bit addition. Each time it is loaded into the cache it will take its full 12 cycles, with no pairing. The looping code presented earlier would take 16 to 21 cycles.

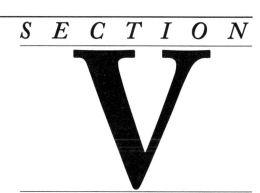

Advanced Topics

Floating-Point Math

16

*"If I have seen further it is by standing
on the shoulders of Giants."*

—Sir Isaac Newton

I n this chapter we'll discuss the operation of the floating-point unit (FPU). After briefly reviewing the basics of FPU operation, we'll get right into the advanced optimizations. If you've never programmed the FPU before, be sure to review the material about the FPU pipeline in Chapter 10.

To start, I must thank Harlan Stockman, the programmer who wrote most of the floating-point routines and did the timings contained in this chapter. Harlan did a tremendous amount of work to optimize some basic low-level routines to help write scientific applications. From Harlan's shoulders I saw how to apply superscalar techniques for the FPU. We did some final fine-tuning for this book together, but there are still several unsolved Pentium FPU mysteries. Perhaps you can see their solutions from our shoulders.

FPU Basics

The 8087 family includes the floating-point co-processors (8087, 80287 and 80387) and the floating-point units in the 486 and Pentium. We will refer to all of these as the

FPU, even though this term is technically correct only for the 486 and Pentium. The FPU has a stack architecture (as described in Chapter 10). Instructions are included for

- loading and storing data (**FLD**, **FST**, etc.)
- performing arithmetic calculations (**FADD**, **FMUL**, etc.)
- controlling program flow (**FCOM**, **FTST**, etc.)

The example program in Listing 16.1 shows some of the basic FPU programming techniques.

Table 16.1 shows the floating-point instructions from Listing 16.1 and their effect on the floating-point stack. Remember, the FPU stack is the register set for floating-point programming. It is helpful to trace the stack as shown in Table 16.1 when first learning FPU programming and when performing complex operations.

Table 16.1 Floating-Point Stack Operation for Listing 16.1

		;	st(0)	st(1)	st(2)	...1	st(7)
		;	—	—	—	—	—
fld	radius	;	2.0	—	—		—
fmul	st, st	;	4.0	—	—		—
fldpi		;	3.14+	4.0	—		—
fmul		;	12.56+	—	—		—
fld	side	;	3.0	12.56+	—		—
fmul	st, st	;	9.0	12.56+	—		—
fcom		;	9.0	12.56+	—		—
fstsw	ax	;	9.0	12.56+	—		—
fstp	square	;	12.56+	—	—		—
fstp	circle	;	—	—	—		—

(radius dd2.0)

(side dd3.0)

```
                          ; calculate area of circle        (Listing 16.1)
                          ;   (pi * r * r)

        fld   radius      ; load the radius
        fmul  st, st      ; square the radius
        fldpi             ; load pi
        fmul              ; multiply to get area

; calculate area of square

        fld   side        ; load side of a square
        fmul  st, st      ; square the side

; compare the areas

        fcom              ; compare
        fstsw ax          ; load FPU status into AX

; store the results
        fstp  square      ; store area of square and pop from stack
        fstp  circle      ; store area of circle and pop from stack

; branch based on previously obtained compare status

        sahf              ; put FPU flags into main CPU flags
        jp    fperr       ; parity flag is C2 FPU flag
                          ;   (when this is set an error occurred)
        je    comp_equal
        jc    circle_larger
        jmp   square_larger

fperr:
        ...

comp_equal:
        ...

circle_larger:
        ...

square_larger:
        ...

  mov ah, 4ch
  int21h

main endp

.data

radius dd 1.2            ; radius of a circle
side   dd 2.1            ; side of a square
circle dd 0             ; result area of circle
square dd 0             ; result area of square
```

FPU Matrix Optimizations

The Pentium FPU is much faster than the 486 FPU at basic arithmetic. This improvement is mostly due to better algorithms that reduce instruction cycle times, and these gains are automatic. However, additional performance gains of significant magnitude can be realized with proper instruction scheduling and pipeline pairing. The benefits of these techniques are most obvious in loops with many iterations. An excellent example that requires many iterations and careful coding is a double-precision matrix multiplication. We'll start by using a C program to multiply two double-precision matrices to form a product matrix (**c[][]** = **a[][]** * **b[][]**). See Listing 16.2.

```
void normal()                                              (Listing 16.2)
{
  int i,j,k;
  for (i=0;i<N;i++){
    for (j=0;j<N;j++){
      c[i][j] = 0.0;
      for (k=0;k<N;k++){
        c[i][j] += a[i][k] * b[k][j];
      }
    }
  }
}
```

This algorithm wouldn't be too bad if the matrices that we wanted to manipulate would all fit in the Pentium's 8K data cache. Each double-precision number requires 8 bytes, so an array of 1024 numbers can fit into the cache, or a 32 by 32 matrix. However, our data consists of three matrices (**a[]**, **b[]** and **c[]**) plus stack and variable space. This reduces the maximum matrix size down to about 18 by 18. This is insignificant for most scientific applications. For this example we will handle large matrices (i.e., up to 500 by 500 elements). Three 500 by 500 matrices requires about 6 MB of memory. Definitely too large for the cache.

This brings up the problem with the code in Listing 16.2. The cache on the Pentium is divided into 128 two-line sets, each containing 32 bytes (or four double-precision numbers). Each time a matrix element is read from memory, the processor attempts to fill a line in the data cache with that element and some of its neighboring elements; the cache design assumption being that the data will be accessed sequentially. However, the cache size is limited, so if a program reads elements from widely separated places in memory, a cache line will rarely be reused before it needs to be replaced with new data.

The **b[][]** elements are accessed along the *j*th column, and each element is separated by $8N$ bytes (N is the number of elements in a row). Each time we read an element from **b[][]**, the cache reads three neighbors, assuming they will soon be used. However, these neighbors are in the next three columns, and the program won't try to fetch them until it cycles through the next outer loop—by then, the cache line will have been overwritten. Translating the inner loop to assembly would have little effect, since the time taken to read data into the CPU far overshadows the time for addition and multiplication.

In contrast, the inner loops of the next two examples access the matrices along rows, thus using the cache more efficiently.

The matrix multiplication example provides two fundamental lessons. First, write routines so the innermost loops operate on array rows whenever possible, or at least reuse data while it is in the cache. Second, before you spend a lot of time writing assembly language, make sure the overall algorithm is cache-efficient.

Some applications are based on smaller matrices, and Listing 16.2 is appropriate. Assembly speeds up the code in Listing 16.2, but not by as much as it speeds up the code in Listings 16.3 and 16.4. Table 16.2 contains the timed results of various methods for writing the matrix multiply (timings include a comparison with the MIPS R4000).

While searching for the most efficient C algorithm, be aware that many methods are implicitly optimized for RISC chips and may not be suited for the Pentium. An example is the **WARNER()** method (lines 11 and 12 of Table 16.2). In the pure C version, this algorithm does not substantially improve Pentium performance over the much simpler

```
void transpose()                              (Listing 16.3)
{
  int i,j,k;
  double temp;
  for (i=0;i<N;i++){
    for (j=0;j<N;j++){
      bt[j][i] = b[i][j];
    }
  }
  for (i=0;i<N;i++){
    for (j=0;j<N;j++){
#ifndef asmloop
      temp = a[i][0] * bt[j][0];
      for (k=1;k<N;k++){
        temp += a[i][k] * bt[j][k];
      }
      c[i][j] = temp;
#else
      c[i][j] = ddot(N, a[i], bt[j]);
#endif
    }
  }
}
```

```
void reg_loops()                                    (Listing 16.4)
{
  int i,j,k;
  double a_entry;
  for (i=0;i<N;i++){
    for (j=0;j<N;j++){
      c[i][j] = 0.0;
    }
  }
  for (i=0;i<N;i++){
    for (k=0;k<N;k++){
#ifndef asmloop
      a_entry = a[i][k];
      for (j=0;j<N;j++){
        c[i][j] += a_entry * b[k][j];
      }
#else
      daxpy(N, a[i]+k, b[k], c[i]);
#endif
    }
  }
}
```

Table 16.2 Matrix Multiply Times, in Seconds
(Two Double-Precision 500 x 500 Matrices)

		60 MHz Pentium	100MHz MIPS R4000
(1)	normal()	145.7	76.39
(2)	normal(), **a	186.2	128.6
(3)	normal(), asm inner loop	121.6	—
(4)	transpose()	58.66	30.96
(5)	transpose(), **a	61.08	30.61
(6)	transpose(), asm ddot() inner loop	21.59	—
(7)	reg_loops()	43.44	37.00
(8)	reg_loops(), asm daxpy() inner loop	23.79	—
(9)	tiling()	53.28	40.29
(10)	tiling(), asm daxpy() inner loop	20.59	—
(11)	warner()	42.89	19.40
(12)	warner(), asm inner loop	18.13	—

REG_LOOPS() method. However, the MIPS R4000 speed is greatly improved by **WARNER()**. The latter algorithm copies array elements into numerous temporary variables, to keep the program from constantly recalculating addresses in the innermost loop; this approach works well on a RISC machine, since the compiler will keep these variables in registers. The Pentium has far fewer registers than the R4000, so the C compiler tends to keep the temporary variables in memory; thus, the Pentium sees little benefit from the Warner method unless one uses hand-optimized assembly language for the inner loop, carefully keeping the temporary variables on the FPU stack.

WHICH ARRAY DECLARATION IS BEST?

It is often supposed that two-dimensional arrays are much more efficient when declared as pointers to pointers to double—that is, as

```
double **a
```

instead of

```
double a[500][500]
```

The latter declaration requires a multiplication by the row length to calculate the address of an element; since integer multiplications are comparatively slow (10 or 11 cycles on a Pentium or R4000), it is reasonable to assume that the **a[500][500]** declaration would be less efficient. However, the second and fifth lines of Table 16.2 tell a different story. For the normal algorithm, the ****a** type declaration produces substantially slower code, on both the Pentium and the R4000; on both processors, the **a[]**, **b[]** and **c[]** pointers must be read from memory, adding to cache thrashing. The speed loss is much smaller with the transpose algorithm (line 5 in Table 16.2), since only one **a[]**, **b[]** and **c[]** pointer need be read for each dot product.

OPTIMIZING WITH ASSEMBLY

To eke more performance out of the Pentium, we can replace the inner loops with two simple assembly routines. The function **ddot()**, Listing 16.3, returns the dot product of the vectors X and Y; **daxpy()**, Listing 16.1, forms the vector sum $ax + y$, where a is a scalar, replacing the old y values with the new. Both **ddot()** and **daxpy()** process n elements per call. Eventually, each function will process n elements in an unrolled loop of $n/4$ iterations, relying on a cleanup block to process the last (n mod 4) elements.

These low-level assembly functions have wide application and are at the core of packages such as the LINPACK linear algebra package.

From an assembly language programmer's perspective, the Pentium FPU looks much like its 80x87 predecessors, with a few exceptions. First, it is difficult to achieve simultaneous execution of integer and FPU instructions on the Pentium (see later explanation). Second, with the Pentium it is much more important to avoid data dependencies—that is, successive FPU operations that reference the same location in memory and stall the pipeline. Third, the **FXCH** instruction can be paired with another FPU instruction (see Table 10.6), making it execute in zero cycles.

Simultaneous execution of FPU and integer instructions is difficult on the Pentium because many of the common FPU instructions are so fast that there is no "delay" time in which an integer instruction can execute. For example, on the 486 **FMUL** takes 14–16 cycles, while on the Pentium **FMUL** takes 1–3 cycles.

Listing 16.5 shows a typical assembly-language attempt at writing the **daxpy()** function. The listings show cycle counts based on cache hits. We know this is not true because at least one out of four data reads will miss (one eight-byte double in a 32-byte cache line).

(Listing 16.5)

```
; void daxpy(int n, double *aptr, double *xptr, double *yptr)
;       forms the sum of a*x[i] + y[i], and stores in y[]

    push ebp
    mov  ebp, esp

    mov  ecx, dword ptr [ebp+8]      ;              count
    mov  eax, dword ptr [ebp+12]     ;              aptr
    fld  qword ptr [eax]             ;
    mov  eax, dword ptr [ebp+16]     ;              xptr
    mov  ebx, dword ptr [ebp+20]     ;              yptr

lbl:                                 ; cycles
    fld  qword ptr [eax]             ; 1            load double
    fmul st, st(1)                   ; 1+2          multiply
    fadd qword ptr [ebx]             ; 1+2          add double
    fstp qword ptr [ebx]             ; 2+1          store in memory and pop
    add  eax, 8                      ; 1            advance ptr to next double
    add  ebx, 8                      ; 0            advance ptr to next double
    loop lbl                         ; 5            loop
                                     ; ---
    fstp st(0)                       ; 16 cycles per double (cache hit)
    pop  ebp
    ret
```

The **FMUL** instruction takes only one cycle if the following instructions are not dependent on the result of the multiply; otherwise, there is a two-cycle delay while the **FMUL** completes. The same is true for **FADD**. In addition, **FSTP** takes an additional cycle when the result is being calculated in the previous instruction. Optimized FPU code can eliminate all of these delays. We'll start in in Listing 16.6 by unrolling the loop, performing two operations per loop:

```
lbl:                        ; cycles               (Listing 16.6)
  fld    qword ptr [eax]    ; 1
  fmul   st, st(1)          ; 1+2
  fadd   qword ptr [ebx]    ; 1+2
  fstp   qword ptr [ebx]    ; 2+1

  fld    qword ptr [eax+8]  ; 1
  fmul   st, st(1)          ; 1+2
  fadd   qword ptr [ebx+8]  ; 1+2
  fstp   qword ptr [ebx+8]  ; 2+1

  add    eax, 16            ; 1
  add    ebx, 16            ; 0
  dec    ecx                ; 1
  jnz    lbl                ; 0
                            ; ---
                            ; 22 cycles, 11 per double
```

Interleaving FPU instructions is not quite as easy as it is for the integer instructions. This is because the FPU operates with its registers arranged as a stack. One way to arrange the instructions is to just let the results "stack" up on the stack, then pop them off when they are done. This eliminates an **FADD** delay:

```
lbl:                        ; cycles               (Listing 16.7)
  fld    qword ptr [eax]    ; 1
  fmul   st, st(1)          ; 1+2
  fadd   qword ptr [ebx]    ; 1

  fld    qword ptr [eax+8]  ; 1
  fmul   st, st(2)          ; 1+2
  fadd   qword ptr [ebx+8]  ; 1+2

  fstp   qword ptr [ebx+8]  ; 2+1
  fstp   qword ptr [ebx]    ; 2

  add    eax, 16            ; 1
  add    ebx, 16            ; 0
  dec    ecx                ; 1
  jnz    lbl                ; 0
                            ; ---
                            ; 19 cycles, 9.5 cycles per double
```

Using the pairing capability of the **FXCH** instruction can eliminate the **FSTP** delay on one instruction by exchanging the top two stack elements:

```
lbl:                                 ; cycles                    (Listing 16.8)
    fld    qword ptr [eax]           ; 1
    fmul   st, st(1)                 ; 1+2
    fadd   qword ptr [ebx]           ; 1

    fld    qword ptr [eax+8]         ; 1
    fmul   st, st(2)                 ; 1+2
    fadd   qword ptr [ebx+8]         ; 1

    fxch   st(1)                     ; 0
    fstp   qword ptr [ebx]           ; 2
    fstp   qword ptr [ebx+8]         ; 2+1

    add    eax, 16                   ; 1
    add    ebx, 16                   ; 0
    dec    ecx                       ; 1
    jnz    lbl                       ; 0
                                     ; ---
                                     ; 16 cycles, 8 cycles per double
```

However, performing this first half of each operation, then the second half eliminates all the delays:

```
lbl:                                 ; cycles                    (Listing 16.9)
    fld    qword ptr [eax]           ; 1
    fmul   st, st(1)                 ; 1
    fld    qword ptr [eax+8]         ; 1
    fmul   st, st(2)                 ; 1
    fxch   st(1)                     ; 0
    fadd   qword ptr [ebx]           ; 1
    fxch   st(1)                     ; 0

    fadd   qword ptr [ebx+8]         ; 1
    fxch   st(1)                     ; 0
    fstp   qword ptr [ebx]           ; 2
    fstp   qword ptr [ebx+8]         ; 2

    add    eax, 16                   ; 1
    add    ebx, 16                   ; 0
    dec    ecx                       ; 1
    jnz    lbl                       ; 0
                                     ; ---
                                     ; 12 cycles, 6 per double
```

Expanding the loop to four operations per iteration improves performance still a little bit more. See Listing 16.10.

```
lbl:                            ; cycles            (Listing 16.10)
    fld   qword ptr [eax]       ;  1
    fmul  st, st(1)             ;  1
    fld   qword ptr [eax+8]     ;  1
    fmul  st, st(2)             ;  1
    fxch  st(1)                 ;  0

    fadd  qword ptr [ebx]       ;  1
    fxch  st(1)                 ;  0
    fadd  qword ptr [ebx+8]     ;  1
    fxch  st(1)                 ;  0
    fstp  qword ptr [ebx]       ;  2
    fstp  qword ptr [ebx+8]     ;  2

    fld   qword ptr [eax+16]    ;  1
    fmul  st, st(1)             ;  1
    fld   qword ptr [eax+24]    ;  1
    fmul  st, st(2)             ;  1
    fxch  st(1)                 ;  0
    fadd  qword ptr [ebx+16]    ;  1
    fxch  st(1)                 ;  0

    fadd  qword ptr [ebx+24]    ;  1
    fxch  st(1)                 ;  0
    fstp  qword ptr [ebx+16]    ;  2
    fstp  qword ptr [ebx+24]    ;  2

    add   eax, 32               ;  1
    add   ebx, 32               ;  0
    dec   ecx                   ;  1
    jnz   lbl                   ;  0
                                ; ---
                                ; 22 cycles, 5.5 per double
```

Just as with the integer instructions, looking at the atomic operations tells us, approximately, the best performance we can achieve:

- load a number
- multiply
- add
- store (2)

In this case five cycles seems the best we can do, not including loop management. (However, timing tests showed six cycles. I haven't quite worked out why.)

Just like the **daxpy** function, the **ddot** function can also be optimized. The following is a typical assembly language implementation of the **ddot()** function. See Listing 16.11.

```
; double ddot(int n, double *xptr, double *yptr)        (Listing 16.11)
;       forms the dot product of two row vectors
;       returns in edx:eax and __fac

push    ebp
mov     ebp, esp

mov     ecx, dword ptr [ebp+8]        ;   count
mov     eax, dword ptr [ebp+12]       ;   xptr
mov     ebx, dword ptr [ebp+16]       ;   yptr
fldz

lbl:                                  ; cycles
  fld   qword ptr [eax]               ;   1         load double
  fmul  qword ptr [ebx]               ;   1+2       multiply
  fadd                                ;   1         add
  add   eax, 8                        ;   1         advance ptr to next double
  add   ebx, 8                        ;   0         advance ptr to next double
  loop  lbl                           ;   5         loop
                                      ; ---
  fstp  __fac                         ; 11 cycles per double (cache hit)
  mov   eax, dword ptr __fac
  mov   edx, dword ptr __fac+4
  pop   ebp
  ret
```

The **ddot** function returns the result in a global variable named **__fac** and also in the EDX:EAX registers. Different C compilers follow different conventions for returning the result of the function. You may not need to load the result back into EDX:EAX, but the **FSTP** instruction always needs to store the result in a global variable or local stack variable. Some compilers require the function result to be left on the FPU stack in **ST(0)**.

The first steps for optimizing this code is to use simple integer instructions and use two pipelines as much as possible.

```
lbl:                                  ; cycles             (Listing 16.12)
  fld   qword ptr [eax]               ;   1         load A1
  fmul  qword ptr [ebx]               ;   1+2       multiply A1 * A2
  fadd                                ;   1         add sum+A1*A2
  fld   qword ptr [eax+8]             ;   1         load B1
  fmul  qword ptr [ebx+8]             ;   1+2       multiply B1 * B2
  fadd                                ;   1         add sum+B1*B2
  add   eax, 16                       ;   1
  add   ebx, 16                       ;   0         dec
  ecx                                 ;   1
  jnz
lbl                                   ;   0
                                      ; ---
                                      ; 12 cycles, 6 per double
```

This increases performance but does not solve the problem of the extra delays caused by using the result of a **FMUL** in the next instruction. Keep in mind that the Pentium can execute only a single FPU instruction at a time (except for the **FXCH** instruction). The goal in programming the Pentium FPU is to optimize the operation of the pipeline by eliminating data dependencies. Utilization of the two pipelines only applies to integer instructions. However, unrolling the loop to operate on two (or more) sets of data is advantageous because the FPU delays are eliminated when the results of an operation are not needed until one or two cycles later.

Listing 16.13 shows a simple way to eliminate one of the two delays.

```
        jmp    lbl2              ; cycles                    (Listing 16.13)
lbl:
        fadd                     ; 1        add sum+A1*A2
lbl2:
        fld    qword ptr [eax]   ; 1        load A1
        fmul   qword ptr [ebx]   ; 1        multiply A1 * A2
        fld    qword ptr [eax+8] ; 1        load B1
        fmul   qword ptr [ebx+8] ; 1+2      multiply B1 * B2
        fadd                     ; 1        add sum+B1+B2
        add    eax, 16           ; 1
        add    ebx, 16           ; 0
        dec    ecx               ; 1
        jnz    lbl               ; 0
        fadd                     ; ---
                                 ; 10 cycles, 5 per double
```

Delaying the second **FADD**, for each iteration, until the start of the next loop allows the loop management overhead to execute during the two cycles required for the first **FADD** result to become available. This technique is advantageous because it generates no additional cycles on the 486 (and earlier) processors.

Listing 16.14 uses the **FXCH** instruction to eliminate the delay on the first **FADD** instruction.

```
        jmp    lbl2              ; cycles                    (Listing 16.14)
lbl:
        fadd                     ; 1        add sum+B1*B2
lbl2:
        fld    qword ptr [eax]   ; 1        load A1
        fmul   qword ptr [ebx]   ; 1        multiply A1*A2
        fld    qword ptr [eax+8] ; 1        load B1
        fmul   qword ptr [ebx+8] ; 1        multiply B1*B2
        fxch                     ; 0        exchange st(0) and st(1)
        faddp  st(2), st         ; 1        add sum+A1*A2
        add    eax, 16           ; 1
        add    ebx, 16           ; 0
        dec    ecx               ; 1
        jnz    lbl               ; 0
        fadd                     ; ---
                                 ; 8 cycles, 4 per double
```

Table 16.3 Floating-Point Stack Operation for Listing 16.14

	;	st(0)	st(1)	st(2)	...	st(7)
	;	sum	–	–		–
fld	;	A1	sum	–		–
fmul	;	A1*A2	sum	–		–
fld	;	B1	A1*A2	sum		–
fmul	;	B1*B2	A1*A2	sum		–
fxch	;	A1*A2	B1*B2	sum		–
faddp st(2), st	;	B1*B2	sum+A1*A2	–		–
...						
fadd	;	sum+A1*A2 +B1*B2	–	–		–

The key to Listing 16.14 is the use of the **FXCH** and **FADDP** instructions to change the order that the additions are performed. Table 16.3 shows the details of the FPU stack for these operations.

As a final step, the loop can be unrolled to operate on four sets of data in each iteration, as shown in Listing 16.15.

```
        jmp    lbl2              ; cycles              (Listing 16.15)
lbl1:
        fadd                     ;    1      add sum+D1*D2
lbl2:
        fld    qword ptr [eax]   ;    1      load A1
        fmul   qword ptr [ebx]   ;    1      multiply A1*A2
        fld    qword ptr [eax+8] ;    1      load B1
        fmul   qword ptr [ebx+8] ;    1      multiply B1*B2
        fxch                     ;    0      exchange st(0) and st(1)
        faddp st(2), st          ;    1      add sum+A1*A2

        fld    qword ptr [eax+16]  ;  1      load C1
        fmul   qword ptr [ebx+16]  ;  1      multiply C1*C2
        fxch                     ;    0      exchange st(0) and st(1)
        faddp st(2), st          ;    1      add sum+B1*B2

        fld    qword ptr [eax+24]  ;  1      load D1
        fmul   qword ptr [ebx+24]  ;  1      multiply D1*D2
        fxch                     ;    0      exchange st(0) and st(1)
        faddp st(2), st          ;    1      add sum+C1*C2

        add    eax, 32           ;    1
        add    ebx, 32           ;    0
        dec    ecx               ;    1
        jnz    lbl1              ;    0
        fadd                     ;    ---
                                 ; 14 cycles, 3.5 per double
```

Table 16.4 shows the details of the FPU stack for Listing 16.15.

Table 16.4 Floating-Point Stack Operation for Listing 16.15

	;	st(0)	st(1)	st(2)	...	st(7)
	;	sum	-	-		-
fld	;	A1	sum	-		-
fmul	;	A1*A2	sum	-		-
fld	;	B1	A1*A2	sum		-
fmul	;	B1*B2	A1*A2	sum		-
fxch	;	A1*A2	B1*B2	sum		-
faddp st(2), st	;	B1*B2	sum+A1*A2	-		-
fld	;	C1	B1*B2	sum+A1*A2		-
fmul	;	C1*C2	B1*B2	sum+A1*A2		-
fxch	;	B1*B2	C1+C2	sum+A1*A2		-
faddp st(2), st	;	C1*C2	sum+A1*A2	-		-
	;		+B1*B2			
fld	;	D1	C1*C2	sum+A1*A2		-
	;			+B1*B2		
fmul	;	D1*D2	C1*C2	sum+A1*A2		-
	;			+B1*B2		
fxch	;	C1*C2	D1*D2	sum+A1*A2		-
	;			+B1*B2		
faddp st(2), st	;	D1*D2	sum+A1*A2	-		-
	;		+B1*B2			
	;		+C1*C2			
...						
fadd	;	sum+A1*A2	-	-		-
		+B1*B2				
		+C1*C2				
		+D1*D2				

Just as with the integer instructions and the **daxpy** FPU example, looking at the atomic operations tells us, approximately, the best performance we can achieve:

- load a number
- multiply
- add

In this case three cycles is the best we can do, not including loop management, and we obtained 3.5 cycles.

The actual timing results shown in Table 16.2 show that the performance of C and C++ numeric applications can be significantly improved through the use of just a small amount of optimized assembly on the Pentium. FPU performance increases of 100% are not uncommon when taking full advantage of the Pentium over unoptimized use of the Pentium. And this was after we had already used an algorithm that made better use of the Pentium's cache. In the next chapter we'll explore several methods for interfacing assembly language with C and C++.

Interfacing to C

17

*"I pass with relief from the tossing sea of
Cause and Theory to the
firm ground of Result and Fact."*
—Sir Winston Churchill

I n this chapter we will discuss various techniques for including assembly language routines in C or C++ programs. There are three methods that we'll be discussing:

- in line assembly
- separately linked ASM and C modules
- separately linked ASM and C modules with fastcall

I'll describe the interface requirements of each method, give some examples and then discuss the advantages and disadvantages. Finally, we'll see how to time the code we've written using the timer from Chapter 12.

INLINE ASSEMBLY

Probably the easiest way to include assembly language in a C or C++ program is to use inline assembly. Inline assembly is a feature of a C compiler that allows you to put assembly code right in your C or C++ programs. Listing 17.1 shows an example of how it works for Microsoft C/C++ 7.0 and above (including Visual C++):

```
int add2c( int x, int y)      /* sample C function */        (Listing 17.1)
{
  return x+y;
}
                              /* same C function in assembly */
{
__asm{
  mov ax, y
  add ax, x
  }
}
```

or the assembly function can be written this way:

```
int add2a( int x, int y)                                      (Listing 17.2)
{
  __asm  mov ax, y
  __asm  add ax, x
}
```

For Borland C/C++ it would be written as:

```
#pragma inline   /* some Borland compilers require this */ (Listing 17.3)

int add2( int x, int y)
{
asm   mov ax, y
asm   add ax, x
}
```

The use of #**ifdef**'s can allow the same code to be compiled with either compiler, such as:

```
#ifdef (_MSC_VER >= 700)
# define asm   __asm
#endif
```

However, for clarity, I'll use the block structure allowed by the Microsoft C/C++ 7.0 and above, (__asm{...} keyword) in examples. You can place __asm or asm on each line of your code, as required.

The choice between inline assembly and assembly code in separate files is largely a matter of style and personal preference. However, there are some specific strengths of each method. The advantages of using inline assembly are:

- quick and simple to use
- does not require a separate assembler (i.e. MASM or TASM)
- allows easy use of C variables and functions
- version control may be easier
- can mix C and assembly in the same function
- knowledge of C++ name mangling not required
- little knowledge of calling conventions required

Some disadvantages of using inline assembly are:

- does not have the power and capacity of a full assembler
- full segmentation control not available
- full power of data declarations and macros not available

INLINE ASSEMBLY EXAMPLE

In this example we'll replace the standard C library **strcpy** function with the code from Chapter 13 that copies strings. Of course, we're assuming that this code will be faster, and we'll test that theory later. Here is how you might currently be using **strcpy**, in a simple program:

```
#include <string.h>
void main()
{
 char buffer1[80] = "A sample string";
 char buffer2[80];
 strcpy(buffer2, buffer1);
 printf("string 2 = %s\n", buffer2);
}
```

To change the program we must add the new **strcpy** function, as follows:

```
#include<string.h>                                    (Listing 17.5)
void main()
{
 char buffer1[80] = "A sample string";
 char buffer2[80];

 strcpy(buffer2, buffer1);
 printf("string 2 = %s\n", buffer2);
}
char *strcpy(char *string1, const char *string2);
 {
 __asm{
   mov   di, string1
   mov   si, string2
  lbl:
   mov   ax, [si]
   add   si, 2
   cmp   al, 0h
   je    exit2
   mov   [di], ax
   add   di, 2
   cmp   ah, 0h
   jne   lbl
  exit:
   jmp   exit3
  exit2:
   mov   [di], al
  exit3:
   mov   ax, string1  ; return ptr to destination
 }
 }
```

LINKING SEPARATE MODULES

Keeping assembly code separate from C or C++ code may be helpful for version control. Many times it is necessary because the full power of the assembler is required. In either case it is a fairly simple matter to write the code and assemble it, then link it in with the C or C++ object modules. One possible difficulty is the passing of parameters from the C or C++ code to the assembly routine. To do this we must have an understanding of the calling conventions. With inline assembly we were able to get by without knowing much about the conventions.

There are several steps to writing an assembly-language procedure to be called from a high level language program. Some of these steps may not apply in all situations, but you can use this list as a guide:

- declare the procedure name
- set up the stack frame
- allocate local stack space, if required
- save registers being used

- load or access the stack parameters
- perform the core purpose of the function
- determine the function's value, if any
- restore registers
- deallocate local stack space, if any
- restore from stack frame
- exit via a return

We'll discuss each of these items in detail, but first we need to get a general understanding of how different languages handle some of these steps.

CALLING CONVENTIONS

Different languages have different names for subroutines, procedures and functions. In C the term *function* is used, and in C++ there are functions and methods. In other languages there is a differentiation between functions that return a result and other types of routines that don't. Generally we'll use the terms routine, subroutine and procedure interchangeably. Functions are any of those that return a value.

High-level languages pass parameters to subroutines and functions by using the system stack. To be able to write a function that accepts input parameters, we must know several things about how the language puts the items on the stack and how they are removed. Table 17.1 shows the conventions for various languages on the PC.

The parameter order refers to the sequence in which items are pushed onto the stack. In C and C++ they are pushed in the reverse order (right to left). The stack reset refers to how the stack pointer is reset to its original position. In C and C++ the parent function pushes parameters on the stack, calls the child function and then resets the stack pointer to its initial value. In other languages the child function must return by executing a

Table 17.1 HLL Calling Conventions

	Parameter Order	Parameter Val/Ref	Stack Reset	Naming Convention
BASIC	forward	offsets	ret #	type info (%, &, !, #, $) removed
C	reverse	values	caller	underscore prefix, case sensitive
Fortran	forward	far ptrs	ret #	N/A
Pascal	forward	values	ret #	N/A

RET # instruction, where **#** is the number of bytes pushed onto the stack by the calling function. The naming convention specifies that C functions must be declared with a leading underscore, and the function names are case-sensitive.

Parameters can be pushed on the stack by value or by reference. Table 17.1 shows the general conventions for each language. Each data type in each language may have its own convention. Passing by value means the actual value of a variable is passed on the stack. Passing by reference means that a pointer to the variable is passed on the stack. Pointers can be only offsets (near pointers) or segments and offsets (far pointers). When only an offset is passed, the data segment (DS) is assumed. The advantage of passing by value is that it is faster (for small data items), takes less code and prevents the subroutine from changing the value of the actual variable. The disadvantage is that the subroutine cannot change the value. The advantage of passing by reference is that it is faster and takes less stack space for large data items.

C passes all arrays by reference because performance would be terribly slow, for example, to push a 10,000-element array. Arrays can be passed by value by being declared as the only member of a structure. Passing all other data types by value instead of by reference is not a problem in C because the **&** (address of) operator may be placed in front of any variable to pass by reference.

The size of a parameter passed by reference (a pointer) in C depends on the memory model. In the tiny, small and medium memory models, pointers are two bytes, and therefore only the offset is passed. In compact, large and huge memory models pointers are four bytes and include the segment and offset. In 32-bit flat model all pointers are 32-bit near offsets.

Setting up the Stack Frame

A stack frame must be set up if any parameters are passed on the stack or if the stack will be used for local variables. The term stack frame is used to describe the temporary instance of a data structure on the stack. The BP (or EBP) register is used as a pointer to the stack frame. When using BP as pointer, the stack segment is the default segment (specifically for this purpose). Here is how it is done for 16-bit code:

```
push  bp
mov   bp, sp
```

Here is how to set up a stack frame for 32-bit code:

```
push  ebp
mov   ebp, esp
```

Allocating Local Stack Space

If space is needed on the stack for variables local to the assembly subroutine it can easily be done after the stack frame is setup. Space is allocated by just subtracting the required number of bytes from the stack pointer (SP or ESP) as follows:

```
sub    esp, 8          ; allocate 8 bytes of stack space
                       ; for local variables
```

Saving Registers

The C compilers expect certain registers to have their values left intact upon return from a function call. These registers are BP, SI, DI and DS. For a proper return to the calling program, the CS and SS segment registers must also have been preserved. Assembly procedures are free to modify AX, BX, CX and DX. In addition, if a procedure modifies the direction flag (using CLD or STD) the flags register must be pushed and popped.

Loading and Accessing arameters

Once the stack frame is set, local storage allocated and registers are saved, the main body of the procedure can be written. Within this code it will be necessary to load or access the values of the passed parameters. Table 17.2 shows the location of the first parameter for each of the memory models. The location of the first parameter relative to BP (or EBP) is based on the size of the return address and the fact that BP (or EBP) was pushed onto the stack to save it before the stack frame was set.

Table 17.2 Location of First Parameter on the Stack by Memory Model

Model	First parameter
tiny	[bp+4]
small	[bp+4]
compact	[bp+4]
medium	[bp+6]
large	[bp+6]
huge	[bp+6]
32-bit flat	[ebp+8]

Table 17.3 Return Value Conventions for C

Data Type	Return Method
(unsigned) character	AL
(unsigned) integer	AX
(unsigned) long integer	DX:AX
Near pointer	AX
Far pointer	DX:AX
Float	__fac (Microsoft), FPU ST(0) (Borland)
Double	__fac (Microsoft), FPU ST(0) (Borland)
Long double (10 bytes)	FPU st(0)
Near structures	AX ptr to structure
Far structures	DX:AX ptr to structure

Return Values

Values returned from C functions (written in C or assembly) must also follow a convention. Table 17.3 shows how to return various data types from a C function. For example, to return an integer, the integer value is placed in the AX register.

The method for returning floating-point values is quite different. For Microsoft C, floats (single-precision) and doubles (double-precision) are returned in the global variable, __**fac** (floating-point accumulator). Long double values are returned on the FPU stack. For Borland C, floats, doubles and long doubles are all returned on the FPU stack. A long double is the ten-byte format used internal to the FPU. [All 32-bit C functions using __**fastcall** (see later discussion) use the FPU stack for all floating-point data types.]

When a function must return a structure to a C program, a pointer to the structure is returned. This means that a copy of the structure must be in global variable. In the Pascal and Fortran convention, the compilers allocate space on the stack of the calling program for the structure and pass a pointer as an extra parameter for the result.

Restoring the Stack Frame and Exiting

After the goal of the function is complete, the stack pointer must be returned to the value it had before space for any local variables was allocated. This can be done by adding the same value to SP (ESP) that was subtracted when the space was allocated. However, since the BP (EBP) register contains a copy of the SP (ESP) register from just before the space was allocated, it is just as easy (and sometimes faster) to just copy BP (EBP) into SP (ESP). The BP (EBP) register must then be restored from the initial stack frame setup. Finally, there must be a **RET** instruction. For the C calling convention, it is just a plain **RET**. For all other calling conventions, the **RET** must include an operand that is the number of bytes to remove from the stack after the return is executed.

```
mov     sp, bp              ; restore SP from local variable use
pop     bp                  ; restore BP
ret                         ; C style return
```

Here is how to return for 32-bit code:

```
mov     esp, ebp
pop     ebp
ret
```

Here is how to return for all calling conventions other than C. In this example, the routine accepted four bytes on the stack (i.e., two integers, two near pointers, etc.):

```
mov     sp, bp
pop     bp
ret     4
```

FULL C-TO-ASSEMBLY TEMPLATES

Now we'll put all this together. Here is a full C-to-assembly template for small model:

```
push    bp                  ; save BP for stack frame      (Listing 17.6)
mov     bp, sp              ; setup stack frame
sub     sp, 2               ; 2 bytes of local storage
push    di                  ; save registers
push    si

...
mov     ax, [bp+4]          ; access passed parameter

...
inc     ax
mov     [bp-2], ax          ; use local storage

...
mov     ax, [bp-2]          ; return integer value

...
pop     si                  ; restore registers
pop     di
mov     sp, bp              ; de-allocate local storage
pop     bp                  ; restore BP
ret                         ; return
```

We can write a similar template for 32-bit flat model as shown in Listing 17.7.

```
push  ebp                      ; save EBP for stack frame       (Listing 17.7)
mov   ebp, esp                 ; setup stack frame
sub   esp, 4                   ; 4 bytes of local storage
push  edi                      ; save registers
push  esi

...
mov   eax, [ebp+8]             ; access passed parameter

...
inc   eax
mov   [ebp-4], eax             ; use local storage

...
mov   eax, [ebp-4]             ; return long integer value

...
pop   esi                      ; restore registers
pop   edi
mov   esp, ebp                 ; de-allocate local storage
pop   ebp                      ; restore EBP
ret                            ; return
```

When writing 32-bit code it is possible to use ESP for the stack frame instead of EBP for simple functions (simple based on the use of the stack frame). Both EBP and ESP use the SS segment as the default segment.

```
push  edi                      ; save registers                 (Listing 17.8)
push  esi

...
mov   eax, [esp+12]            ; access first dword
mov   ebx, [esp+16]            ; access second dword

...
pop   esi                      ; restore registers
pop   edi
ret                            ; return
```

EXAMPLES OF CALLING ASSEMBLY ROUTINES FROM C

Now that we've covered the C to ASM calling mechanism it's time to try some examples. Here is a modified version of Listing 17.4 for using an external assembly function.

```
extern char * strcpy2(char *, const char *);          (Listing 17.9)
void main()
{
 char buffer1[80] = "A sample string";
 char buffer2[80];
 strcpy2(buffer2, buffer1);
 printf("string 2 = %s\n", buffer2);
}
```

In a C++ the extern declaration must written as

```
extern "C" char * strcpy2(char *, const char *);
```

The following example is the same strcpy from Listing 17.5 converted to a stand-alone **.ASM** file:

```
.model small                                          (Listing 17.10)
.code
_strcpy2 proc near

    push   bp
    mov    bp, sp
    push   di
    push   si

    mov    di, [bp+4]          ; string1
    mov    si, [bp+6]          ; string2
lbl:
    mov    ax, [si]
    add    si, 2
    cmp    al, 0
    je     exit2
    mov    [di], ax
    add    di, 2
    cmp    ah, 0h
    jne    lbl
exit:
    jmp    exit3
exit2:
    mov    [di], al
exit3:
    mov    ax, [bp+4]          ; return ptr to string1

    pop    si
    pop    di
    pop    bp
    ret
_strcpy2 endp
```

Here is a large model version of **strcpy** in a stand-alone. **ASM** file:

```
.model large                                          (Listing 17.11)
.code
_strcpy2 proc far            ; large model strcpy

    push  bp
    mov   bp, sp
    push  di
    push  si
    push  ds
    push  es

    les   di, [bp+6]         ; string1
    lds   si, [bp+10]        ; string2
lbl:
    mov   ax, [si]
    add   si, 2
    cmp   al, 0
    je    exit2
    mov   ES:[di], ax
    add   di, 2
    cmp   ah, 0h
    jne   lbl
exit:
    jmp   exit3
exit2:
    mov   ES:[di], al
exit3:
    mov   ax, [bp+6]         ; return ptr to string1
    mov   dx, es

    pop   es
    pop   ds
    pop   si
    pop   di
    pop   bp
    ret

_strcpy2 endp
```

In the large model procedure, the first parameter is six bytes from BP (instead of four) because the stack has a far return address from the procedure call. The second parameter is four bytes from the first (instead of two) because the pointers are four bytes (not two) in large model. Three other changes needed to be made in the code. First, both segments and offsets needed to be read from the stack. This is easily done using LDS and LES. Second, because far pointers are loaded, the DS and ES segment registers needed to be

Table 17.4 Summary of Details for Passing Two Pointers in C

Model	string1 location	string2 location	load far ptrs, save/restore DS/ES and ES override
tiny	[bp+4]	[bp+6]	no
small	[bp+4]	[bp+6]	no
compact	[bp+4]	[bp+8]	yes
medium	[bp+6]	[bp+8]	no
large	[bp+6]	[bp+10]	yes
huge	[bp+6]	[bp+10]	yes

pushed and popped. Third, an ES segment override needed to be placed on each **[DI]** memory reference.

For this **strcpy** example, Table 17.4 is a summary of the changes for each memory model.

USING THE EXTENDED PROC DIRECTIVE

There are some extensions to the **PROC** directive that make interfacing C and assembly much more convenient than the preceding examples may lead you to believe. In the **proc** directive, we can specify each parameter and its data type and each register that must be pushed and popped. In the **.model** directive, we specify the memory model and the high-level calling convention we are using. The language controls the following three items:

- naming convention (for underscore in C)
- parameter order to be expected from the stack
- whether the **RET** instruction also clean up the stack

This allow us to write procedures with very few differences between memory models and languages. The code in Listing 17.12 can be used for any model and any language to copy ASCIIZ strings.

An assembler feature, conditional assembly, is shown for the first time in Listing 17.12. Conditional assembly allows an assembler to evaluate the value of a symbol (or some other expression) to determine whether or not a particular section of code should be assembled into the object file. The built-in symbols, **@codesize** and **@datasize**, are defined by the assembler based on the memory model.

```
.model small, C; change "small" to any model          (Listing 17.12)
.code

strcpy2 PROC USES di, si, string1:ptr, string2:ptr

if @datasize
    push ds
    push es
    les  di, string1
    lds  si, string2
else
    mov  di, string1
    mov  si, string2
endif
 lbl:
    mov  ax, [si]
    add  si, 2
    cmp  al, 0
    je   exit2
if @datasize
    mov  ES:[di], ax
else
    mov  [di], ax
endif
    add  di, 2
    cmp  ah, 0h
    jne  lbl
 exit:
    jmp  exit3
 exit2:
if @datasize
    mov  ES:[di], al
else
    mov  [di], al
endif
 exit3:
    mov  ax, string1
if @datasize
    mov  dx, es
    pop  es
    pop  ds
endif
     ret

strcpy2 endp
```

FASTCALL

We've seen how to use the power of the Pentium to optimize assembly-language routines and how to interface those routines in C and C++ programs. There are still more optimizations that we can make when combining assembly and C. One of the reasons that assembly language is faster and more compact than high-level languages is that assembly-language procedures are usually called with parameters passed in registers. Many times the parameters are already in registers, but if not, it is always faster to move data into a register than to push it onto the stack. Setting up the stack frame and moving the parameters off the stack into registers also takes a lot of code and CPU cycles.

High-level languages are designed this way because one of their purposes is to hide the details of the underlying CPU architecture. Hiding the number and size of registers forces everything into the general solution of using the stack for parameters. Don't be misled by this explanation—using the stack for passing parameters is a brilliant and elegant software innovation. However, many function calls require only a few parameters, well within the number of available registers on the 80x86.

The C and C++ compilers support a fastcall convention that allow passing as many parameters as possible in registers. Compiling with the **/Gr** command line option enables fastcall for an entire file. Using the **_fastcall** keyword enables fastcall for a specific function. Fastcall is most beneficial if the called functions have fewer than four parameters and the function(s) are in a loop or are called recursively. Borland C/C++ 3.0 and above compilers support fastcall with the keyword **_fastcall**. Because of a naming convention error in the Borland 3.0 fastcall, I recommend using Borland C/C++ 3.1 or above when using a Borland compiler. The Microsoft C 6.0 compiler supports fastcall with the keyword **_fastcall**. The Microsoft C/C++ 7.0 and Visual C++ compilers support fastcall with the keyword **__fastcall**. (The following examples use **__fastcall**.)

Listing 17.13 is an example with the **strcpy** function from Listing 17.5.

I timed this example and, unexpectedly, it was measured at exactly the same speed as without the **__fastcall** keyword. After inspecting the assembly code generated by the compiler, I discovered some curious code. The compiler pushed the two parameters onto the stack at the start of the function. The Microsoft manual states, "don't use the **__fastcall** calling convention for functions with **__asm** blocks." It also states that the registers assigned to a particular parameter may change in future releases of the compiler. So, I wondered, does **__fastcall** provide any benefit when using assembly? What appears to happen is the compiler detects the **__asm** block in the function and decides to push the parameters on the stack. Functions written entirely in C will still benefit.

To get the performance gains from assembly language and from the fastcall convention, it is necessary to write the assembly-language function as a separately linked module. The separate module can be written in C or assembly. When writing the code in assembly language, note that the C naming convention of adding a leading underscore is changed to adding a leading at sign (**@**). In addition, the calling convention for parameters that are not passed in registers is changed to the Pascal convention.

```
char * __fastcall strcpy2(char *, const char *);          (Listing 17.13)
void main()
{
 char buffer1[80] = "A sample string";
 char buffer2[80];

 strcpy2(buffer2, buffer1);
 printf("string 2 = %s\n", buffer2);
}
char * __fastcall strcpy2(char *string1, const char *string2)
 {
 __asm{
   mov   di, string1
   mov   si, string2
 lbl:
   mov   ax, [si]
   add   si, 2
   cmp   al, 0h
   je    exit2
   mov   [di], ax
   add   di, 2
   cmp   ah, 0h
   jne   lbl
 exit:
   jmp   exit3
 exit2:
   mov   [di], al
 exit3:
   mov   ax, string1        ; return ptr to destination
 }
}
```

CAUTION

When taking advantage of the fastcall convention with assembly language code you must be sure to retest each function when you change compiler versions.

FASTCALL REGISTERS

To effectively use the fastcall convention, we must know what parameters are passed in each register. Table 17.5 is a summary of registers used by both the Borland and Microsoft compilers for 16-bit code. When writing 32-bit assembly code with fastcall, see the documentation with the current version of your compiler, since they are different.

Table 17.5 Fastcall Registers (16-Bit Code)

Data types	Possible registers
char	AL, DL, BL
unsigned char	AL, DL, BL
int	AX, DX, BX
unsigned int	AX, DX, BX
long int	DX:AX
unsigned long int	DX:AX
near pointer	BX, AX, DX (Microsoft)
near pointer	AX, DX, BX (Borland)
far pointer	on the stack only
float, double & others	on the stack only

TIMING C CODE

Using the timer library to time C or C++ code is simple. You must be sure to time code of a long enough duration to obtain an accurate measurement. Listing 17.14 shows an example of timing the C library **strcpy** function:

```
void main()                                    (Listing 17.14)
{
 int i;
 char buffer1[20] = "A sample string ";
 char buffer2[20];
 timer_on();                    /* start the timer */
 for(i=0;i<1000;i++)
 {
  strcpy(buffer2, buffer1);
 }
 timer_off();                   /* stop the timer */
 timer_show();                  /* display the results */
}
```

Table 17.6 shows the timing results of the **strcpy** functions developed in Chapter 13 and used in various configurations in this chapter.

From Table 17.6 we can see that our assembly-language routine speeds up string copies by 37% on a 486 and 150% on a Pentium. When the fastcall is used, the speed-up is even greater: 42% on a 486 and 166% on a Pentium. The timings in Table 17.6 are

Table 17.6   Timing for Small Model strcpy, in Microseconds
(55 Characters Copied 1000 Times)

	Pentium-60	486-33	386-25
C library **strcpy**	6002	13350	32950
strcpy inline ASM	2367	9716	38300
strcpy fastcall	2251	9343	34560

based on string lengths of 55 characters. I believe this string length is a good measurement after trying many lengths, as shown in the graphs in Figure 17.1.

From the graphs in Figure 17.1, it can be seen that shorter strings have a greater speed-up, as much as two or three times as much. Longer strings have a speed-up that decreases a few percent at 100 or 200 characters.

Figure 17.1   String Length vs. Speed

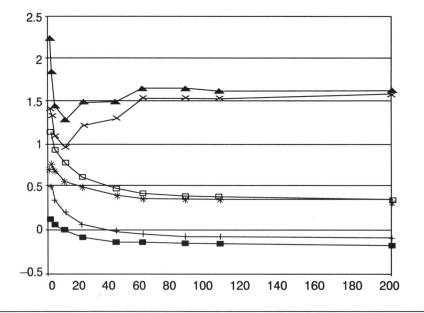

Performance on a 386 is degraded by our **strcpy** (5% to 14% for 55 characters). 386 performance is actually improved for small strings and is about equal in the 10- to 35-character range.

There are many opportunities to improve the performance of C and C++ programs through the use of assembly language. This is true on the 486 and even more so on the Pentium. When you are interested in high performance, do not be lulled by the "let the compiler optimize it for you" theory. We were all born with an optimizing compiler. Measure and isolate the hot spots in your C or C++ code so that you can optimize from the firm ground of results and facts.

Protected-Mode Programming

18

> *"… to boldly go where no*
> *man has gone before."*
> —William Shatner
> (Captain Kirk™ , Star Trek™)

I n this chapter we will take a voyage into the realms of protected-mode programming. Although you may have been there before, Captain Kirk was also preceded by others to the distant places he and the crew of the Enterprise™ visited. We'll also learn how to write "invisible" software like a cloaked Klingon spaceship.

INTRODUCTION TO PROTECTED MODE

There are many environments that can be used to run protected-mode programs, including Windows, Windows NT, OS/2 and DOS extenders. In addition, other operating systems, such as SCO UNIX and the like, can be used. The most widely available platforms are DOS and Windows, so I'll limit this protected-mode discussion to these environments.

DOS runs in real mode (always 16-bit) or virtual 8086 mode (also 16-bit) under the control of a memory manager. Windows 3.0 or 3.1 running in enhanced mode is running in 16-bit protected mode. Windows 4.0 and Windows NT run in 32-bit protected mode.

The difference between 16-bit protected mode and 32-bit protected mode is that a 32-bit operating system must recognize and allow programs containing 32-bit code to be loaded and executed. Such programs contain segments that are declared as **USE32**. A segment declared as **USE32** is set up differently by the operating system before execution begins.

The segment descriptors on the 386 and above contain a bit called the D bit. The D bit, in a code segment, indicates the default length for operands and effective addresses. When the D bit is set, then 32-bit operands and 32-bit effective addressing modes are assumed. If the D bit is clear, then 16-bit operands and addressing modes are assumed. The operand size and/or the effective address size can be overridden, on an instruction-by-instruction basis, by using the operand-size prefix (**66h**) and/or the address size prefix (**67h**). These prefixes are automatically inserted by the assembler based on the operands of each instruction and whether or not **USE32** was specified for the code segment.

DOS extenders, such as the Phar Lap TNT DOS-extender, allow DOS programs to run in protected mode by translating DOS and BIOS system service calls back into 16-bit real mode requests to DOS and the BIOS. Some DOS extenders allow only 16-bit protected-mode code; others allow both 16- and 32-bit protected-mode code. Vendors of DOS extenders provide special toolkits and usually charge royalties for the run-time libraries that you must ship with your products.

DPMI, DOS PROTECTED-MODE INTERFACE

The development environment you choose will be based on user preferences, market size, installed base, etc. These issues are not relevant for this discussion because we will be using an environment that is widely available and is an excellent test platform for other environments. This platform is DPMI or DOS Protected-Mode Interface. DPMI (briefly described in Chapter 6) is a specification for allowing DOS programs to access the advanced features of the 80286 (and above) in a well-behaved fashion.

Although applications that use DPMI directly might have a limited commercial value, using DOS DPMI programs to measure and test code, especially for the Pentium, can be quite productive. Here is why. When running in a multitasking environment, such as Windows, NT or OS/2, it is difficult to maintain complete control over the CPU, which is usually required to get accurate timing measurements.

Suppose you want to write a routine like one of the string routines in Chapter 14. This isn't a problem when you are writing 16-bit code because you can write and test the code in DOS. However, what happens if you want to write 32-bit code? You can write and test the code in DOS, but your timing will be way off. When you assemble the code for DOS, the assembler creates 16-bit code for 16-bit segments. This means any 32-bit operations will have operand size and/or address size override prefixes mixed throughout the code. Recall rule 6 from Table 9.2:

- Prefixed instructions can only execute in the U pipe
  (except for **0F** prefix in **Jcc**).

For example:

```
mov    eax, 1
mov    ebx, 2
```

These instructions can pair in 32-bit code and take only one cycle to execute. But in 16-bit code, these instructions do not pair, and the prefix on each instruction takes an extra cycle. The final result is two instructions taking two cycles each—four times as long in16-bit code than in 32-bit code.

Using a DPMI server you can write, test and accurately measure true 32-bit code and run it from DOS. The tools you'll need are:

- an assembler and linker that will generate 32-bit code
- a memory manager containing a DPMI server

TASM 1.0 (or above) and MASM 5.1 (or above, MASM 6.0 or above preferred) will both generate 32-bit code and their linkers (TLINK and LINK) will produce a 32-bit .EXE file. 386MAX version 6.01 or 7.0 is the memory manager I used for a DPMI server.

PROTECTED-MODE SEGMENTS

In protected mode (both 16-bit and 32-bit), the value in the segment registers are called selectors. They are actually pointers into a descriptor table which contain information about the segment, such as the starting address, total length, the D bit (discussed earlier) and more. All the information in the descriptor table is copied into internal registers when a segment register is loaded. This is why loading segment registers in protected mode takes longer than in real mode. Every time an address is calculated in real mode, the segment and offset are combined, with the segment shifted left by four bits. In protected mode the starting address of the segment is combined with the offset.

CONVERTING CODE TO PROTECTED MODE

Because of the change in the way selectors operate versus segment values, there are generally no valid operations that may be performed on selectors. Real mode code being converted to protected mode must be modified to remove any "segment arithmetic" code sequences.

Other changes must be made when converting to protected mode, such as:

- Data cannot be written to the code segment
- Certain instructions may cause protection violations, such as **CLI**, **STI**, **IN**, **OUT**

MIXED 16-BIT AND 32-BIT PROTECTED-MODE PROGRAMMING

Mixing 16-bit and 32-bit code in the same program is primarily done when writing operating system software and utilities, and for testing 32-bit code in a 16-bit environment, as we will do here. The reason for mixing 16-bit and 32-bit code in an application would primarily be to allow 32-bit code to be run from a 16-bit environment. A 16-bit application could then, optionally, run 32-bit code if required and if possible in the user's environment. The following terminology is sometimes used to describe the various combinations of segments, selectors and offsets:

16:16	segment:offset	real mode
16:16	selector:offset	16-bit protected mode
16:32	segment:offset	virtual 8086 with address override
16:32	selector:offset	32-bit protected mode
0:32	offset	32-bit flat model

FULL SEGMENT DEFINITIONS

Full segment definitions are required when you need complete control over segments. Simplified segments can be used in combination with full segment definitions, but they must not conflict with the automatic segment definitions the assembler uses. Simplified segmentation directives can be used to create **USE32** segments by placing the **.386**, **.486** or **.586** directive before the **.model** directive. (The **.586** directive allows use of the new Pentium instructions.) This sets the default to **USE32**, which can be overridden by using **USE16**.

Table 18.1 describes the full syntax of the **SEGMENT** directive in the latest versions of MASM (version 6.0 and above) and TASM (version 3.1 and above).

Table 18.1 Defining segments with the **SEGMENT** directive

```
seg SEGMENT [align] [READONLY] [combine] [use] ['class']

  code and/or data

seg ENDS
```

where:

[ ]	Items in brackets are optional.
seg	The name you choose for the segment.
SEGMENT	The required directive name.
align	Alignment type (byte, word, dword, para or page). (default is para)
READONLY	Keyword declaring the segment as **readonly**. An assembler error will be generated for any instruction that modifies any item in the segment.
combine	Determines how the linker combines segments. Must be one of: **PRIVATE**, **PUBLIC**, **STACK**, **COMMON**, **MEMORY** or **AT** address.
use	**USE16** or **USE32**
class	Specifies a class name for the segment. The linker groups segments with the same class name together.
ENDS	Required directive to end a segment.

All optional parameters after the **SEGMENT** keyword may be specified in any order.

Combine types:

PRIVATE	(default) The segment is not combined with others with the same name in other modules.
PUBLIC	Combines segments with the same name from other modules into one contiguous segment. Normally this is what you want.
STACK	For, possibly, uninitialized data for the stack.
COMMON	Overlaps segments. The final length is the largest of the combined segments. Not for initialized data.
MEMORY	same as **PUBLIC**.
AT addr	Places the segment at the specified address. For real mode only. Not linked by the linker, only used to define data or structures at specific far memory locations.

Continued

Table 18.1 Defining segments with the **SEGMENT** directive *(Continued)*

Use types:

USE16	16-bit offsets and operands are the default.
USE32	32-bit offsets and operands are the default.
FLAT	

If **.386**, **.486** or **.586** is specified before a **.model** directive, then **USE32** is the default use type; otherwise, **USE16** is the default use type.

PROTECTED MODE TIMING

The 32-bit version of the timing library (see Chapter 12) must be used when timing protected mode code. This library (**TIMER32.LIB**) contains the proper segment declarations for 32-bit code. In protected mode the **CLI** (clear interrupt flag) and **STI** (set interrupt flag) will normally generate a general protection fault in an application program. Because of this, disabling interrupts is not easily done. So it is important to time many events and take into account that interrupts may be occurring on the system.

32-BIT PROTECTED-MODE CODE TEMPLATE

The code in Listing 18.1 is a template for writing 16-bit and/or 32-bit protected-mode code.

```
.model small                                                      (Listing 18.1)
.stack
.486

.data

intro_msg               db 'Switching into protected mode.',13,10,0
in16_msg                db 'In protected mode, 16-bit segment.',13,10,0
in32_msg                db 'In protected mode, 32-bit segment.',13,10,0
; data returned from INT 2Fh function 1687h

DPMI_flags              db 0
CPU_type                db 0
DPMI_major_version      db 0
DPMI_minor_revision     db 0
```

```
DPMI_mem             dw 0
DPMI_entry           dd 0
code32_selector      dw 0          ; filled with selector for CODE32 segment
main32_address       df main32

cs_descriptor label dword
cs_limit             dw 0          ; descriptor limit
cs_low_addr          db 0,0,0      ; low order 3 bytes of address
cs_access            dw 0          ; descriptor access bytes
cs_high_addr         db 0          ; high order byte of address

; error messages

err_msg1             db 'DPMI host not detected',13,10,0
err_msg2             db 'Could not allocate real-mode memory
                         requested',13,10,0
err_msg3             db 'The switch to protected mode did not work',13,10,0

.code

main proc

  mov     ax, @data
  mov     ds, ax


; (1) ;   re-size memory allocated
; ↑    Note: Shaded numbers keyed to description in text
  mov     bx, ss                   ; start of stack segment
  mov     ax, es                   ; start of PSP
  sub     bx, ax                   ; para for code & data
  mov     ax, sp                   ; get stack size
  shr     ax, 4                    ; divide by 16 to get para
  add     bx, ax
  inc     bx                       ; BX = total para needed
  mov     ah, 4ah                  ; modify memory allocation
  int     21h

; (2)    check to see if DPMI is available
  call    DPMI_check               ; check for a DPMI server
  jc      error1                   ; exit if none

; (3)    Print intro message
  lea     si, intro_msg            ; intro message
  call    print_string

; (4)    Allocate memory for DPMI server
  mov     ax, 0                    ; use seg=0 if no memory required
```

```
        mov     bx, DPMI_mem            ; get para count required for DPMI
        test    bx, bx
        jz      main_2                  ; skip down if none required
        mov     ah, 48h                 ; allocate memory
        int     21h
        jc      error2                  ; check for allocate error
; (5)    switch to protected mode
main_2:
  mov     es, ax
  mov     ax, 1                   ; indicate 32-bit application
  call    dword ptr DPMI_entry    ; switch to protected mode
  jc      error3                  ; if CF set, error in switching
; (6)    print message on entry to protected mode
  lea     si, in16_msg            ; 16-bit protected mode message
  call    print_string
; <<< call any 16-bit PM code here >>>

;======================================
; begin setup to switch to 32-bit PM
;======================================
; (7)    allocate a descriptor for use32 segment
  mov     ax, 0                   ; allocate LDT descriptor
  mov     cx, 1                   ; 1 descriptor
  int     31h                     ; call DPMI host
  mov     code32_selector,ax      ; selector to use32 segment
  mov     word ptr main32_address+2, ax    ; store selector
; (8)    get copy of LDT entry
  mov     bx, cs                  ; get current CS descriptor
  mov     di, offset cs_descriptor         ; point to result buffer
  movzx   edi, di                 ; (convert to 32 bits)
  push    ds                      ; ES:EDI => buffer
  pop     es                      ;
  mov     ax, 000bh               ; get descriptor request
  int     31h                     ; call DPMI host
; (9)    set segment base address
  mov     ax, seg code32          ; linear address of code32
  movzx   eax, ax                 ;
  shl     eax, 4                  ; segment value times 16
  mov     dx, ax                  ; move to cx:dx
  mov     ecx, eax                ;
  shr     ecx, 16                 ;
  mov     bx, code32_selector     ; identify selector
  mov     ax, 7                   ; set segment base address
```

```
        int     31h                     ; call DPMI host
; (10)   set segment limit
        mov     cx, 0000h               ; set segment limit to 64K
        mov     dx, 0ffffh              ;
        mov     bx, code32_selector     ; identify selector
        mov     ax, 8h                  ; set segment limit request
        int     31h                     ; call DPMI host
; (11)   switch to 32-bit mode by changing the D bit
        mov     cx, cs_access           ; start with current cs access
        or      ch, 40h                 ; change to 32 bit default
        mov     bx, code32_selector     ; identify selector
        mov     ax, 0009h               ; set access rights request
        int     31h                     ; call DPMI host
; (12)   Execute a 16:16 far call to 32-bit code
        call    dword ptr main32_address
; When we return we are still in 16-bit PM.
main_exit:
        mov     ax, 4c00h               ; DOS exit
        int     21h
; error messages
error1:
        lea     si, err_msg1            ; DPMI host not found
        jmp     err0
error2:
        lea     si, err_msg2            ; could not allocate memory
        jmp     err0

error3:
        lea     si, err_msg3            ; could not switch to PM
err0:
        call    print_string
        jmp     main_exit

main endp
DPMI_check proc near

;----------------------------------------
; Check for a DPMI server
;
; outputs: CF set if no DPMI server installed
;----------------------------------------

        push    ax
        push    bx
```

```
        push    cx
        push    dx
        push    di
        push    si
        push    es

        mov     ax, 1687h               ; request DPMI host address
        int     2fh                     ; via multiplex interrupt (2Fh)
        test    ax, ax                  ; AX = 0 if success
        jnz     not_found               ; exit with error if not found

        and     bl, 00000001b           ; check bit 1 to see if 32-bit
        setne   al                      ; code supported
        mov     DPMI_flags, al
        mov     CPU_type, cl
        mov     DPMI_major_version, dh
        mov     DPMI_minor_revision, dl
        mov     DPMI_mem, si
        mov     word ptr DPMI_entry[0], di
        mov     word ptr DPMI_entry[2], es
        clc                             ; success
dc_ret:
        pop     es
        pop     si
        pop     di
        pop     dx

        pop     cx
        pop     bx
        pop     ax
        ret

not_found:
        stc
        jmp     dc_ret

DPMI_check endp

public print_string
print_string proc near

;-------------------------------------
; Print ASCIIZ string
;
; inputs: DS:SI ptr to string
;-------------------------------------
        push    ax
        push    bx
```

```
        push    cx
        push    dx

        call    str_len
        mov     dx, si
        mov     bx, 1               ; stdout
        mov     ah, 40h             ; DOS write handle
        int     21h

        pop     dx
        pop     cx
        pop     bx
        pop     ax
        ret

print_string endp
public str_len
str_len proc near
;--------------------------------------
; Get length of string
;
; inputs: DS:SI ptr to string
;
; outputs: CX length
;--------------------------------------

        push    ax
        push    si

        lea     cx, [si+2]
sl_1:
        mov     ax, [si]
        add     si, 2
        test    al, al

        je      sl_2
        test    ah, ah
        jne     sl_1
        inc     si
sl_2:
        sub     si, cx
        mov     cx, si

        pop     si
        pop     ax
        ret
```

```
str_len endp

code32    segment public para use32 'code'
          assume  cs:code32
public main32
main32 proc far
;----------------------------------------
; 32-bit code main entry point
;
; DS = @data from 16-bit code
;----------------------------------------

  pusha

; (13)    display message that we're in 32-bit mode
          esi, offset in32_msg
  mov
  call    print_string32

; (14)    call any 32-bit code from here
  call    do_test

; restore registers

  popa

; (15)    return to the 16-bit code segment we came from
  db      66h                    ; operand size prefix (see note below)
  ret


;--------------------------------------------------------------------
;    Note: If we used a RET without the operand size prefix the assembler
;    would generate a normal RETF for 32-bit code (16:32). We need
;    this return to match the CALL that got us here (16:16).
;--------------------------------------------------------------------

main32 endp

do_test proc

  ret    ; this example does nothing

do_test endp

public print_string32
print_string32 proc near
  ;----------------------------------------
```

```
       ; 32-bit Print ASCIIZ string
       ;
       ; inputs: DS:ESI ptr to string
       ;------------------------------------

         push    eax
         push    ebx
         push    ecx
         push    edx

         call    str_len32
         mov     edx, esi
         mov     ebx, 1                  ; stdout
         mov     ah, 40h                 ; DOS write handle
         int     21h

         pop     edx
         pop     ecx
         pop     ebx
         pop     eax
         ret

print_string32 endp

public str_len32
str_len32 proc near
;------------------------------------
; 32-bit Get length of string
;
; inputs: DS:ESI ptr to string
;
; outputs: ECX length
;------------------------------------

         push    eax
         push    esi

         lea     ecx, [esi+2]
s132_1:
         mov     eax, [esi]
         add     esi, 2
         test    al, al
         je      s132_2
         test    ah, ah
         jne     s132_1
         inc     esi
```

```
sl32_2:
  sub     esi, ecx
  mov     ecx, esi

  pop     esi
  pop     eax
  ret

str_len32 endp

code32 ends

end main
```

Notes: The DPMI functions used in Listing 18.1 are documented in the DPMI Specification version
1.0 (available from Intel, order number 240977-001).

Here is a brief explanation of the code in Listing 18.1. Comments in the code corresponding to the numbers.

1. The program starts by resizing memory to the amount actually used by the program.
   If you change the segment configuration, be sure to change this calculation. It is
   based on the stack being at the end of the memory image.
2. Check for the presence of a DPMI server. If none, then the program exits with an
   error message.
3. A startup message is displayed.
4. Memory is allocated, if required, for the DPMI server. When the check is made for
   the presence of a DPMI server, the number of paragraphs of memory is returned. It
   may be zero.
5. Switch to protected mode. When the check is made for the presence of a DPMI server, the far address for the procedure used to enter protected mode is returned. This
   entry point is used only for the first switch into protected mode by an application.

   When the switch to protected mode is complete the application gains control
   with the following results:

   CS = selector matching CS on entry with size of 64K
   DS = selector matching DS on entry with size of 64K
   SS = selector matching SS on entry with size of 64K
   ES = selector for PSP with a size of 100h
   FS = 0
   GS = 0

If SS and DS are the same on entry, there will be only one descriptor allocated and SS and DS will be the same on return. The environment pointer (at **PSP:2Ch**) in the PSP is automatically converted to a valid selector if it is not 0 on entry.

6. A message is displayed if protected mode is successfully entered.

7. Allocate a descriptor for **USE32** segment. Although our 32-bit code is in memory, the DPMI host does not know about it. We must allocate a descriptor for this segment.

8. After the descriptor is allocated we must get a copy of the LDT (local descriptor table) entry so that we may make modifications to it.

9. Set segment base address. The first modification is to specify the starting address of our 32-bit code segment.

10. Set segment limit. The second modification is to specify the size of our 32-bit code segment. Because this code was loaded by DOS, in low memory, the code size is limited to less than 640K, just like DOS programs. To run a larger program you must allocate memory beyond 1 MB and load the program into the allocated memory.

11. The final modification is to identify our 32-bit code segment as a 32-bit code segment by changing the D bit in the access rights/type bytes. When a DPMI server allocates a descriptor, the default value for the D bit is zero, which is for 16-bit code segments.

12. The next step is to execute a call to our 32-bit code. This call is a protected-mode 16:16 far call. This means we have an address in memory that is a 16-bit offset followed by a 16-bit selector. This address is stored in the data segment in a variable named **main32_address**. The data type of **main32_address** always needs to be a dword (DD), even if you change memory models. Various versions of assemblers may generate errors and require a DF declaration. This is not a problem because **main32_address** is declared as a pointer to **main32**, but the second word is always overwritten with the actual selector, always providing a correct dword ptr for 16-bit code.

13. A message is displayed from the 32-bit code. It is important to note that the utility routines used for this are different from the 16-bit utility routines.

14. This is where you would place a call to your own 32-bit code to be tested.

15. This is the return to the 16-bit code segment where we came from. This return may seem odd, but is very important. The return must match the call. A near return for a **USE32** segment is a 32-bit offset. A far return for a **USE32** segment is a 6-byte far pointer (32-bit offset and 16-bit selector). The call to the **main32** procedure is a 16-bit far call (16-bit offset and 16-bit selector). To execute the proper **RET** instruction requires using an operand-size prefix byte (**66h**). In most cases, MASM and TASM can automatically generate prefix bytes when required. In this case I could find no way other than inserting the prefix byte manually.

   This operand-size-prefixed return instruction is only required if you need to return to the original 16-bit protected mode code. If not, you can just issue an **INT 21h, function 4Ch** and exit back to DOS.

LARGE DATA SEGMENTS

As written, the example code template only has access to 32-bit code that is loaded by DOS in the lower 640K of memory. In addition, this example uses only a data segment that has a size of 64K (or less) that is accessible from real or virtual 8086 mode, 16-bit protected mode and from 32-bit protected-mode code. To use a data segment larger than 64K requires the use of one of two techniques.

First, the data can be declared in the source file in a segment declared as **USE32** with the required length. This method is limited in that the data must fit in the lower 640K when DOS loads the program. (To mix **USE16** segments and **USE32** segments in a program that has a segment larger than 64K appears to require that simplified segments not be used.)

The second method is to allocate a block of extended memory via DPMI services. This is not as straightforward as allocating memory from DOS. The memory must be allocated with one function call, and then the selector is obtained with another function call to allocate a descriptor. Finally, the descriptor base address and size must be set.

```
large_allocate proc                                       (Listing 18.2)
  ; inputs:  BX:CX      32-bit block size
  ;                     (use 4K page increments)
  ; outputs: AX         selector
  ;          SI:DI      memory block handle
  ;                     (used to deallocate)

  mov     temp_size, cx
  mov     temp_size[2], bx

; allocate memory from DPMI

  mov     ax, 0501h                ; allocate memory
  int     31h                      ; DPMI
  jc      la_ret

  mov     temp_base, cx            ; store results in
  mov     temp_base[2], bx         ; temporary variables
  mov     temp_handle, di
  mov     temp_handle[2], si

; allocate a descriptor for use32 segment

  mov     ax, 0                    ; allocate LDT descriptor
  mov     cx, 1                    ; descriptor count
  int     31h                      ; DPMI
  jc      la_ret
```

```
        mov     temp_selector, ax       ; temp save

; set segment base address

    mov     bx, ax                  ; selector
    mov     dx, temp_base
    mov     cx, temp_base[2]
    mov     ax, 7                   ; set segment base address
    int     31h                     ; DPMI

; set segment limit

    mov     dx, temp_size
    mov     cx, temp_size[2]

    mov     bx, temp_selector
    mov     ax, 8h                  ; set segment limit
    int     31h                     ; DPMI

    mov     ax, temp_selector
    mov     di, temp_handle
    mov     si, temp_handle[2]

la_ret:
  ret
large_allocate endp

large_deallocate proc
  ; inputs: SI:DI memory block handle
  ; BX   selector
    mov     ax, 1                   ; free LDT descriptor
    int     31h                     ; DPMI
    mov     ax, 0502h               ; free memory block
    int     31h                     ; DPMI
  ret
large_deallocate endp
```

To use the **large_allocate** procedure in Listing 18.2, the size of the block of memory to be allocated must be specified in the BX:CX register pair. Because memory is allocated in 4K pages, the size should be an even increment of 4K (lower 12 bits of CX are equal to zero).

```
        mov bx, 2                           ; BX:CX size of block
        mov cx, 0
        call large_allocate
        jc  alloc_err
```

If an error occurs while allocating memory, the carry flag (**CF**) is set and AX is returned with an error code. (See the DPMI specification for a complete list of error codes.) The following errors can occur when allocating memory:

8012h	linear memory unavailable
8013h	physical memory unavailable
8014h	backing store unavailable
8016h	no more handles
8021h	invalid size (BX:CX = 0)

Deallocating a block of memory requires the selector to be deallocated and then the memory to be deallocated. This is done by the **large_deallocate** procedure in Listing 18.2.

TIMING 32-BIT CODE

Timing 32-bit code is the same as for 16-bit code, except the library **TIMER32.LIB** (provided on the disk) must be linked. This library is a 32-bit small model and works with the sample code in Listing 18.1. The **do_test** procedure in the following listing shows how to test the speed of different versions of a procedure using the timing library.

```
do_test proc                                           (Listing 18.3)
; allocate memory for test (two 68K byte strings)

    mov     bx, 2                   ; BX:CX size of block
    mov     cx, 2000h
    call    large_allocate
    jc      dt_exit
    mov     data_selector1, ax
    mov     data_handle1, di
    mov     data_handle1[2], si

; setup and perform testing

    call    test_init               ; fill string with test data
    call    timing_test             ; perform tests

; deallocate memory

    mov     bx, data_selector1
    mov     di, data_handle1
    mov     si, data_handle1[2]
    call    large_deallocate
```

```
dt_exit:
  ret

do_test endp

test_init proc

  push       ds
  push       es

  mov        ds, ax              ; DS=ES=allocated memory selector
  mov        es, ax


; fill first string with data

  mov        edi, 0
  mov        eax, 01020304h
  mov        ecx, (68*1024/4)-1
  rep        stosd
  xor        eax, eax
  stosd

  pop        es
  pop        ds
  ret

test_init endp

timing_test proc

; test 1: copy one byte per loop

  mov        esi, 0
  mov        edi, 72*1024
  push       ds
  push       es
  call       timer_on
  mov        es, data_selector1
  mov        ds, data_selector1
  call       str_copy1
  pop        es
  pop        ds
  call       timer_off
  call       timer_show
```

```
        ; test 2: copy four bytes per loop

        mov         esi, 0
        mov         edi, 72*1024

        push        ds
        push        es
        call        timer_on
        mov         es, data_selector1
        mov         ds, data_selector1
        call        str_copy2
        pop         es
        pop         ds
        call        timer_off
        call        timer_show

        ; test 3: copy four bytes per loop

        mov         esi, 0
        mov         edi, 72*1024
        push        ds
        push        es
        call        timer_on
        mov         es, data_selector1
        mov         ds, data_selector1
        call        str_copy4
        pop         es
        pop         ds
        call        timer_off
        call        timer_show

        ret

timing_test endp

str_copy1 proc                      ; string copy 1 byte per loop

    lbl1:                           ; Pent    486      386
        mov     al, [esi]           ;  1       1        4
        inc     esi                 ;  0       1        2
        mov     [edi], al           ;  1       1        2
        inc     edi                 ;  0       1        2
        cmp     al, 0               ;  1       1        2
        jne     lbl1                ;  0       3        7+2
    exit1:                          ; ---     ---      ---
                                    ;  3       8        21
        ret
```

```
str_copy1 endp
str_copy2 proc                    ; string copy two bytes per loop

   lbl2:                          ; Pent    486      386
      mov    eax, [esi]           ;  1       1        4
      add    esi, 2               ;  0       1        2
      cmp    al, 0                ;  1       1        2
      jz     exit2                ;  0       1        3
      mov    [edi], ax            ;  1+1     1+1      2+1     (prefix delay)
      add    edi, 2               ;  0       1        2
      cmp    ah, 0                ;  1       1        2
      jne    lbl2                 ;  0       3        7+2
   exit2:                         ;  ---     ---      ---
                                  ;  5       11       27
                                  ;  2.5     5.5      13.5    cycles per byte

      ret
str_copy2 endp

str_copy4 proc                    ; string copy four bytes per loop
   lbl4:                          ; Pent    486      386
      mov    eax, [esi]           ;  1       1        4
      add    esi, 4               ;  0       1        2
      mov    [edi], eax           ;  1       1        2
      add    edi, 4               ;  0       1        2
      cmp    al, 0                ;  1       1        2
      jz     exit4                ;  0       1        3
      cmp    ah, 0                ;  1       1        2
      jz     exit4                ;  0       1        3
      ror    eax, 16              ;  1       1        7
      cmp    al, 0                ;  0       1        2
      jz     exit4                ;  1       1        3
      cmp    ah, 0                ;  1       1        2
      jne    lbl4                 ;  0       3        7+2

   exit4:                         ;  ---     ---      ---
                                  ;  7       15       43
                                  ;  1.75    3.75     10.75   cycles per byte

      ret
str_copy4 endp
```

Table 18.2 shows the timings results for Listing 18.3. There are two important factors affecting theses results. First, because interrupts cannot easily be disabled when in protected mode, the results are not as precise as when in real mode. Second, this test copies strings larger than the cache. There is a two-cycle penalty on the 486 and a three-cycle penalty on the Pentium when reading from memory, and there is a cache miss. On a 386 the cache-miss penalty varies because the cache is external and there are many different cache designs. There can also be delays when the write buffers are full. The first portion of Table 18.2 shows the timings results (microseconds) and the cycles per byte copied. The second portion of Table 18.2 has the minimum theoretical cycles per byte copied. For copies beyond the size of the internal cache, the cycles per byte do not vary more than a few percent for different size strings. The example shows a 68K string.

Table 18.2 Timings for Large 32-Bit String Copies (Microseconds and Cycles/Byte)

	Pentium-60		486-33		386-25	
`str_copy1`	5487	4.7	21884	10.4	67648	24.3
`str_copy2`	3725	3.2	14228	6.7	47516	16.6
`str_copy4`	2593	2.2	10947	5.2	32356	11.6

Minimum theoretical cycles per byte (no cache miss penalty)

	Pentium-60	486-33	386-25
`str_copy1`	3	8	21
`str_copy2`	3	6	13.5
`str_copy4`	1.75	3.75	10.75

Notes: cycles = (time * MHz)/(byte length)
byte length = 68K

Cloaking Developers Toolkit

Another interesting way to write a protected mode program is to use the Cloaking Developer's Toolkit from Helix Software, the makers of the NetRoom memory manager. With this toolkit you can develop what is called a "cloaked program." Primarily for writing device drivers and TSR (terminate and stay resident) programs, the toolkit works by loading and running your code in protected mode, ring 0. DPMI applications run in ring 3, the lowest privilege level. Ring 0 is the highest privilege level, therefore providing capabilities not allowed by other environments such as DPMI. It is also dangerous, because serious bugs will surely crash the system. But this is not much different from DOS real-mode programming, where the same thing happens.

Cloaked programs that hook interrupts, as do most device drivers and TSRs, leave a small stub in conventional memory. When an interrupt occurs, this 11-byte stub activates the host, which then calls your protected-mode code. The host can be Helix's NetRoom memory manager, or a Helix-provided device driver. There are separate drivers for DOS and Windows, and both must be licensed from Helix.

In 1986 when the first 386 systems were shipped, it seemed like 16-bit applications would soon be relics. It hasn't happened very fast. However, by writing code for 32-bit protected mode, you are more likely to live long and prosper.

CHAPTER

Final Notes and Optimizations

19

"Few things are harder to put up with than the annoyance of a good example."

—Mark Twain

A book on programming would be incomplete if it did not leave you with more than a few techniques and a load of reference material. In Chapters 13 to 15 we discovered a process for converting single-instruction-stream algorithms into highly optimized loops firing with two cylinders. This chapter is primarily about finding and aligning the right instructions to feed into these cylinders.

Appendix B contains an abundance of information about various optimizations for the entire 80x86 family. In this chapter we will explore a few of these optimizations and try to discover techniques for finding similar enhancements. We'll also take a look at another optimization that is easy to overlook: code alignment.

SPEED VS. CODE SIZE

Many code selection optimizations boil down to a trade-off between code size and speed. Many widely known optimizations have both a code-size and a speed advantage.

Two of the most widely known and used optimizations are setting a register to zero and multiplying by two:

```
mov  ax, 0          ; three ways to set a register to zero
xor  ax, ax
sub  ax, ax

mov  eax, 0         ; (32-bit)
xor  eax, eax
sub  eax, eax
```

Here are three ways to multiply a 16-bit register by two:

```
mov  bx, 2
mul  bx             ; multiplies AX by 2

shl  ax, 1          ; also multiplies AX by 2

add  ax, ax         ; also multiplies AX by 2
```

Here are four ways to multiply a 32-bit register by two:

```
mov  ebx, 2
mul  ebx

shl  eax, 1

add  eax, eax

lea  eax, [eax+eax]
```

In 32-bit mode, other interesting code-size optimization opportunities arise because some instructions use only 32-bit immediate data. For example:

```
mov  eax, 1         ; 5 bytes
xor  eax, eax       ; 2 bytes
inc  eax            ; 1 byte
```

Let's back up and look at the details of the various ways to set a register to zero. See Table 19.1.

Although there may be many ways to "do the same thing," it is a rarity when two instructions or instruction sequences actually produce a completely identical set of results. **XOR** and **SUB** are a rare case. The cycle counts and Pentium pairing details are

Table 19.1   Details of the Different Ways to Zero a Register

	Code Size	Flags Affected	Pairing	Cycles		
				Pentium	486	386
mov	5	none	UV	1	1	2
xor	2	all arith	UV	1	1	2
sub	2	all arith	UV	1	1	2

the same for all three instructions. The only differences are the effect on the flags and the code size.

Now let's look at the details of the different ways to multiply by two. See Table 19.2.

As you can see from Table 19.2, none of these ways of multiplying by two is the same as another. Each instruction sequence may have its own uses.

The steps I use to find optimum instruction sequences are

- compare the effects of two or more alternatives for your situation
- determine the code size bytes
- count the cycles for each target CPU for baseline info
- time the sequences on each target CPU
- time the sequences in your code for each target CPU

These steps tell you several things. First, you can identify whether two code sequences produce the same results, or at least the same effective results for your situation. Second, it tells you the code size of each choice of instructions. These are all important, as we will see later.

Table 19.2   Details of the Different Ways to Multiply by Two (32-Bit)

	Code Size	Flags Affected	Pairing	Cycles		
				Pentium	486	386
mov/mul	5+2	CF OF	UV/NP	1/10	/131	2/9
shl	2	all arith	PU	1	1	2
add	2	all arith	UV	1	1	2
lea	3	none	UV	1	1	2

Another more complicated example is multiplying by two with identical data results. **MUL** and **SHL** leave the flags in a different state. But more important, they do not produce the same data. **MUL** accepts operands of 8, 16 or 32 bits and returns a 16-, 32- or 64-bit result. **SHL** accepts operands of the same size, but returns results of the same size. The carry flag must be shifted into a zeroed register to get the same result for large initial values. If we needed **SHL** to allow for large values we would need to use one of these examples:

```
mov  ah, 0            ; 8->9 bits (16- or 32-bit code)
shl  ax, 1


xor  dx, dx           ; 16->17 bits (16-bit code)
shl  ax, 1
rcl  dx, 1


and  eax, 0FFFFh      ; 16->17 bits (32-bit code)
shl  eax, 1


xor  edx, edx         ; 32->33 bits (32-bit code)
shl  eax, 1
rcl  edx, 1
```

Of course, all this complication shows that it really pays to know your data—and we haven't even discussed multiplying by four when using **SHL**.

Let's look at another example. In this one we'll advance a pointer by two. Here are three ways of doing this:

```
add  si, 2            ; add method


inc  si               ; inc method
inc  si


lea  si, [si+2]       ; lea method
```

Table 19.3   Details of the Different Ways to Advance a Pointer by 2

				Cycles		
	Code Size	Flags Affected	Pairing	Pentium	486	386
inc/inc	2	all but CF	UV	2	2	4
add	3	all arith	UV	1	1	2
lea	3	none	UV	1	1	2

Of course, the **INC** method is only smaller when advancing a pointer by one or two. **LEA** has the advantage of not affecting the flags, when this is required. But **LEA** is much more powerful than just this.

LEA, THE MULTI-PURPOSE INSTRUCTION

The **LEA**, load effective address, instruction is an optimizer's delight. **LEA** can be used for many things, such as

- pointer addition without changing the flags
- fast multiplications
- two-, three- and four-operand addition

The only hidden disadvantage of LEA is that it uses the address generation unit. (The Pentium has one for each pipeline.) This means that it is possible to have an **LEA** instruction delayed due to an **AGI** when an **ADD** would not have the same delay, because the execution of the **LEA** occurs earlier in the pipeline than an **ADD**. However, only in a rare coding sequence would this occur.

LEA is especially useful in 32-bit mode code. Here are some sample uses:

Using **LEA** to multiply:

```
lea eax, [eax+eax]        ; mult by 2
lea eax, [eax+eax*2]      ; mult by 3
lea eax, [eax*4]          ; mult by 4
lea eax, [eax+eax*4]      ; mult by 5
lea eax, [eax*8]          ; mult by 8
lea eax, [eax+eax*8]      ; mult by 9

add eax, eax
lea eax, [eax+eax*2]      ; mult by 6

add eax, eax
lea eax, [eax+eax*4]      ; mult by 10

add eax, eax
lea eax, [eax+eax*8]      ; mult by 18

mov ebx, eax
lea ebx, [ebx+ebx*8]
lea eax, [eax+ebx*2]      ; mult by 19
```

```
mov  ebx, eax
lea  ebx, [ebx+ebx*8]
lea  eax, [eax+ebx*4]   ; mult by 37

mov  ebx, eax
lea  ebx,[ebx+ebx*8]
lea  eax, [eax+ebx*8]   ; mult by 73
```

Using **LEA** to add:

```
lea  eax, [eax+ebx]     ; two operands

lea  eax, [ebx+ecx]     ; three operands
                        ; replaces MOV and ADD

lea  eax, [ebx+ecx+4]   ; four operands, 1 immediate
                        ; replaces MOV, ADD and ADD

lea  eax, [eax+1]       ; replaces INC
lea  eax, [eax+4]       ; replaces pointer addition

lea  eax, [eax-1]       ; replaces DEC
lea  eax, [eax-4]       ; replaces pointer subtraction
```

CODE AND DATA ALIGNMENT

Aligning data is more difficult than it may seem at first, as we shall see. It is simple to align data on word boundaries because all segments are always automatically aligned on an even word boundary or better. To ensure even word alignment of a data element, you place the **EVEN** directive before the start of the item, as follows:

```
even                 ; even word alignment
dw 100 dup(0)        ; 100 words on even word boundary
```

Aligning dwords is not as simple. The **ALIGN** directive can be used to align to any location that is a power of two. The following code would appear to align an array of dwords on a dword boundary:

```
align 4              ; dword alignment
dd 100 dup(0)        ; 100 dwords on even dword boundary
```

However, there are other factors that affect how the alignment will work. For the dword alignment to work, the segment must be declared with an alignment type of dword or above (see Table 18.1). The default alignment type is **PARA** (paragraph) or 16 bytes when using the **SEGMENT** directive. When using the simplified segmentation directives, the alignment type is **WORD** for code segments and data segments. When using the simplified segmentation directives, MASM 5.1 will allow specifying an alignment with the **ALIGN** directive that is greater than the segment alignment (which is a word). This will only work for single-module programs, or when the **ALIGN** directive is in the first module to be linked. Otherwise, it is hit-or-miss. TASM and MASM 6.0 and above will generate an error when you attempt to use an **ALIGN** that cannot be guaranteed.

It is possible to use a mix of simplified segmentation directives and the full **SEGMENT** declaration directives to insure proper alignment. However, it would not be wise to rely on this method if you intend to upgrade assemblers. Declare a paragraph aligned data segment as follows:

```
_data  segment public para 'data'

data1  dw 0            ; sample data

align  16
data2  dd 100 dup(0) ; sample data para aligned

_data  ends
```

Once the segments are properly declared, there are several techniques that can be used for aligning data:

- declare global data with proper alignment
- use structures with proper alignment
- align large string operations by address alignment in code (discussed later)

LOCAL STACK VARIABLES

Allocating stack space for local variables that must be aligned can be difficult. In real mode and 16-bit protected mode you can assume that the stack pointer (SP) is aligned to an even word boundary, although it is possible that it is not. It is possible to manipulate the BP register, if required, to gain alignment, as follows:

```
push   bp

mov    bp, sp
sub    sp, local_space + 4
```

```
; (push required registers)

; (access passed parameters, if required)

; align BP for local variables

push  bp
mov   ax, bp          ; align BP to dword boundary
and   ax, 3           ; or use: and   bp, 0fffch
sub   bp, ax

...

pop  bp

; pop saved registers

mov   sp, bp
pop   bp
ret
```

When programming in 32-bit protected-mode, every **PUSH** and **POP** uses four bytes of stack space. This is true even when pushing and popping segment registers. When pushing a segment register, the high word is pushed as a zero, keeping pure 32-bit code from misaligning ESP from a dword boundary. However, it is still possible to push word values by using an operand-size prefix. This could occur in any 32-bit program. Align EBP to a dword boundary in a 32-bit procedure as follows:

```
push  ebp
mov   ebp, esp
sub   esp, local_space + 4

; (push required registers)

; (access passed parameters, if required)

; align EBP for local variables

push  ebp
mov   eax, ebp        ; align EBP to dword boundary
and   eax, 3          ; or use: and   ebp, 0fffffffch
sub   ebp, eax

...
```

```
pop     ebp

; pop saved registers

mov     esp, ebp
pop     ebp
ret
```

MEASURING AND CORRECTING
THE DATA MISALIGNMENT PENALTY

So now that we've seen how to align data, you may be wondering: is it really worth it? It is easy enough to test. Table 19.4 shows the misalignment penalty for the **REP MOVSW** instruction.

Table 19.4 Data Misalignment Penalty for **REP MOVSW**

		DI aligned	**DI misaligned**
Pentium cache hit	SI aligned	0%	50%
	SI misaligned	0%	50%
Pentium cache miss	SI aligned	0%	45%
	SI misaligned	0%	45%
486 cache hit	SI aligned	0%	26%
	SI misaligned	36%	67%
486 cache miss	SI aligned	0%	20%
	SI misaligned	40%	50%
386 cache hit	SI aligned	0%	8%
	SI misaligned	36%	70%
386 cache miss	SI aligned	0%	13%
	SI misaligned	46%	57%
386SX no cache	SI aligned	0%	73%
	SI misaligned	73%	123%

Notes: Delays calculated as a percentage increase in execution time from the case where SI and DI are aligned.

From Table 19.4 we can see that the penalty for misalignment can be quite large (50–100 %). The largest penalty is when both the source and the destination are misaligned. It is a simple matter to correct this case. On the 386 and 486 it is always most advantageous to read from aligned data and write to misaligned data (except on the 386SX, where there is no difference.) This is because the CPU must wait for a read operation to complete, but may buffer write operations to be completed later. On the Pentium the opposite is true—it is best to write to aligned addresses.

The exact numerical results of Table 19.4 apply to the **REP MOVSW** instruction. The following code shows how to align SI for the **REP MOVSW**:

```
test      si, 1           ; check for odd address          (Listing 19.1)
jz        ok
movsb                     ; move one byte at odd SI
dec       cx              ; reduce word count
jz        mv              ; branch down if only 1 word to move
stc                       ; CF set for odd start
ok:
  rep     movsw           ; move words
  jnc     done
mv:
  movsb                   ; move final remaining odd byte
done:
```

The same tests can be performed on the **REP MOVSD** instruction, as shown in Table 19.5.

Table 19.5 Data Misalignment Penalty for **REP MOVSD**

		DI aligned	DI+1	DI+2	DI+3
Pentium cache hit	SI aligned	0%	100%	100%	100%
	SI +1	0%	100%	100%	100%
	SI +2	0%	100%	100%	100%
	SI +3	0%	100%	100%	100%
Pentium cache miss	SI aligned	0%	80%	80%	80%
	SI +1	0%	80%	80%	80%
	SI +2	0%	80%	80%	80%
	SI +3	0%	80%	80%	80%

(continued)

Table 19.5   Data Misalignment Penalty for **REP MOVSD** *(Continued)*

		DI aligned	DI+1	DI+2	DI+3
486 cache hit	SI aligned	0%	36%	36%	27%
	SI +1	55%	96%	96%	96%
	SI +2	55%	96%	96%	96%
	SI +3	60%	96%	96%	96%
486 cache miss	SI aligned	0%	18%	18%	18%
	SI +1	36%	60%	60%	60%
	SI +2	36%	60%	60%	60%
	SI +3	36%	60%	60%	60%
386 cache hit	SI aligned	0%	33%	33%	33%
	SI +1	66%	116%	116%	116%
	SI +2	66%	116%	116%	116%
	SI +3	66%	116%	116%	116%
386 cache miss	SI aligned	0%	17%	17%	17%
	SI +1	50%	66%	66%	66%
	SI +2	50%	66%	66%	66%
	SI +3	50%	66%	66%	66%
386SX no cache	SI aligned	0%	25%	0%	25%
	SI +1	25%	50%	40%	66%
	SI +2	20%	40%	33%	57%
	SI +3	25%	66%	57%	66%

Notes: Delays calculated as a percentage increase in execution time from the case where SI and DI are aligned.

Again, the timing results shown in Table 19.5 show that aligning the source register (**SI** or **ESI**) can minimize the misalignment penalty. The string instructions tend to show the greatest data misalignment penalty because the instructions are optimized to utilize the memory bus near its maximum capacity. Most other operations would not be using as much bus bandwidth.

Table 19.6 shows the misalignment penalty for independent data read and writes.

Table 19.6   Read and Write Misalignment Penalty

	16-bit read	16-bit write
Pentium cache hit	70%	50%
Pentium cache miss	40%	50%
486 cache hit	20%	25%
486 cache miss	22%	25%
386 cache hit	12%	23%
386 cache miss	15%	23%
386SX no cache	17%	14%

CODE ALIGNMENT

We've seen that performance can be significantly degraded by having data misaligned, but what about code alignment? In other words, can procedures and loops be aligned on even word, dword or paragraph boundaries to improve performance? It certainly can. Each 80x86 CPU fetches instructions on certain boundaries. Aligning a frequently fetched instruction will improve performance. The prefetch units on the 80x86 CPUs fetch instructions on differing boundaries, as shown in Table 19.7.

Because of the branch prediction on the Pentium, there is little need to perform code alignment for the Pentium (except to even word boundaries). Aligning for the 486 is the worse case that should be taken into account. Branch prediction eliminates the need for code alignment on the Pentium because the only time that alignment is a real concern is when a section of code is repeatedly the target of a branch. The branch prediction will detect this and begin prefetching in the second prefetch queue in advance.

Table 19.7   Prefetch Boundaries

8088/188	byte
8086/186	word
80286	word
80386SX	word
80386	dword
80486	paragraph (cache-line boundary)
Pentium	32-byte (cache-line boundary)

On the 486, the performance penalty can be as high as 50%, as shown in Listing 19.2.

```
        mov      cx, 1000                                          (Listing 19.2)

        align    16              ; align to paragraph

        rept     15              ; insert 15 NOP's to get
        nop                      ; the worst alignment for the 486
        endm
loop1:
        sub      cx, 1
        jnz      loop1

        align    16
loop2:
        sub      cx, 1
        jnz      loop2
```

The first loop in Listing 19.2 takes 50% longer than the second loop on the 486. The performance is so bad because this is the worst-case code alignment problem for the 486. The loop is small and the first instruction in the loop, the **SUB**, is two bytes in length, with one byte on each side of a prefetch boundary.

On the 386, instructions are prefetched four bytes at a time on dword boundaries. The first loop in Listing 19.2 takes only 7% longer than the second loop on the 386.

Listing 19.3 contains a more typical loop with the worst-case code alignment.

```
        mov      cx, 1000                                          (Listing 19.3)

        align    16              ; align to paragraph

        rept     15              ; insert 15 NOP's to get
        nop                      ; the worst alignment for the 486
        endm
loop1:
        add      ax, [si]
        add      si, 2
        dec      cx
        jnz      loop1

        align 16
loop2:
        add      ax, [si]
        add      si, 2
        dec      cx
        jnz      loop2
```

In this example, the 486 takes 25% longer on the first loop than the second loop. The 386 takes only 3% longer for this loop.

Now that you've heard all the bad news about code alignment on the 486, it's time for some good news. It is usually not necessary to paragraph align procedures and loops. Near-optimum performance can be attained by positioning the first instruction to be contained within a paragraph boundary. And better yet, running the code on a Pentium eliminates the problem.

One final note on code alignment. You may have seen or written code that uses a software delay loop, such as

```
    mov    cx, 100
  delay:
    loop   delay
```

Whether the **LOOP** instruction straddles a prefetch boundary or not can cause the delay to vary by large amounts—8% on the 386 and 30% on the 486. Simply using the **EVEN** directive eliminates the variance.

```
    mov    cx, 100
    even
  delay:
    loop   delay
```

Further Reading

For additional tips and techniques for optimizing code for the 80x86 family, see the excellent book by Michael Abrash, *Zen of Code Optimization*. This book provides a unique insight into many system performance issues, advanced algorithms and more.

Assembly Language Step by Step, by Jeff Duntemann, is an excellent beginning assembly-language book for those readers who need to develop more experience with the basic 8088 instruction set before feeling comfortable with the advanced superscalar techniques presented in this book.

Where We've Been

We've seen a lot in this book—from the history of the 80x86 and some strange instructions for 8080 compatibility to high-performance text and numeric programming for the Pentium. Hopefully, you've learned a few things you didn't know before you started on this journey. We've seen that once you've optimized your design there may still be lots of room for improvement, if required, by using some or all of the following techniques:

- instruction scheduling for superscalar programming
- careful instruction selection
- data alignment
- loop and procedure code alignment
- testing and measuring your code

For me, the learning process will begin again, as you, the readers, tell me what you liked and disliked, what you found useful and where I messed up. You can reach me on CompuServe at 76347,3661.

Now that you're an expert on the Pentium's superscalar architecture, you may be interested in other superscalar architectures and what will be coming in the future. In the final chapter we'll take a look at the PowerPC and how it compares to the Pentium.

PowerPC vs. Pentium

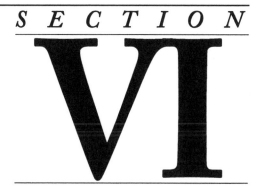

PowerPC vs. Pentium

20

> *"Wall Street indexes predicted nine*
> *out of the last five recessions."*
> —Paul Samuelson

> *"And that's the way it is."*
> —Walter Cronkite

IBM, Apple and Motorola teamed up in the early 1990s to form a partnership that produced the PowerPC family of RISC microprocessors. IBM and Motorola are collaborating on the chip design, and IBM and Apple are selling complete systems based on this new chip architecture. The PowerPC design is based on a previous CPU design in IBM's RS-6000 workstation computers. There have been many predictions from Wall Street to Main Street on the future success of the PowerPC. Here we'll discuss the background and technical capabilities of the PowerPC vs. the Pentium and their future technical directions.

WHAT IS RISC?

RISC stands for Reduced Instruction Set Computing. This basically describes a computer designed with a CPU that has a reduced number of instructions. However, this is not what RISC computers are really about. In the late 1970s computer designers realized CPUs were becoming more and more complex, but most software spent about 80% of execution time using about 20% of the available instructions. This led to the theory that it would be possible to build a very fast and powerful CPU with fewer instructions if they were highly optimized.

RISC CPU chips would be smaller (thus less expensive to manufacture) and would result in lower-cost systems. These ideas were pitched throughout the 1980s but never materialized. Yes, the machines appeared and were cheaper than minicomputers, but they were much more expensive than PCs. RISC systems were the domain of the high-priced (relative to PCs) workstation market in the $10,000 to $100,000 range.

WHAT IS CISC?

CISC, or Complex Instruction Set Computing, is a term coined by the RISC camp to describe the older design methods of ever-increasing CPU instruction-set complexity in mainframes (i.e., the IBM 370), minicomputers (i.e., the DEC VAX) and microprocessors like the 80x86 and the 680x0.

WHAT IS RISC, REALLY?

RISC is really not a mnemonic for Reduced anything. If you look at the instruction sets of any RISC processor you'll find over a hundred instructions. The real characteristics of what designers call RISC processors are this:

- load and store architecture
- highly regular instruction set that can easily be pipelined
- lots of registers
- registers, data bus and address bus with 32 bits (or more)

A load and store architecture is a design where data operations (i.e., add, sub, cmp, etc.) are separate from loading data into registers or storing data into memory. Two or three instructions are required to operate on data in memory. (By contrast, the 80x86 processors have single instructions that can operate on memory items.)

RISC instruction sets are highly regular because most every instruction has the same format, with certain bits specifying certain operations. Because of the regularity of the instruction set, relatively little decoding logic is required to efficiently pipeline the instruction stream. Likewise, it is also simpler to build superscalar processors.

RISC CPUs tend to have many registers. The PowerPC has 32 32-bit general-purpose registers and 32 64-bit floating-point registers. (By contrast, the 80x86 processors have eight each, and one is the stack pointer.)

WHICH IS BETTER, RISC OR CISC?

From a computer science point of view, the answer is clear. Every major CPU architecture developed in the last decade (or more) is a RISC design, the major ones being the Sun SPARC, MIPS, Hewlett Packard PA, DEC Alpha and PowerPC. From a market share point of view, the 80x86 and 680x0 families have consistently outsold RISC systems because of the installed base of software, the wide variety of software, the low cost of systems and the highly competitive consumer market. If computer components (memory, disks, monitors, etc.) had been more expensive in the late 1970s, the PC sales explosion of the 1980s may have been delayed five years and RISC chips might be selling 50 million per year.

CISC systems do score some technical advantage points. Because RISC systems must perform combinations of simple instructions to perform what one CISC instruction can do, RISC programs tend to be larger than CISC programs. Programs that are 50% larger are not unusual. Larger programs require more memory and larger caches on RISC systems. The impetus for complex instructions in the 1960s and 1970s was the quest to do many operations for each instruction fetched, since the fetch time was long compared to the execution time.

A major consideration in a multitasking system is the amount of time it takes to perform a context switch. A major factor affecting the context switch time is the number of registers that must be saved. The PowerPC has about three times the number of bytes to be saved in a context switch as the Pentium. It is ironic that RISC systems have been widely used in the workstation market, where they run UNIX, a multitasking operating system, and 80x86 systems, historically, have been used to run single-tasking DOS applications and non-preemptive multitasking in Windows.

IS THE PENTIUM RISC OR CISC?

When Intel announced the 486 they claimed the core components of the 386 were completely redesigned in developing the 486. Basic operations were carried out by a RISC core, and complex instructions were handled by separate logic. The 486 was pipelined, and all simple instructions took only one cycle. With the Pentium they have shown that this subset of instructions can be executed in parallel in two pipelines. So maybe the Pentium is the best of both RISC and CISC. This is almost true, except the number of registers on the Pentium may be quite a limiting factor, as we shall see.

SUPERSCALAR PROCESSORS

Pipelining allows a CPU to perform most (simple) operations in a single cycle. The most effective way to improve performance after pipelining is to have multiple pipelines. This technique is known as a superscalar architecture. A single pipeline is a scalar architecture. Scalar architectures are in contrast to parallel architectures. In general, parallel-architecture machines are suited for problems that can use many processors (dozens to thousands) working on the same problem with independent portions of the data. Superscalar architectures are designed for the same general-purpose computing as scalar architectures—a single stream of instructions working on a single stream of data.

The concept of multiple pipelines is simple. When you double the number of pipelines, you double the overall performance. When you have four pipelines, you get four times the performance. But not quite. As we've seen from the examples in previous chapters, many simple loops must be completely reworked to obtain double the performance. At some point the results of some instructions must be used for a subsequent instruction. When the average distance between these dependencies is large, many pipelines can be kept in use.

There is an inherent limitation in the number of pipelines that can be effectively used in a superscalar machine. Typically, researchers seem to agree on six pipelines as a practical limit. Entire books have been devoted to the reasons for these limits, a good one being *Superscalar Microprocessor Design* by Mike Johnson, published by Prentice Hall (1991). Simply put, the six-processor limit is based on the fact that CPU operations on general-purpose applications must wait for the results of previous operations. The number of data-independent operations that can be performed simultaneously is limited to a maximum of about six in the studied algorithms. Some algorithms may be able to use more and some less. (It is curious that Intel named the Pentium's pipelines U and V, leaving W, X, Y and Z available.)

Microprocessor designs have many trade-offs. For example, should there be four pipelines and 256K of cache, or six pipelines and 32K of cache? This is a contrived example, but the number of algorithms that use five or six pipelines may be small and the performance gain insignificant compared to having only four pipelines and the larger cache.

This is similar to the memory trade-off many of us make when optimizing DOS and Windows machines. Should I have 2MB of disk cache and 14MB for programs to run in, or should I have 6MB of disk cache and only 10MB for software? It depends a lot on what software you run. The difference is you can reboot and try something else till you find an optimum configuration. Once a chip is built it can't be changed—until a newer chip is designed.

As chip technology advances, it becomes possible to put more and more transistors on a single chip. Moore's Law states that the number of transistors on a chip doubles about every 18 months. And while this is not a law of physics, it has been an observable fact of technological history over the past 25 years. In our previous example, the next generation may have six pipelines and 512K of cache. There is a balance, I suppose, among memory bandwidth, cache size and the number of pipelines that can be kept full for a given clock speed and transistor count on a chip. Because of Moore's Law, the transistor count seems to be fairly predictable. But Moore's Law cannot go on forever. At some point the laws of physics will prevent further reductions when a circuit becomes only a few atoms wide, and probably sooner. Current technology has circuits that are 0.6 microns wide, or 6×10^{-7} meters. A hydrogen atom is about 10^{-10} meters in diameter. Based on these numbers we still have 10 to 20 years before we approach atomic limitations. It is fairly easy to predict that in six years chips will have about 16 times as many transistors, and in 12 years, 256 times as many.

SUPERSCALAR TECHNIQUES AND TERMINOLOGY

Scalar processors achieve their maximum performance through the use of pipelining. The maximum performance of one cycle per instruction could not be achieved otherwise. (See Chapter 10 for a detailed explanation.) The one cycle per instruction is actually the throughput, not the elapsed execution time for a single instruction. To obtain the performance of more than one instruction per cycle requires only the addition of an additional pipeline. However, to maintain a performance level of two or more instructions per cycle requires techniques beyond merely additional pipelines because of the following fundamental limitations:

- data dependencies
- procedural dependencies
- resource conflicts

Data dependencies occur when the results of an operation must be used before the next operation may proceed. AGIs (address generation interlocks) are examples of a case where the result of an operation is needed in the cycle before an operation can proceed. Read-after-write and write-after-write conflicts (see Chapter 9) are data dependencies.

Procedural dependencies occur when a branch occurs because the processor must wait until the branch occurs to know what instructions to execute next.

Resource conflicts can occur in many stages of pipelined execution. This is because there are various circuits in the computer that are shared. These include such items as memory, cache memory, buses, registers, shifters, and adders. A conflict arises when two instructions require the use of the same resource during the same cycle.

There is no easy hardware solution to the data dependency problem. The primary solution is the main topic of this book—clever programming. But the other two limitations have many hardware design techniques that can be used to overcome them:

- branch prediction
- resource duplication
- out-of-order execution
- register renaming
- branch folding
- speculative execution
- Very Long Instruction Word (VLIW) Processors

The Pentium uses branch prediction to allow many conditional branches to execute in a single cycle; zero cycles when paired with another instruction. The Pentium even overcomes the mild data dependency implied with conditional branches by ignoring the data and making the prediction based on a history of branches. If the prediction is incorrect, then there is a delay.

Resource duplication is a solution for eliminating execution bottlenecks. For example, the Pentium can execute two instructions in the same cycle that access memory because there are two circuits for accessing memory.

Out-of-order execution is the capability of a processor to execute instructions in a different order from those specified in the program and still obtain the same results as if they had been executed in order. Here is a brief explanation of this extremely advanced feature. Instructions are fetched and decoded, then placed in a buffer called the instruction window or instruction queue. The processor looks at the instructions available to be executed and the resources available and matches up as many as possible. Logically, the instruction window is in the pipeline between the decode and execution stages. The processor fetches and decodes instructions attempting to keep the instruction window full. At the same time, instructions must be examined to detect data dependencies and enforce in-order execution when required. The resources to be matched with the instructions are execution units, of which there can be two or more. One key feature of this type of architecture is that the execution units can have a narrow purpose, such as being capable of executing only branch instructions or only a load instruction. The PowerPC has out-of-order execution capability, and the Pentium does not.

Register renaming is a technique that keeps the internal registers from becoming scrambled when an out-of-order execution architecture is employed. For example, instruction number one may require the use of a register as a pointer to memory and may be waiting in the instruction window because of a memory bus resource conflict. A second instruction could execute out-of-order (ahead of the first instruction) and be allowed to modify this register (a write after a read) through the use of register renaming. Register renaming works by providing additional registers that are used to reestablish the proper relationships between registers and values. Some PowerPC processors employ register renaming.

Branch folding is a technique where unconditional branch instructions are eliminated from the instruction window and instruction fetching continues from the branch destination. The advantage is that no execution unit time is ever required. The PowerPC has this capability, and the Pentium does not. Conditional jumps cannot be folded because they must actually be executed to determine their outcome.

Speculative execution is the technique of predicting a branch destination and executing the instructions at the destination, assuming that their results will be needed. If it turns out the branch prediction is incorrect, then the results of the speculatively executed instructions are disregarded. A more advanced technique is to execute both paths at a conditional branch. Neither the Pentium nor the PowerPC currently has this feature.

Very Long Instruction Word (VLIW) Processors belong to a design class beyond a normal superscalar architecture. Traditional superscalar designs discussed so far execute multiple independent instructions at the same time when they are determined to be non-conflicting at execution time. A VLIW processor executes multiple concurrent operations that are all specified in a single instruction. The programmer and/or compiler determines several operations to be executed by each instruction. These operations are then coded into one very long instruction. The CPU can easily execute all the encoded operations, because they must be arranged to not conflict. VLIW processors, in a way, are the reinvention of CISC, the difference being that each instruction can be unique, made up of many smaller instructions. As of this writing, Intel and Hewlett Packard have announced intentions to build a VLIW processor compatible with the HP PA RISC architecture and the 80x86 architecture.

WHAT IS IN THE POWERPC?

The PowerPC is a RISC CPU family of processors based on the IBM POWER architecture. The PowerPC 601 is the first chip in this series and is used in the Power Macintosh computers. Some PowerPC 601 features:

- 32-bit addressing
- 32 32-bit general purpose registers
- 32 64-bit floating point registers
- 3 execution units with out-of-order execution
- 32K cache (data and code combined)

The most interesting feature is that the 601 has three execution units and can execute instructions out-of-order. The execution units are each different:

- integer unit
- branch processing unit
- floating-point unit

This means the 601 can execute three instructions in the same cycle, as long as one is a branch, one is a floating-point instruction and one is anything else (integer operation). Without doing any testing, I would tend to think this is not as powerful as the Pentium, which can execute two integer instructions in the same cycle as well as an integer and branch in the same cycle (with branch prediction). It would seem the 601 has an advantage in floating-point performance because the Pentium tends to have delays when mixing FPU and integer instructions and the 601 can execute them in the same cycle.

The real advantage to the out-of-order architectures is the ability to add additional execution units. The PowerPC 603 has five:

- integer unit (IU)
- load/store unit (LSU)
- system register unit (SRU)
- branch processing unit (BPU)
- floating-point unit (FPU)

The LSU executes all load and store instructions and transfers between general-purpose registers, floating-point registers and memory. The SRU executes various system instructions such as moves to/from system registers and condition register (like the 80x86 flags) operations.

Another PowerPC advantage is the number of registers. As we have seen in optimizing Pentium programs, we usually used all or nearly all of the seven general-purpose registers on the Pentium. More complex programs, with nested loops, for example, would tend to suffer more on the Pentium.

IS THE POWERPC LESS EXPENSIVE?

There are two ways to look at this question. The first is from a manufacturing point of view. IBM and Motorola state that the die size of the chip is less than half that of the first Pentium chips (see Table 20.1). All other factors being equal (i.e. manufacturing yields, overhead, etc.) this would make the PowerPC less than half the price. From a product life-cycle point of view, the Intel chips have some (current) advantages. First, Intel sells more chips, perhaps 10 times as many. This gives them some economies of scale in building chip fabrication plants (FABs) and spreading the research and development costs to more units. Also, at about the same time the first PowerPC 601 systems were shipped, Intel began shipping a second generation of Pentiums with a 0.6 micron process (reduced from 0.8 microns). This reduced the die size and the manufacturing costs (see Table 20.1).

Probably the most important design feature of the PowerPC architecture is the choice of using multiple execution units that execute different classes of instructions. This is in contrast to the Pentium architecture, in which most pairable instructions can execute in either pipe. This means the Pentium has duplicated many resources in anticipation of simultaneous use. The PowerPC architecture has taken the concept of a single execution unit and broken it into several smaller execution units. This technique takes less chip real estate because there is less duplication of resources. This design may allow the use of additional chip real estate for other performance-enhancing features and/or duplication of some execution units. In my mind this concept produces a less expensive chip. It is not clear that this concept (alone) scales to a more powerful chip at the same price. Keep in mind Moore's Law: in six years chips will have 16 times as many transistors.

Table 20.1 Pentium and PowerPC Comparison

	Pentium	**Pentium**	**PPC 601**	**PPC 603**
Speed, Mhz	60, 66	90, 100	66, 80	60, 75
Ship Date	Q2 93	Q1 94	Q3 93	Q3 94
Transistors	3.1M	3.3M	2.8M	1.6M
Process Tech.	0.8 micron	0.6 micron	0.6 micron	0.5 micron
	BICMOS	BICMOS	CMOS	CMOS
Die Size (mm^2)	294	163	121	85

FUTURE PROCESSOR DESIGNS

It is important to note that all the superscalar techniques that we've discussed are not exclusive to one architecture or another. For example, it would be possible for a future Intel processor to have out-of-order execution with three integer execution units, a branch processing unit and a floating-point unit. Likewise, a PowerPC could have two load/store units and two integer units. Branch folding could be added to the Pentium, and branch prediction added to the PowerPC.

The only major limitation in either architecture is the number of registers in the 80x86 family. There is no easy way to overcome this limitation. There are ways to add more general-purpose registers, such as providing additional longer instructions and/or extensions to the addressing modes. Another method is to use a bit in the code segment descriptor to trigger the use of a modified instruction set. These methods have a disadvantage in that some chip real estate is providing compatibility with older software, and other chip real estate is attempting to gain maximum performance. But it takes only 18 months to double chip density. It can take much longer than this to rewrite software. On the other hand, IBM is working on a version of the PowerPC (615) that includes hardware to run the 80x86 instruction set.

Benchmarks for the PowerPC are most likely done with PowerPC optimized code vs. old 80x86 code running on the Pentium. As we've seen in this book, it is possible to improve the performance of old 80x86 code by 100% to 500% for some routines. And many routines like those in this book are likely to be in many programs. It is not valid to argue that rewriting the old 80x86 code is a disadvantage because the PowerPC is starting with very little installed base of software.

There is one lesson we keep relearning in the computer industry: Customers are always demanding more and more speed, but it had better be compatible, too.

There are many performance-improving features Intel can add in the next one or two generations to keep close to the PowerPC in performance. But beyond that, the Intel CPU architects will have to come up with some ingenious designs and/or technology to keep the 80x86 architecture competitive—and that's the way it is.

Instruction Set Reference

This appendix is divided into two sections. The first section contains the integer instructions; the second section contains the floating-point instructions.

Part I

80x86 Instruction Set (8088–Pentium)

This section includes instruction length and timing for all instruction forms (excluding floating point) and pairing information for Pentium. See the legend on p. 289 for an explanation of the abbreviations used.

AAA	**ASCII adjust after addition**						
	bytes	*8088*	*186*	*286*	*386*	*486*	*Pentium*
aaa	1	8	8	3	4	3	3 NP

AAD	ASCII adjust AX before division (second byte is divisor)						
	bytes	8088	186	286	386	486	Pentium
aad	2	60	15	14	19	14	10 NP

AAM	ASCII adjust AX after multiply (second byte is divisor)						
	bytes	8088	186	286	386	486	Pentium
aam	2	83	19	16	17	15	18 NP

AAS	ASCII adjust AL after subtraction						
	bytes	8088	186	286	386	486	Pentium
aas	1	8	7	3	4	3	3 NP

ADC		Integer add with carry						
		bytes	8088	186	286	386	486	Pentium
adc reg, reg		2	3	3	2	2	1	1 PU
adc mem, reg		2+ d (0,2)	24+EA	10	7	7	3	3 PU
adc reg, mem		2+ d (0,2)	13+EA	10	7	6	2	2 PU
adc reg, imm		2+ i (1,2)	4	4	3	2	1	1 PU
adc mem, imm		2+ d (0,2)						
		+ i (1,2)	23+EA	16	7	7	3	3 PU*
adc acc, imm		1+ i (1,2)	4	4	3	2	1	1 PU

* = not pairable if there is a displacement and immediate

ADD		Integer addition						
		bytes	8088	186	286	386	486	Pentium
add reg, reg		2	3	3	2	2	1	1 UV
add mem, reg		2+ d (0,2)	24+EA	10	7	7	3	3 UV
add reg, mem		2+ d (0,2)	13+EA	10	7	6	2	2 UV
add reg, imm		2+ i (1,2)	4	4	3	2	1	1 UV
add mem, imm		2+ d (0,2)						
		+ i (1,2)	23+EA	16	7	7	3	3 UV*
add acc, imm		1+ i (1,2)	4	4	3	2	1	1 UV

* = not pairable if there is a displacement and immediate

AND		Logical AND						
		bytes	8088	186	286	386	486	Pentium
and reg, reg		2	3	3	2	2	1	1 UV
and mem, reg		2+ d (0,2)	24+EA	10	7	7	3	3 UV
and reg, mem		2+ d (0,2)	13+EA	10	7	6	2	2 UV
and reg, imm		2+ i (1,2)	4	4	3	2	1	1 UV
and mem, imm		2+ d (0,2)						
		+ i (1,2)	23+EA	16	7	7	3	3 UV*
and acc, imm		1+ i (1,2)	4	4	3	2	1	1 UV

* = not pairable if there is a displacement and immediate

ARPL Adjust RPL field of selector (286+)

	bytes		286	386	486	Pentium
arpl reg, reg	2		10	20	9	7 NP
arpl mem, reg	2+ d (0–2)		11	21	9	7 NP

BOUND Check array index against bounds (186+)

	bytes	186	286	386	486	Pentium
bound reg, mem	4	35	13	10	7	8 NP

BSF Bit scan forward (386+)

	bytes		386	486	Pentium
bsf r16, r16	3		10+3n	6–42	6–34 NP
bsf r32, r32	3		10+3n	6–42	6–42 NP
bsf r16, m16	3+ d (0,1,2)		10+3n	7–43	6–13 NP
bsf r32, m32	3+ d (0,1,2,4)		10+3n	7–43	6–43 NP

BSR Bit scan reverse (386+)

	bytes		386	486	Pentium
bsf r16, r16	3		10+3n	6–103	7–39 NP
bsf r32, r32	3		10+3n	7–104	7–71 NP
bsf r16, m16	3+ d (0,1,2)		10+3n	6–103	7–40 NP
bsf r32, m32	3+ d (0,1,2,4)		10+3n	7–104	7–72 NP

BSWAP Byte swap (486+)

	bytes		486	Pentium
bswap r32	2		1	1 NP

BT Bit test (386+)

	bytes		386	486	Pentium
bt reg, reg	3		3	3	4 NP
bt mem, reg	3+ d (0,1,2,4)		12	8	9 NP
bt reg, imm8	3+ i (1)		3	3	4 NP
bt mem, imm8	3+ d (0,1,2,4)+i(1)		6	3	4 NP

BTC Bit test and complement (386+)

	bytes		386	486	Pentium
btc reg, reg	3		6	6	7 NP
btc mem, reg	3+ d (0,1,2,4)		13	13	13 NP
btc reg, imm8	3+ i (1)		6	6	7 NP
btc mem, imm8	3+ d (0,1,2,4)+i(1)		8	8	8 NP

BTR Bit test and reset (386+)

	bytes		386	486	Pentium
btr reg, reg	3		6	6	7 NP
btr mem, reg	3+ d (0,1,2,4)		13	13	13 NP

BTR   **Bit test and reset (386+)**

	bytes	386	486	Pentium
btr reg, imm8	3+ *i* (1)	6	6	7 NP
btr mem, imm8	3+ *d* (0,1,2,4)+*i* (1)	8	8	8 NP

BTS   **Bit test and set (386+)**

	bytes	386	486	Pentium
bts reg, reg	3	6	6	7 NP
bts mem, reg	3+ *d* (0,1,2,4)	13	13	13 NP
bts reg, imm8	3+ *i* (1)	6	6	7 NP
bts mem, imm8	3+ *d* (0,1,2,4)+*i* (1)	8	8	8 NP

CALL   **Call subroutine**

	bytes	8088	186	286	386	486	Pentium
call near	3	23	14	7+*m*	7+*m*	3	1 PV
call reg	2	20	13	7+*m*	7+*m*	5	2 NP
call mem16	2+ *d* (0–2)	29+EA	19	11+*m*	10+*m*	5	2 NP
call far	5	36	23	13+*m*	17+*m*	18	4 NP
call mem32	2+ *d* (0–2)	53+EA	38	16+*m*	22+*m*	17	4 NP

Protected Mode

	bytes	286	386	486	Pentium
call far	5	26+*m*	34+*m*	20	4–13 NP
call mem32	2+ *d* (0–2)	29+*m*	38+*m*	20	5–14 NP

cycles not shown for calls through call and task gates

CBW   **Convert byte to word (AL → AX)**

	bytes	8088	186	286	386	486	Pentium
cbw	1	2	2	2	3	3	3 NP

CDQ   **Convert double to quad (EAX → EDX:EAX)**

	bytes	386	486	Pentium
cdq	1	2	3	2 NP

CLC   **Clear the carry flag**

	bytes	8088	186	286	386	486	Pentium
clc	1	2	2	2	2	2	2 NP

CLD   **Clear the direction flag (set to forward direction)**

	bytes	8088	186	286	386	486	Pentium
cld	1	2	2	2	2	2	2 NP

CLI   **Clear the interrupt flag (disable interrupts)**

	bytes	8088	186	286	386	486	Pentium
cli	1	2	2	3	3	5	7 NP

CLTS   Clear task switched flag in CR0 (286+)

	bytes			286	386	486	Pentium
clts	2			2	5	7	10 NP

CMC   Complement carry flag

	bytes	8088	186	286	386	486	Pentium
cmc	1	2	2	2	2	2	2 NP

CMP   Compare two operands

	bytes	8088	186	286	386	486	Pentium
cmp reg, reg	2	3	3	2	2	1	1 UV
cmp mem, reg	2+ d (0,2)	13+EA	10	7	5	2	2 UV
cmp reg, mem	2+ d (0,2)	13+EA	10	6	6	2	2 UV
cmp reg, imm	2+ i (1,2)	4	4	3	2	1	1 UV
cmp mem, imm	2+ d (0,2)						
	+ i (1,2)	14+EA	10	6	5	2	2 UV*
cmp acc, imm	1+ i (1,2)	4	4	3	2	1	1 UV

* = not pairable if there is a displacement and immediate

CMPS/CMPSB/   Compare string operands
CMPSW/CMPSD   (compare DS:[SI] with ES:[DI])

	bytes	8088	186	286	386	486	Pentium
cmpsb	1	30	22	8	10	8	5 NP
cmpsw	1	—	—	—	10	8	5 NP
cmpsd	1	—	—	—	10	8	5 NP
repX cmpsb	2	9+30n	5+22n	5+9n	5+9n	7+7n*	9+4n NP
repX cmpsw	2	9+30n	5+22n	5+9n	5+9n	7+7n*	9+4n NP
repX cmpsd	2	—	—	—	5+9n	7+7n*	9+4n NP

repX = repe, repz, repne or repnz

* = 5 if n = 0

CMPXCHG   Compare and Exchange (486+)

	bytes		486	Pentium
cmpxchg reg, reg	3		6	5 NP
cmpxchg mem, reg	3+ d (0–2)		7–10	6 NP

CMPXCHG8B   Compare and Exchange 8 bytes (Pentium)

	bytes	Pentium
cmpxchg8b mem	3+ d (0–2)	10 NP

CPUID   CPU identification (Pentium)

	bytes	Pentium
cpuid	2	14 NP

CWD — Convert word to double (AX → DX:AX)

	bytes	8088	186	286	386	486	Pentium
cwd	1	5	4	2	2	3	2 NP

CWDE — Convert word to dword (386+) (AX → EAX)

	bytes				386	486	Pentium
cwde	1				3	3	3 NP

DAA — Decimal adjust AL after addition

	bytes	8088	186	286	386	486	Pentium
daa	1	4	4	3	4	2	3 NP

DAS — Decimal adjust AL after subtraction

	bytes	8088	186	286	386	486	Pentium
das	1	4	4	3	4	2	3 NP

DEC — Decrement

	bytes	8088	186	286	386	486	Pentium
dec r8	2	3	3	2	2	1	1 UV
dec r16	1	3	3	2	2	1	1 UV
dec r32	1	3	3	2	2	1	1 UV
dec mem	2+d (0,2)	23+EA	15		6	3	3 UV

DIV — Unsigned divide

	bytes	8088	186	286	386	486	Pentium
div r8	2	80–90	29	14	14	16	17 NP
div r16	2	144–162	38	22	22	24	25 NP
div r32	2	—	—	—	38	40	41 NP
div mem8	2+d (0–2)	86–96+EA	35	17	17	16	17 NP
div mem16	2+d (0–2)	150–168+EA	44	25	25	24	25 NP
div mem32	2+d (0–2)	—	—	—	41	40	41 NP

implied dividend		operand		quotient	remainder
AX	÷	byte	=	AL	AH
DX:AX	÷	word	=	AX	DX
EDX:EAX	÷	dword	=	EAX	EDX

ENTER — Make stack frame for procedure parameters (186+)

	bytes	8088	186	286	386	486	Pentium
enter imm16, 0	3	—	15	11	10	14	11 NP
enter imm16, 1	4	—	25	15	12	17	15 NP
enter imm16, imm8	4	—	22+16n	12+4n	15+4n	17+3i	15+2i NP

n = imm8-1; i = imm8

ESC Escape

escape opcodes D8–DF are used by floating point instructions

HLT Halt

	bytes	8088	186	286	386	486	Pentium
hlt	1	2	2	2	5	4	4 NP

IDIV Signed divide

	bytes	8088	186	286	386	486	Pentium
idiv r8	2	101–112	44–52	17	19	19	22 NP
idiv r16	2	165–184	53–61	25	27	27	30 NP
idiv r32	2	—	—	—	43	43	46 NP
idiv mem8	2+d (0–2)	107–118+EA	50–58	20	22	20	22 NP
idiv mem16	2+d (0–2)	171–190+EA	59–67	28	30	28	30 NP
idiv mem32	2+d (0–2)	—	—	—	46	44	46 NP

implied dividend		operand		quotient	remainder
AX	÷	byte	=	AL	AH
DX:AX	÷	word	=	AX	DX
EDX:EAX	÷	dword	=	EAX	EDX

IMUL Signed multiply

Accumulator Multiplies

	bytes	8088	186	286	386	486	Pentium
imul r8	2	80–98	25–28	13	9–14	13–18	11 NP
imul r16	2	128–154	34–37	21	9–22	13–26	11 NP
imul r32	2	—	—	—	9–38	13–42	10 NP
imul mem8	2+d (0–2)	86–104+EA	32–34	16	12–17	13–18	11 NP
imul mem16	2+d (0–2)	134–160+EA	40–43	24	12–25	13–26	11 NP
imul mem32	2+d (0–2)	—	—	—	12–41	13–42	10 NP

implied multiplicand		operand (multiplier)		result
AL	×	byte	=	AX
AX	×	word	=	DX:AX
EAX	×	dword	=	EDX:EAX

2 and 3 Operand Multiplies

	bytes	186	286	386	486	Pentium
imul r16, imm	2+i (1,2)	—	21	9–14/ 9–22	13–18/ 13–26	10 NP
imul r32, imm	2+i (1,2)	—	—	9–38	13–42	10 NP
imul r16,r16,imm	2+i (1,2)	22/29	2	9–14/ 9–2	13–18/ 13–26	10 NP
imul r32,r32,imm	2+i (1,2)			9–38	13–42	10 NP

IMUL　　　Signed multiply

	bytes	8088	186	286	386	486	Pentium
imul r16,m16,imm	2+ d (0–2) + i (1,2)		25/32	2	12–17/ 12–25	13–18/ 13–26	10 NP
imul r32,m32,imm	2+ d (0–2)+i (1,2)			—	12–41	13–42	10 NP
imul r16, r16	2+ i (1,2)			—	—	9–22	13–18/ 13–26	10 NP
imul r32, r32	2+ i (1,2)			—	—	9–38	13–42	10 NP
imul r16, m16	2+ d (0–2)+i (1,2)			—	—	12–25	13–18/ 13–26	10 NP
imul r32, m32	2+ d (0–2)+i (1,2)			—	—	12–41	13–42	10 NP

all forms:　　**dest, src**　　　　　cycles for:　byte/word
　　　　　　　or
　　　　　　　dest, src1, src2

IN　　　Input from port

	bytes	8088	186	286	386	486	Pentium
in al, imm8	2	14	10	5	12	14	7 NP
in ax, imm8	2	14	10	5	12	14	7 NP
in eax, imm8	2	—	—	—	12	14	7 NP
in al, dx	1	12	8	5	13	14	7 NP
in ax, dx	1	12	8	5	13	14	7 NP
in eax, dx	1	—	—	—	13	14	7 NP

Protected Mode

	bytes	386	486	Pentium
in acc, imm	2	6/26/26	9/29/27	4/21/19 NP
in acc, dx	1	7/27/27	8/28/27	4/21/19 NP

cycles for: CPL $\leq$ IOPL / CPL > IOPL / V86

INC　　　Increment

	bytes	8088	186	286	386	486	Pentium
inc r8	2	3	3	2	2	1	1 UV
inc r16	1	3	3	2	2	1	1 UV
inc r32	1	3	3	2	2	1	1 UV
inc mem	2+d (0,2)	23+EA	15	7	6	3	3 UV

INS/INSB/INSW/INSD　Input from port to string; input byte from port DX into ES:DI

	bytes	8088	186	286	386	486	Pentium
insb	1	—	14	5	15	17	9 NP
insw	1	—	14	5	15	17	9 NP
insd	1	—	—	—	15	17	9 NP

INS/INSB/INSW/INSD Input from port to string;
input byte from port DX into ES:DI

Protected Mode

	bytes				*386*	*486*	*Pentium*
`ins`	1				9/29/29	10/32/30	6/24/22 NP

cycles for: CPL ≤ IOPL / CPL > IOPL / V86

INT Call interrupt procedure

	bytes	*8088*	*186*	*286*	*386*	*486*	*Pentium*
`int 3`	1	72	45	23+*m*	33	26	13 NP
`int imm8`	2	71	47	23+*m*	37	30	16 NP

Protected Mode

	bytes	*8088*	*186*	*286*	*386*	*486*	*Pentium*
`int`	1	—	—	(40–78)+*m*	59–99	44–71	27–82 NP

INTO Call interrupt procedure if overflow

	bytes	*8088*	*186*	*286*	*386*	*486*	*Pentium*
`into`	1	4/73	4/48	3/24+*m*	3/35	3/28	4/13 NP

Protected Mode

	bytes			*286*	*386*	*486*	*Pentium*
`into`	1			(40–78)+*m*	59–99	44–71	27–56 NP

Task switch clocks not shown

INVD Invalidate cache (486+)

	bytes	*8088*	*186*	*286*	*386*	*486*	*Pentium*
`invd`	2	—	—	—	—	4	15 NP

INVLPG Invalidate TLB entry (486+)

	bytes					*486*	*Pentium*
`invlpg mem32`	5					12	25 NP

IRET Return from interrupt

	bytes	*8088*	*186*	*286*	*386*	*486*	*Pentium*
`iret`	1	44	28	17+*m*	22	15	8–27 NP

Task switch clocks not shown

IRETD 32-bit return from interrupt (386+)

	bytes				*386*	*486*	*Pentium*
`iretd`	1				22	15	10–27 NP

Task switch clocks not shown

Jcc	Jump on condition code						
	bytes	8088	186	286	386	486	Pentium
Jcc near8	2	4/16	4/13	3/7+m	3/7+m	1/3	1 PV
Jcc near16	3	—	—	—	3/7+m	1/3	1 PV

cycles for: no jump/jump

conditional jump instructions

ja	jump if above	jnbe	jump if not below or equal
jae	jump if above or equal	jnb	jump if not below
jb	jump if below	jnae	jump if not above or equal
jbe	jump if below or equal	jna	jump if not above
jg	jump if greater	jnle	jump if not less or equal
jge	jump if greater or equal	jnl	jump if not less
jl	jump if less	jnge	jump if not greater or equal
jle	jump if less or equal	jng	jump if not greater
je	jump if equal	jz	jump if zero
jne	jump if not equal	jnz	jump if not zero
jc	jump if carry	jnc	jump if not carry
js	jump if sign	jns	jump if not sign
jnp	jump if no parity (odd)	jpo	jump if parity odd
jo	jump if overflow	jno	jump if not overflow
jp	jump if parity (even)	jpe	jump if parity even

JCXZ/JECXZ	Jump if CX/ECX = 0						
	bytes	8088	186	286	386	486	Pentium
jcxz dest	2	6/18	5/16	4/8+m	5/9+m	5/8	5/6 NP
jecxz dest	2				5/9+m	5/8	5/6 NP

cycles for: no jump/jump

JMP	Unconditional jump						
	bytes	8088	186	286	386	486	Pentium
jmp short	2	15	13	7+m	7+m	3	1 PV
jmp near	3	15	13	7+m	7+m	3	1 PV
jmp far	5	15	13	11+m	12+m	17	3 NP
jmp r16	2	11	11	7+m	7+m	5	2 NP
jmp mem16	2+ d (0,2)	18+EA	17	11+m	10+m	5	2 NP
jmp mem32	2+ d (4)	24+EA	26	15+m	12+m	13	4 NP
jmp r32	2	—	—	—	7+m	5	2 NP
jmp mem32	2+ d (0,2)	—	—	—	10+m	5	2 NP
jmp mem48	2+ d (6)	—	—	—	12+m	13	4 NP

cycles for jumps through call gates not shown

LAHF   Load flags into AH

	bytes	8088	186	286	386	486	Pentium
lahf	1	4	2	2	2	3	2 NP

LAR   Load access rights byte (286+)

	bytes			286	386	486	Pentium
lar r16, r16	3			14	15	11	8 NP
lar r32, r32	3			—	15	11	8 NP
lar r16, m16	3			16	16	11	8 NP
lar r32, m32	3			—	16	11	8 NP

LDS   Load far pointer

	bytes	8088	186	286	386	486	Pentium
lds reg, mem	2+d (2)	24+EA	18	7	7	6	4 NP

LES   Load far pointer

	bytes	8088	186	286	386	486	Pentium
les reg, mem	2+d (2)	24+EA	18	7	7	6	4 NP

LFS   Load far pointer (386+)

	bytes				386	486	Pentium
lfs reg, mem	3+d (2,4)				7	6	4 NP

LGS   Load far pointer (386+)

	bytes				386	486	Pentium
lgs reg, mem	3+d (2,4)				7	6	4 NP

LSS   Load stack segment and offset

	bytes				386	486	Pentium
lss reg, mem	3+d (2,4)				7	6	4 NP

LEA   Load effective address

	bytes	8088	186	286	386	486	Pentium
lea r16, mem	2+d (2)	2+EA	6	3	2	1–2	1 UV
lea r32, mem	2+d (2)	—	—	—	2	1–2	1 UV

LEAVE   High-level procedure exit (186+)

	bytes		186	286	386	486	Pentium
leave	1		8	5	4	5	3 NP

LGDT   Load global descriptor table register (286+)

	bytes			286	386	486	Pentium
lgdt mem48	5			11	11	11	6 NP

LIDT   Load interrupt descriptor table register (286+)

	bytes			286	386	486	Pentium
lidt mem48	5			12	11	11	6 NP

LLDT   Load local descriptor table register (286+)

	bytes			286	386	486	Pentium
lldt r16	3			17	20	11	9 NP
lldt mem16	3+d (0–2)			19	24	11	9 NP

LMSW   Load machine status word (286+)

	bytes			286	386	486	Pentium
lmsw r16	3			3	10	13	8 NP
lmsw mem16	3+d (0–2)			6	13	13	8 NP

LOCK   Lock bus on next instruction (prefix)

	bytes	8088	186	286	386	486	Pentium
lock opcode	1	2	2	0	0	1	1 NP

LODS/LODSB/LODSW/LODSD   Load string operand

	bytes	8088	186	286	386	486	Pentium
lodsb	1	16	10	5	5	5	2 NP
lodsw	1	16	10	5	5	5	2 NP
lodsd	1	—	—	—	5	5	2 NP

LOOP   Loop control with CX counter

	bytes	8088	186	286	386	486	Pentium
loop short	2	5/17	5/15	4/8+m	11+m	6/7	5/6 NP
loopw short (uses CX in 32-bit mode)							
loopd short (uses ECX in 16-bit mode)							

LOOPE   Loop while equal (or zero)

	bytes	8088	186	286	386	486	Pentium
loope short	2	6/18	5/16	4/8	11+m	6/9	7/8 NP
loopz short							
loopew short (uses CX in 32-bit mode)							
loopzw short (uses CX in 32-bit mode)							
looped short (uses ECX in 16-bit mode)							
loopzd short (uses ECX in 16-bit mode)							

LOOPZ   Loop while zero (or equal)

See: **loope** (**loope** and **loopz** are synonyms)

LOOPNE   Loop while not equal (or not zero)

	bytes	8088	186	286	386	486	Pentium
loopne short	2	5/19	5/16	4/8	11+m	6/9	7/8 NP
loopnz short							
loopnew short	(uses CX in 32-bit mode)						
loopnzw short	(uses CX in 32-bit mode)						
loopned short	(uses ECX in 16-bit mode)						
loopnzd short	(uses ECX in 16-bit mode)						

LOOPNZ   Loop while not zero (or not equal)

See: **loopne** (**loopne** and **loopnz** are synonyms)

LSL   Load segment limit (286+)

	bytes	286	386	486	Pentium
lsl r16, r16	3	14	20/25	10	8 NP
lsl r32, r32	3	—	20/25	10	8
lsl r16, m16	3+d (0,2)	16	21/26	10	8
lsl r32, m32	3+d (0,2)	—	21/26	10	8

LTR   Load task register (286+)

	bytes	286	386	486	Pentium
ltr r16	3	17	23	20	10 NP
ltr mem16	3+d (0,2)	19	27	20	10

MOV   Move data

	bytes	8088	186	286	386	486	Pentium
mov reg, reg	2	2	2	2	2	1	1 UV
mov mem, reg	2+ d (0–2)	13+EA	9	3	2	1	1 UV
mov reg, mem	2+ d (0–2)	12+EA	12	5	4	1	1 UV
mov mem, imm	2+ d (0–2)						
	+ i (1,2)	14+EA	12–13	3	2	1	1 UV*
mov reg, imm	2+ i(1,2)	4	3–4	2	2	1	1 UV
mov acc, mem	3	14	8	5	4	1	1 UV
mov mem, acc	3	14	9	3	2	1	1 UV

* = **mov** **mem+disp,** **imm** not pairable, pairable UV if displacement = 0

Segment register moves

Real Mode

	bytes	8088	186	286	386	486	Pentium
mov seg, r16	2	2	2	2	2	3	2–11 NP
mov seg, m16	2+ d (0,2)	12+EA	9	5	5	3	3–12 NP
mov r16, seg	2	2	2	2	2	3	1 NP
mov m16, seg	2+ d (0,2)	13+EA	11	3	2	3	1 NP

MOV — Move data

Protected Mode Differences

	bytes		286	386	486	Pentium
mov seg, r16	2		17	18	9	2–11* NP
mov seg, m16	2+d (0,2)		19	19	9	3–12* NP

*= add 8 if new descriptor; add 6 if SS

MOVE to/from special registers (386+)

	bytes			386	486	Pentium
mov r32, cr32	3			6	4	4 NP
mov cr32, r32	3			4/10*	4/16*	12/22* NP
mov r32, dr32	3			14/22*	10	2/12* NP
mov dr32, r32	3			16/22*	11	11/12* NP
mov r32, tr32	3			12	3/4*	—
mov tr32, r32	3			12	4/6*	—

*= cycles depend on which special register

MOVS/MOVSB/MOVSW/MOVSD — Move data from string to string

	bytes	8088	186	286	386	486	Pentium
movsb	1	18	9	5	7	7	4 NP
movsw	1	26	9	5	7	7	4 NP
movsd	1	—	—	—	7	7	4 NP
rep movsb	2	9+17n	8+8n	5+4n	7+4n	12+3n*	3+n NP
rep movsw	2	9+25n	8+8n	5+4n	7+4n	12+3n*	3+n NP
rep movsd	2	—	—	—	7+4n	12+3n*	3+n NP

*= 5 if $n=0$, 13 if $n=1$, else $12+3n$
(n = count of bytes, words or dwords)

MOVSX — Move with sign-extend (386+)

	bytes		386	486	Pentium
movsx reg, reg	3		3	3	3 NP
movsx reg, mem	3+d (0,1,2,4)		6	3	3 NP

MOVZX — Move with zero-extend (386+)

	bytes		386	486	Pentium
movzx reg, reg	3		3	3	3 NP
movzx reg, mem	3+d (0,1,2,4)		6	3	3 NP

MUL — Unsigned multiply

	bytes	8088	186	286	386	486	Pentium
mul r8	2	70–77	26–28	13	9–14	13–18	11 NP
mul r16	2	118–133	35–37	21	9–22	13–26	11 NP
mul r32	2	—	—	—	9–38	13–42	10 NP

MUL	Unsigned multiply							
mul mem8		2+d (0–2)	76–83+EA	32–34	16	12–17	13–18	11 NP
mul mem16		2+d (0–2)	124–139+EA	41–43	24	12–25	13–26	11 NP
mul mem32		2+d (0–2)	—	—	—	12–41	13–42	10 NP

implied multiplicand		operand (multiplier)		result
AL	×	byte	=	AX
AX	×	word	=	DX:A
EAX	×	dword	=	EDX:EAX

NEG	Twos complement negation						
	bytes	*8088*	*186*	*286*	*386*	*486*	*Pentium*
neg reg	2	3	3	2	2	1	1 NP
neg mem	2+d(0–2)	24+EA	13	7	6	3	3 NP

NOP	No operation						
	bytes	*8088*	*186*	*286*	*386*	*486*	*Pentium*
nop	1	3	3	3	3	1	1 UV

NOT	Ones complement negation						
	bytes	*8088*	*186*	*286*	*386*	*486*	*Pentium*
not reg	2	3	3	2	2	1	1 NP
not mem	2+d(0–2)	24+EA	13	7	6	3	3 NP

OR	Logical inclusive or						
	bytes	*8088*	*186*	*286*	*386*	*486*	*Pentium*
or reg, reg	2	3	3	2	2	1	1 UV
or mem, reg	2+d (0,2)	24+EA	10	7	7	3	3 UV
or reg, mem	2+d (0,2)	13+EA	10	7	6	2	2 UV
or reg, imm	2+i (1,2)	4	4	3	2	1	1 UV
or mem, imm	2+d (0,2) +i (1,2)	23+EA	16	7	7	3	3 UV*
or acc, imm	1+i (1,2)	4	4	3	2	1	1 UV

* = not pairable if there is a displacement and immediate

OUT	Output to port						
	bytes	*8088*	*186*	*286*	*386*	*486*	*Pentium*
out imm8, al	2	14	9	3	10	16	12 NP
out imm8, ax	2	14	9	3	10	16	12 NP
out imm8, eax	2	—	—	—	10	16	12 NP
out dx, al	1	12	7	3	11	16	12 NP
out dx, ax	1	12	7	3	11	16	12 NP
out dx, eax	1	—	—	—	11	16	12 NP

OUT — Output to port

	bytes			386	486	Pentium
		Protected Mode				
out **imm8, acc**	2			4/24/24	11/31/29	9/26/24 NP
out **dx, acc**	1			5/25/25	10/30/29	9/26/24 NP

cycles for: CPL ≤IOPL / CPL > IOPL / V86

OUTS/OUTSB/OUTSW/OUTSD — Output string to port

	bytes	186	286	386	486	Pentium
outsb	1	14	5	14	17	13 NP
outsw	1	14	5	14	17	13 NP
outsd	1	—	—	14	17	13 NP

	bytes			386	486	Pentium
		Protected Mode				
outs	1			8/28/28	10/32/30	10/27/25 NP

cycles for: CPL <= IOPL / CPL > IOPL / V86

POP — Pop a word/dword from the stack

	bytes	8088	186	286	386	486	Pentium
pop **reg**	1	12	10	5	4	1	1 UV
pop **mem**	2+ *d* (0–2)	25+EA	20	5	5	6	3 NP
pop **seg**	1	12	8	5	7	3	3 NP
pop **FS/GS**	2	—	—	—	7	3	3 NP

	bytes		286	386	486	Pentium
		Protected Mode				
pop **CS/DS/ES**	1		20	21	9	3–12 NP
pop **SS**	1		20	21	9	8–17 NP
pop **FS/GS**	2		—	21	9	3–12 NP

POPA/POPAD — Pop all (186+)/Pop all double (386+)

	bytes	186	286	386	486	Pentium
popa	1	51	19	24	9	5 NP
popad	1	—	—	24	9	5 NP

    popa = **pop** di, si, bp, sp, bx, dx, cx, ax
    popad = **pop** edi, esi, ebp, esp, ebx, edx, ecx, eax
    (sp and esp are discarded)

POPF/POPFD — Pop flags/Pop flags double (386+)

	bytes	8088	186	286	386	486	Pentium
popf	1	12	8	5	5	9	6 NP
popfd	1	—	—	—	5	9	6 NP

POPF/POPFD — Pop flags/Pop flags double (386+)

Protected Mode

	bytes		286	386	486	Pentium
popf	1		5	5	6	4 NP
popfd	1		—	5	6	4 NP

PUSH — push a word/dword to the stack

	bytes	8088	186	286	386	486	Pentium
push reg	1	15	10	3	21		1 UV
push mem	2+ *d* (0–2)	24+EA	16	5	5	4	2 NP
push seg	1	14	9	3	2	3	1 NP
push imm	1+ *i* (1,2)	—	—	3	2	1	1 NP
push FS/GS	2	—	—	—	2	3	1 NP

PUSHA/PUSHAD — Push all (186+)/Push all double (386+)

	bytes	186	286	386	486	Pentium
pusha	1	36	17	18	11	5 NP
pushad	1	—	—	18	11	5 NP

pusha = **push** ax, cx, dx, bx, sp, bp, si, di,

pushad = **push** eax, ecx, edx, ebx, esp, ebp, esi, edi

PUSHF/PUSHFD — Push flags/Push flags double (386+)

	bytes	8088	186	286	386	486	Pentium
pushf	1	14	9	3	4	4	9 NP
pushfd	1	—	—	—	4	4	9 NP

Protected Mode

	bytes		286	386	486	Pentium
pushf	1		3	4	3	3 NP
pushfd	1		—	4	3	3 NP

RCL — Rotate bits left with CF

	bytes	8088	186	286	386	486	Pentium
rcl reg, 1	2	2	2	2	9	3	1 PU
rcl mem, 1	2+ *d* (0,2)	23+EA	15	7	10	4	3 PU
rcl reg, cl	2	8+4*n*	5+*n*	5+*n*	9	8–30	7–24 NP
rcl mem, cl	2+ *d* (0,2)	28+EA+4*n*	17+*n*	8+*n*	10	9–3	9–26
rcl reg, imm	3	—	5+*n*	5+*n*	9	8–30	8–25 NP
rcl mem, imm	3+ *d* (0,2)	—	17+*n*	8+*n*	10	9–31	10–27 NP

RCR — Rotate bits right with CF

	bytes	8088	186	286	386	486	Pentium
rcr reg, 1	2	2	2	2	9	3	1 PU
rcr mem, 1	2+ *d* (0,2)	23+EA	15	7	10	4	3 PU
rcr reg, cl	2	8+4*n*	5+*n*	5+*n*	9	8–30	7–24 NP
rcr mem, cl	2+ *d* (0,2)	28+EA+4*n*	17+*n*	8+*n*	10	9–31	9–26 NP

RCR	Rotate bits right with CF							
		bytes	*8088*	*186*	*286*	*386*	*486*	*Pentium*
rcr reg, imm		3	—	5+*n*	5+*n*	9	8–30	8–25 NP
rcr mem, imm		3+ *d* (0,2)	—	17+*n*	8+*n*	10	9–31	10–27 NP

ROL	Rotate bits left							
		bytes	*8088*	*186*	*286*	*386*	*486*	*Pentium*
rol reg, 1		2	2	2	2	3	3	1 PU
rol mem, 1		2+ *d* (0,2)	23+EA	15	7	7	4	3 PU
rol reg, cl		2	8+4*n*	5+*n*	5+*n*	3	3	4 NP
rol mem, cl		2+ *d* (0,2)	28+EA+4*n*	17+*n*	8+*n*	7	4	4 NP
rol reg, imm		3	—	5+*n*	5+*n*	3	2	1 PU
rol mem, imm		3+ *d* (0,2)	—	17+*n*	8+*n*	7	4	3 PU*

* = not pairable if there is a displacement and immediate

ROR	Rotate bits right							
		bytes	*8088*	*186*	*286*	*386*	*486*	*Pentium*
ror reg, 1		2	2	2	2	3	3	1 PU
ror mem, 1		2+ *d* (0,2)	23+EA	15	7	7	4	3 PU
ror reg, cl		2	8+4*n*	5+*n*	5+*n*	3	3	4 NP
ror mem, cl		2+ *d* (0,2)	28+EA+4*n*	17+*n*	8+*n*	7	4	4 NP
ror reg, imm		3	—	5+*n*	5+*n*	3	2	1 PU
ror mem, imm		3+ *d* (0,2)	—	17+*n*	8+*n*	7	4	3 PU*

* = not pairable if there is a displacement and immediate

RDMSR	Read from model-specific register (Pentium)		
		bytes	*Pentium*
rdmsr		2	2–24 NP

REP	Repeat string operation

See: **rep movs**
See: **rep stos**

REPE	Repeat while equal (or zero) string operation

See: **repe cmps**   find non-matching memory items
See: **repe scas**   find non-acc matching byte in memory

REPNE	Repeat while not equal (or not zero) string operation

See: **repne cmps**   find first matching memory items
See: **repne scas**   find first matching memory item to acc

RET/RETN/RETF Return from procedure

RET is coded as **RETN** (return near) or **RETF** (return far) by the assembler

	bytes	8088	186	286	386	486	Pentium
retn	1	20	16	11+m	10+m	5	2 NP
retn imm16	1+ d (2)	24	18	11+m	10+m	5	3 NP
retf	1	34	22	15+m	18+m	13	4 NP
ret imm16	1+ d (2)	33	25	15+m	18+m	14	4 NP

Protected Mode

	bytes	286	386	486	Pentium
retf	1	25+m/55	32+m/62	18/33	4–13/23 NP
retf imm16	1+ d (2)	25+m/55	32+m/68	17/33	4–13/23 NP

cycles for: same privilege level/lower privilege level

RSM Resume from system management mode (Pentium)

	bytes	Pentium
rsm	2	83 NP

SAL/SHL/SAR/SHR Shift bits

	bytes	8088	186	286	386	486	Pentium
sh reg, 1	2	2	2	2	3	3	1 PU
sh mem, 1	2+ d (0,2)	23+EA	15	7	7	4	3 PU
sh reg, cl	2	8+4n	5+n	5+n	3	3	4 NP
sh mem, cl	2+ d (0,2)	28+EA+4n	17+n	8+n	7	4	4 NP
sh reg, imm	3	—	5+n	5+n	3	2	1 PU
sh mem, imm	3+ d (0,2)	—	17+n	8+n	7	4	3 PU*

* = not pairable if there is a displacement and immediate

sh = one of: **sal**, **shl**, **sar**, **shr**

sal = shift arithmetic left	**sar** = shift arithmetic right
shl = shift left (same as **sal**)	**shr** = shift right

SAHF Store AH into flags

	bytes	8088	186	286	386	486	Pentium
sahf	1	4	3	2	3	2	2 NP

SBB Integer subtraction with borrow

	bytes	8088	186	286	386	486	Pentium
sbb reg, reg	2	3	3	2	2	1	1 PU
sbb mem, reg	2+ d (0,2)	24+EA	10	7	7	3	3 PU
sbb reg, mem	2+ d (0,2)	13+EA	10	7	6	2	2 PU
sbb reg, imm	2+ i (1,2)	4	4	3	2	1	1 PU
sbb mem, imm	2+ d (0,2)						
	+ i (1,2)	23+EA	16	7	7	3	3 PU*

SBB	Integer subtraction with borrow						
	bytes	*8088*	*186*	*286*	*386*	*486*	*Pentium*
sbb acc, imm	1+ *i* (1,2)	4	4	3	2	1	1 PU

* = not pairable if there is a displacement and immediate

SCAS/SCASB/SCASW/SCASD	Scan string data						
	bytes	*8088*	*186*	*286*	*386*	*486*	*Pentium*
scasb	1	19	15	7	7	6	4 NP
scasw	1	19	15	7	7	6	4 NP
scasd	1	—	—	—	7	6	4 NP
repX scasb	2	9+15n	5+15n	5+8n	5+8n	7+5n*	8+4n NP
repX scasw	2	9+19n	5+15n	5+8n	5+8n	7+5n*	8+4n NP
repX scasd	2	———	5+8n	7+5n*	8+4n NP		

repX = **repe** or **repz** or **repne** or **repnz**

* = 5 if n=0
(n = count of bytes, words or dwords)

SET	Set byte to 1 on condition else set to 0 (386+)				
	bytes	*386*	*486*	*Pentium*
setCC reg	3	4	4/3	1/2 NP
setCC mem	3+ *d* (0–2)	5	3/4	1/2 NP

Cycles are for: true/false

setCC = one of:

seta	setae	setb	setbe	setc
setg	setge	setl	setle	setna
setnb	setnbe	setnc	setne	setng
setnl	setnle	setno	setnp	setns
seto	setp	setpe	setpo	sets

SGDT	Store global descriptor table register (286+)				
	bytes	*286*	*386*	*486*	*Pentium*
sgdt mem48	5	11	9	10	4 NP

SIDT	Store interrupt descriptor table register (286+)				
	bytes	*286*	*386*	*486*	*Pentium*
sidt mem48	5	12	9	10	4 NP

SHLD	Double precision shift left (386+)			
	bytes	*386*	*486*	*Pentium*
shld reg, reg, imm	4	3	2	4 NP
shld mem, reg, imm	4+ *d* (0–2)	7	3	4 NP
shld reg, reg, cl	4	3	3	4 NP
shld mem, reg, cl	4+ *d* (0–2)	7	4	5 NP

SHRD	Double precision shift right (386+)				
	bytes		*386*	*486*	*Pentium*
`shrd reg, reg, imm`	4		3	2	4 NP
`shrd mem, reg, imm`	4+ *d* (0–2)		7	3	4 NP
`shrd reg, reg, cl`	4		3	3	4 NP
`shrd mem, reg, cl`	4+ *d* (0–2)		7	4	5 NP

SLDT	Store local descriptor table register (286+)				
	bytes	*286*	*386*	*486*	*Pentium*
`sldt reg`	3	2	2	2	2 NP
`sldt mem`	3+ *d* (0–2)	3	2	3	2 NP

SMSW	Store machine status word (286+)				
	bytes	*286*	*386*	*486*	*Pentium*
`smsw reg`	3	2	2	2	4 NP
`smsw mem`	3+ *d* (0–2)	3	3	3	4 NP

STC	Set the carry flag						
	bytes	*8088*	*186*	*286*	*386*	*486*	*Pentium*
`stc`	1	2	2	2	2	2	2 NP

STD	Set direction flag (reverse)						
	bytes	*8088*	*186*	*286*	*386*	*486*	*Pentium*
`std`	1	2	2	2	2	2	2 NP

STI	Set interrupt flag (enable)						
	bytes	*8088*	*186*	*286*	*386*	*486*	*Pentium*
`sti`	1	2	2	2	3	5	7 NP

STOS/STOSB/STOSW/STOSD	Store string data						
	bytes	*8088*	*186*	*286*	*386*	*486*	*Pentium*
`stosb`	1	11	10	3	4	5	3 NP
`stosw`	1	15	10	3	4	5	3 NP
`stosd`	1	—	—	—	4	5	3 NP
`rep stosb`	2	9+10*n*	6+9*n*	4+3*n*	5+5*n*	7+4*n**	3+*n* NP
`rep stosw`	2	9+14*n*	6+9*n*	4+3*n*	5+5*n*	7+4*n**	3+*n* NP
`rep stosd`	2	—	—	—	5+5*n*	7+4*n**	3+*n* NP

$* = 5$ if $n=0$, 13 if $n=1$
(n = count of bytes, words or dwords)

STR	Store task register (286+)				
	bytes	*286*	*386*	*486*	*Pentium*
`str reg`	3	2	2	2	2 NP
`str mem`	3+*d* (0–2)	3	2	3	2 NP

SUB	Integer subtraction							
		bytes	*8088*	*186*	*286*	*386*	*486*	*Pentium*
sub reg, reg		2	3	3	2	2	1	1 UV
sub mem, reg		2+ *d* (0,2)	24+EA	10	7	7	3	3 UV
sub reg, mem		2+ *d* (0,2)	13+EA	10	7	6	2	2 UV
sub reg, imm		2+ *i* (1,2)						
sub mem, imm		2+ *d* (0,2)	4	4	3	2	1	1 UV
		+ *i* (1,2)	23+EA	16	7	7	3	3 UV*
sub acc, imm		1+ *i* (1,2)	4	4	3	2	1	1 UV

* = not pairable if there is a displacement and immediate

TEST	Logical compare							
		bytes	*8088*	*186*	*286*	*386*	*486*	*Pentium*
test reg, reg		2	3	3	2	2	1	1 UV
test mem, reg		2+ *d* (0,2)	13+EA	10	6	5	2	2 UV
test reg, mem		2+ *d* (0,2)	13+EA	10	6	5	2	2 UV
test reg, imm		2+ *i* (1,2)						
test mem, imm		2+ *d* (0,2)	5	4	3	2	1	1 UV
		+ *i* (1,2)	11+EA	10	6	5	2	2 UV*
test acc, imm		1+ *i* (1,2)	4	4	3	2	1	1 UV

* = not pairable if there is a displacement and immediate

VERR	Verify a segment for reading (286+)					
		bytes	*286*	*386*	*486*	*Pentium*
verr reg		3	14	10	11	7 NP
verr mem		3+ *d* (0,2)	16	11	11	7 NP

VERW	Verify a segment for writing (286+)					
		bytes	*286*	*386*	*486*	*Pentium*
verw reg		3	14	15	11	7 NP
verw mem		3+ *d* (0,2)	16	16	11	7 NP

WAIT	Wait for co-processor							
		bytes	*8088*	*186*	*286*	*386*	*486*	*Pentium*
wait		1	4	6	3	6	1–3	1 NP

WBINVD	Write-back and invalidate cache (486+)		
		bytes	*486*	*Pentium*
wbinvd		2	5	2000+ NP

WRMSR	Write to model-specific register (PENTIUM)	
		bytes	*Pentium*
wrmsr		2	30–45 NP

XADD   Exchange and add (486+)

	bytes					486	Pentium
xadd reg, reg	3					3	3 NP
xadd mem, reg	3+ *d* (0–2)					4	4 NP

XCHG   Exchange register/memory with register

	bytes	8088	186	286	386	486	Pentium
xchg reg, reg	2	4	4	3	3	3	3 NP
xchg reg, mem	2+ *d* (0–2)	25+EA	17	5	5	5	3 NP
xchg mem, reg	2+ *d* (0–2)	25+EA	17	5	5	5	3 NP
xchg acc, reg	1	3	3	3	3	3	2 NP
xchg reg, acc	1	3	3	3	3	3	2 NP

acc = AX or EAX only

XLAT/XLATB   Table look-up translation

	bytes	8088	186	286	386	486	Pentium
xlat	1	11	11	5	5	4	4 NP
xlatb							

XOR   Logical exclusive or

	bytes	8088	186	286	386	486	Pentium
xor reg, reg	2	3	3	2	2	1	1 UV
xor mem, reg	2+ *d* (0,2)	24+EA	10	7	7	3	3 UV
xor reg, mem	2+ *d* (0,2)	13+EA	10	7	6	2	2 UV
xor reg, imm	2+ *i* (1,2)	4	4	3	2	1	1 UV
xor mem, imm	2+ *d* (0,2)						
	+ *i* (1,2)	23+EA	16	7	7	3	3 UV*
xor acc, imm	1+ *i* (1,2)	4	4	3	2	1	1 UV

* = not pairable if there is a displacement and immediate

Notes on Timing Layout and Format

acc	=	AL, AX or EAX unless specified otherwise
reg	=	any general register
r8	=	any 8-bit register
r16	=	any general-purpose 16-bit register
r32	=	any general-purpose 32-bit register
imm	=	immediate data
imm8	=	8-bit immediate data

```
imm16 =    16-bit immediate data
mem   =    memory address
mem8  =    8-bit memory address
mem16 =    16-bit memory address
mem32 =    32-bit memory address
```

Timing:

n—generally refers to a number of repeated counts

m—in a jump or call;

   286: bytes in next instruction

   386/486: number of components

      (each byte of opcode) + 1 (if immed data) + 1 (if displacement)

Instruction Length

The byte count includes the opcode length and length of any required displacement or immediate data. If the displacement is optional, it is shown as $d()$ with the possible lengths in parentheses. If the immediate data is optional, it is shown as $i()$ with the possible lengths in parentheses.

Pairing Categories for Pentium

```
NP  =  not pairable
UV  =  pairable in the U pipe or V pipe
PU  =  pairable in the U pipe only
PV  =  pairable in the V pipe only
```

Part II

80x87 INSTRUCTION SET (8087–PENTIUM)

This section includes timing for all floating-point instruction forms and pairing information for Pentium. See the legend at the end of the Appendix for an explanation of the abbreviations used.

F2XM1	Compute $2^x - 1$	8087	287	387	486	Pentium
f2xm1		310–630	310–630	211–476	140–279	13–57 NP

FABS	Absolute value	8087	287	387	486	Pentium
fabs		10–17	10–17	22	3	1 FX

FADD FADDP	Floating point add Floating point add and pop	8087	287	387	486	Pentium
fadd		70–100	70–100	23–34	8–20	3/1 FX
fadd	mem32	90–120+EA	90–120	24–32	8–20	3/1 FX
fadd	mem64	95–125+EA	95–125	29–37	8–20	3/1 FX
faddp		75–105	75–105	23–31	8–20	3/1 FX

FBLD	Load BCD	8087	287	387	486	Pentium
fbld mem		(290–310)+EA	290–310	266–275	70–103	48–58 NP

FBSTP	Store BCD and pop	8087	287	387	486	Pentium
fbstp		(520–540)+EA	520–540	512–534	172–176	148–154 NP

FCHS	Change sign	8087	287	387	486	Pentium
fchs		10–17	10–17	24–25	6	1 FX

FCLEX FNCLEX	Clear exceptions Clear exceptions, no wait	8087	287	387	486	Pentium
fclex		2–8	2–8	11	7	9 NP
fnclex		2–8	2–8	11	7	9 NP

The wait version may take additional cycles

FCOM	Floating-point compare				
FCOMP	Floating-point compare and pop				
FCOMPP	Floating-point compare and pop twice				
	8087	*287*	*387*	*486*	*Pentium*
fcom reg	40–50	40–50	24	4	4/1 FX
fcom mem32	(60–70)+EA	60–70	26	4	4/1 FX
fcom mem64	(65–75)+EA	65–75	31	4	4/1 FX
fcomp	42–52	42–52	26	4	4/1 FX
fcompp	45–55	45–55	26	5	4/1 FX

FCOS	Floating-point cosine (387+)				
	8087	*287*	*387*	*486*	*Pentium*
fcos	—	—	123–772	257–354	18–124 NP

Additional cycles required if operand > $\pi/4$

FDECSTP	Decrement floating-point stack pointer				
	8087	*287*	*387*	*486*	*Pentium*
fdecstp	6–12	6–12	22	3	1 NP

FDISI	Disable interrupts (8087 only, others do fnop)				
FNDISI	Disable interrupts, no wait (8087 only, others do fnop)				
	8087	*287*	*387*	*486*	*Pentium*
fdisi	2–8	2	2	3	1 NP
fndisi	2–8	2	2	3	1 NP

The wait version may take additional cycles

FDIV	Floating divide				
FDIVP	Floating divide and pop				
	8087	*287*	*387*	*486*	*Pentium*
fdiv reg	193–203	193–203	88–91	73	39 FX
fdiv mem32	(215–225)+EA	215–225	89	73	39 FX
fdiv mem64	(220–230)+EA	220–230	94	73	39 FX
fdivp	197–207	197–207	91	73	39 FX

FDIVR	Floating divide reversed and pop				
FDIVRP	Floating divide reversed and pop				
	8087	*287*	*387*	*486*	*Pentium*
fdivr reg	194–204	194–204	88–91	73	39 FX
fdivr mem32	(216-226)+EA	216–226	89	73	39 FX
fdivr mem64	(221–231)+EA	221–231	94	73	39 FX
fdivrp	198–208	198–208	91	73	39 FX

FENI	Enable interrupts (8087 only, others do fnop)				
FNENI	Enable interrupts, nowait (8087 only, others do fnop)				
	8087	*287*	*387*	*486*	*Pentium*
feni	2–8	2	2	3	1 NP
fneni	2–8	2	2	3	1 NP

FFREE	Free register				
	8087	*287*	*387*	*486*	*Pentium*
ffree	9–16	9–16	18	3	1 NP

FIADD	Integer add				
	8087	*287*	*387*	*486*	*Pentium*
fiadd mem16	(102–137)+EA	102–137	71–85	20–35	7/4 NP
fiadd mem32	(108–143)+EA	108–143	57–72	19–32	7/4 NP

FICOM	Integer compare				
FICOMP	Integer compare and pop				
	8087	*287*	*387*	*486*	*Pentium*
ficom mem16	(72–86)+EA	72–86	71–75	16–20	8/4 NP
ficom mem32	(78–91)+EA	78–91	56–63	15–17	8/4 NP
ficomp mem16	(74–88)+EA	74–88	71–75	16–20	8/4 NP
ficomp mem32	(80–93)+EA	80–93	56–63	15–17	8/4 NP

FIDIV	Integer divide				
FIDIVR	Integer divide reversed				
	8087	*287*	*387*	*486*	*Pentium*
fidiv mem16	(224–238)+EA	224–238	136–140	85–89	42 NP
fidiv mem32	(230–243)+EA	230–243	120–127	84–86	42 NP
fidivr mem16	(225–239)+EA	225–239	135–141	85–89	42 NP
fidivr mem32	(231–245)+EA	231–245	121–128	84–86	42 NP

FILD	Load integer				
	8087	*287*	*387*	*486*	*Pentium*
fild mem16	(46–54)+EA	46–54	61–65	13–16	3/1 NP
fild mem32	(52–60)+EA	52–60	45–52	9–12	3/1 NP
fild mem64	(60–68)+EA	60–68	56–67	10–18	3/1 NP

FIMUL	Integer multiply				
	8087	*287*	*387*	*486*	*Pentium*
fimul mem16	(124–138)+EA	124–138	76–87	23–27	7/4 NP
fimul mem32	(130–144)+EA	130–144	61–82	22–24	7/4 NP

FINCSTP	Increment floating-point stack pointer				
	8087	*287*	*387*	*486*	*Pentium*
fincstp	6–12	6–12	21	3	1 NP

FINIT	Initialize floating point processor				
FNINIT	Initialize floating point processor, no wait				
	8087	*287*	*387*	*486*	*Pentium*
finit	2–8	2–8	33	17	16 NP
fninit	2–8	2–8	33	17	12 NP

The wait version may take additional cycles

FIST	Store integer				
FISTP	Store integer and pop				
	8087	*287*	*387*	*486*	*Pentium*
fist mem16	(80–90)+EA	80–90	82–95	29–34	6 NP
fist mem32	(82–92)+EA	82–92	79–93	28–34	6 NP
fistp mem16	(82–92)+EA	82–92	82–95	29–34	6 NP
fistp mem32	(84–94)+EA	84–94	79–93	28–34	6 NP
fistp mem64	(94–105)+EA	94–105	80–97	28–34	6 NP

FISUB	Integer subtract				
FISUBR	Integer subtract reversed				
	8087	*287*	*387*	*486*	*Pentium*
fisub mem16	(102–137)+EA	102–137	71–85	20–35	7/4 NP
fisubr mem32	(108–143)+EA	108–143	57–82	19–32	7/4 NP

FLD	Floating point load				
	8087	*287*	*387*	*486*	*Pentium*
fld reg	17–22	17–22	14	4	1 FX
fld mem32	(38–56)+EA	38–56	20	3	1 FX
fld mem64	(40–60)+EA	40–60	25	3	1 FX
fld mem80	(53–65)+EA	53–65	44	6	3 NP

FLD1	Load constant onto stack, 1.0				
FLDL2E	Load constant onto stack, logarithm base 2 (e)				
FLDL2T	Load constant onto stack, logarithm base 2 (10)				
FLDLG2	Load constant onto stack, logarithm base 10 (2)				
FLDLN2	Load constant onto stack, natural logarithm (2)				
FLDPI	Load constant onto stack, pi (3.14159 ...)				
	8087	*287*	*387*	*486*	*Pentium*
fldz	11–17	11–17	20	4	2 NP
fld1	15–21	15–21	24	4	2 NP
fldl2e	15–21	15–21	40	8	5/3 NP
fldl2t	16–22	16–22	40	8	5/3 NP
fldlg2	18–24	18–24	41	8	5/3 NP
fldln2	17–23	17–23	41	8	5/3 NP
fldpi	16–22	16–22	40	8	5/3 NP

FLDCW	**Load control word**				
	8087	*287*	*387*	*486*	*Pentium*
`fldcw mem16`	(7–14)+EA	7–14	19	4	7 NP

FLDENV	**Load environment state**				
	8087	*287*	*387*	*486*	*Pentium*
`fldenv mem`	(35–45)+EA	35–45	71	44/34	37/32–33 NP

cycles for real mode/protected mode

FMUL	**Floating-point multiply**				
FMULP	**Floating-point multiply and pop**				
	8087	*287*	*387*	*486*	*Pentium*
`fmul reg s`	90–105	90–105	29–52	16	3/1 FX
`fmul reg`	130–145	130–145	46–57	16	3/1 FX
`fmul mem32`	(110–125)+EA	110–125	27–35	11	3/1 FX
`fmul mem64`	(154–168)+EA	154–168	32–57	14	3/1 FX
`fmulp reg s`	94–108	94–108	29–52	16	3/1 FX
`fmulp reg`	134–148	134–148	29–57	16	3/1 FX

s = register with 40 trailing zeros in fraction

FNOP	**no operation**				
	8087	*287*	*387*	*486*	*Pentium*
`fnop`	10–16	10–16	12	3	1 NP

FPATAN	**Partial arctangent**				
	8087	*287*	*387*	*486*	*Pentium*
`fpatan`	250–800	250–800	314–487	218–303	17–173

FPREM	**Partial remainder**				
FPREM1	**Partial remainder (IEEE compatible, 387+)**				
	8087	*287*	*387*	*486*	*Pentium*
`fprem`	15–190	15–190	74–155	70–138	16–64 NP
`fprem1`	—	—	95–185	72–167	20–70 NP

FPTAN	**Partial tangent**				
	8087	*287*	*387*	*486*	*Pentium*
`fptan`	30–540	30–540	191–497	200–273	17–173 NP

Additional cycles required if operand $> \pi/4$

FRNDINT	**Round to integer**				
	8087	*287*	*387*	*486*	*Pentium*
`frndint`	16–50	16–50	66–80	21–30	9–20 NP

FRSTOR	**Restore saved state**				
	8087	*287*	*387*	*486*	*Pentium*
frstor mem	(197–207)+EA	197–207	308	131/120	75–95/70 NP
frstorw mem	—	—	308	131/120	75–95/70 NP
frstord mem	—	—	308	131/120	75–95/70 NP

cycles for real mode/protected mode

FSAVE	**Save FPU state**				
FSAVEW	**Save FPU state, 16-bit format (387+)**				
FSAVED	**Save FPU state, 32-bit format (387+)**				
FSAVE	**Save FPU state, no wait**				
FSAVEW	**Save FPU state, no wait, 16-bit format (387+)**				
FSAVED	**Save FPU state, no wait, 32-bit format (387+)**				
	8087	*287*	*387*	*486*	*Pentium*
fsave	(197–207)+EA	197–207	375–376	154/143	127–151/124 NP
fsavew			375–376	154/143	127–151/124 NP
fsaved			375–376	154/143	127–151/124 NP
fnsave	(197–207)+EA	197–207	375–376	154/143	127–151/124 NP
fnsavew			375–376	154/143	127–151/124 NP
fnsaved			375–376	154/143	127–151/124 NP

Cycles for real mode/protected mode
The wait version may take additional cycles

FSCALE	**Scale by factor of 2**				
	8087	*287*	*387*	*486*	*Pentium*
fscale	32–38	32–38	67–86	30–32	20–31 NP

FSETPM	**Set protected mode (287 only, 387+ = fnop)**				
	8087	*287*	*387*	*486*	*Pentium*
fsetpm	—	2–8	12	3	1 NP

FSIN	**Sine (387+)**				
FSINCOS	**Sine and cosine (387+)**				
	8087	*287*	*387*	*486*	*Pentium*
fsin	—	—	122–771	257–354	16–126 NP
fsincos	—	—	194–809	292–365	17–137 NP

Additional cycles required if operand $> \pi/4$

FSQRT	**Square root**				
	8087	*287*	*387*	*486*	*Pentium*
fsqrt	180–186	180–186	122–129	83–87	70 NP

FST	Floating point store				
FSTP	Floating point store and pop				
	8087	*287*	*387*	*486*	*Pentium*
fst reg	15–22	15–22	11	3	1 NP
fst mem32	(84–90)+EA	84–90	44	7	2 NP
fst mem64	(96-104)+EA	96–104	45	8	2 NP
fstp reg	17–24	17–24	12	3	1 NP
fstp mem32	(86–92)+EA	86–92	44	7	2 NP
fstp mem64	(98–106)+EA	98–106	45	8	2 NP
fstp mem80	(52–58)+EA	52–58	53	6	3 NP

FSTCW	Store control word				
FNSTCW	Store control word, no wait				
	8087	*287*	*387*	*486*	*Pentium*
fstcw mem	12–18	12–18	15	3	2 NP
fnstcw mem	12–18	12–18	15	3	2 NP

The wait version may take additional cycles

FSTENV	Store FPU environment				
FSTENVW	Store FPU environment, 16-bit format (387+)				
FSTENVD	Store FPU environment, 32-bit format (387+)				
FNSTENV	Store FPU environment, no wait				
FNSTENVW	Store FPU environment, no wait, 16-bit format (387+)				
FNSTENVD	Store FPU environment, no wait, 32-bit format (387+)				
	8087	*287*	*387*	*486*	*Pentium*
fstenv mem	(40–50)+EA	40–50	103–104	67/56	48–50 NP
fstenvw mem			103–104	67/56	48–50 NP
fstenvd mem			103–104	67/56	48–50 NP
fnstenv mem	(40–50)+EA	40–50	103–104	67/56	48–50 NP
fnstenvw mem			103–104	67/56	48–50 NP
fnstenvd mem			103–104	67/56	48–50 NP

Cycles for real mode/protected mode
The wait version may take additional cycles

FSTSW	Store status word				
FNSTSW	Store status word, no wait				
	8087	*287*	*387*	*486*	*Pentium*
fstsw mem	12–18	12–18	15	3	2 NP
fstsw ax	–	10–16	13	3	2 NP
fnstsw mem	12–18	12–18	15	3	2 NP
fnstsw ax	–	10–16	13	3	2 NP

The wait version may take additional cycles

FSUB	Floating point subtract					
FSUBP	Floating point subtract and pop					
		8087	*287*	*387*	*486*	*Pentium*
fsub	reg	70–100	70–100	26–37	8–20	3/1 FX
fsub	mem32	(90–120)+EA	90–120	24–32	8–20	3/1 FX
fsub	mem64	(95–125)+EA	95–125	28–36	8–20	3/1 FX
fsubp	reg	75–105	75–105	26–34	8–20	3/1 FX

FSUBR	Floating point reverse subtract					
FSUBRP	Floating point reverse subtract and pop					
		8087	*287*	*387*	*486*	*Pentium*
fsubr	reg	70–100	70-100	26-37	8–20	3/1 FX
fsubr	mem32	(90–120)+EA	90–120	24–32	8–20	3/1 FX
fsubr	mem64	(95–125)+EA	95–125	28–36	8–20	3/1 FX
fsubrp	reg	75–105	75–105	26–34	8-20	3/1 FX

FTST	Floating-point test for zero					
		8087	*287*	*387*	*486*	*Pentium*
	ftst	38–48	38–48	28	4	4/1 FX

FUCOM	Unordered floating-point compare (387+)					
FUCOMP	Unordered floating-point compare and pop (387+)					
FUCOMPP	Unordered floating-point compare and pop twice (387+)					
		8087	*287*	*387*	*486*	*Pentium*
fucom		—	—	24	4	4/1 FX
fucomp		—	—	26	4	4/1 FX
fucompp		—	—	26	5	4/1 FX

FWAIT	Wait while FPU is executing					
		8087	*287*	*387*	*486*	*Pentium*
fwait		4	3	6	1–3	1–3 NP

FXAM	Examine condition flags					
		8087	*287*	*387*	*486*	*Pentium*
fxam		12–23	12–23	30–38	8	21 NP

FXCH	Exchange floating point registers					
		8087	*287*	*387*	*486*	*Pentium*
fxch		10–15	10–15	18	4	0–1 *

* FCXH is pairable in the V pipe with all FX pairable instructions

FXTRACT	Extract exponent and significand				
	8087	*287*	*387*	*486*	*Pentium*
fxtract	27–55	27–55	70–76	16–20	13 NP

FYL2X	Compute $Y * \log^2(x)$				
FYL2XP1	Compute $Y * \log^2(x+1)$				
	8087	*287*	*387*	*486*	*Pentium*
fyl2x	900–1100	900–1100	120–538	196–329	22–111 NP
fyl2xp1	700–1000	700–1000	257–547	171–326	22–103 NP

FPU Instruction Timings

FX   = pairs with FXCH
NP   = no pairing

Timings with a dash indicate a range of possible timings. Timings with a slash (unless otherwise noted) are latency and throughput. Latency is the time between instructions dependent on the result. Throughput is the pipeline throughput between non-conflicting instructions.

FPU Instruction Sizing

All FPU instructions that do not access memory are two bytes in length (except **FWAIT**, which is one byte).

FPU instructions that access memory are four bytes for 16-bit addressing and six bytes for 32-bit addressing.

On the 8087 the assembler automatically inserts a **WAIT** (**FWAIT**) before each FPU instruction.

Optimization Cross-Reference by Instruction

B

T he following is a list of instructions and/or instructions sequences that can be optimized (with their replacements) when programming for maximum speed and/or size.

Key:	
Original Instructions	**Applicable CPUs/modes**
Functional description or replacement instructions	*Description*

aad (imm8)	**all CPUs**
`AL = AL+(AH*imm8)` `AH = 0`	If **imm8** is blank uses 10. Almost always slower, but only 2 bytes long.

aam (imm8)	**all CPUs**
AH = AL/imm8 AL = AL MOD imm8	Same as **AAD**.

adc	**Pentium**
	Pairs only in U pipe.

add	**16-bit CPU modes**
lea reg, [reg+reg+disp]	Use **LEA** to add base + index + disp. Also preserves flags.

add	**32-bit CPU modes**
lea reg, [reg+reg*scale+disp]	Use **LEA** to add base + scaled index + disp. Also preserves flags.

and reg, reg	**Pentium**
test reg, reg	Fewer register conflicts therefore better pairing.

bswap	**Pentium**
ror eax, 16	Pairs in U pipe, BSWAP doesn't pair. Disadvantage: modifies flags.

call	**All CPUs**
	Use near calls.

call dest1 **jmp dest2**	**286+**
push offset dest2 jmp dest1	When **CALL** is followed by a **JMP**, change the return address to the **JMP** destination.

call dest1 **ret**	**All CPUs**
jmp dest1	When a **CALL** is followed by a **RET**, the **CALL** can be replaced by a **JMP**.

cbw	386+
`mov ah, 0`	When you know AL < 128 use **MOV** for speed. **CBW** is smaller (1 byte).
cdq	486+
`xor edx, edx`	When you know EAX is positive. Faster, better pairing. Disadvantage: modifies flags.

cdq
`mov edx, eax`
`sar edx, 31`
	Pentium
	When EAX value could be negative; better pairing.

cmp mem, reg	286
`cmp reg, mem`	reg, mem is 1 cycle faster
cmp reg, mem	386
`cmp mem, reg`	**mem, reg** is 1 cycle faster.
dec reg16	16-bit CPU modes
`lea reg16, [reg16 - 1]`	Use to preserve flags for BX, BP, DI, SI.
dec reg32	32-bit CPU mode
`lea reg32, [reg32 - 1]`	Use to preserve flags for EAX, EBX, ECX, EDX EDI, ESI, EBP.
div <op>	8088
`shr accum, 1`	When <op> resolves to 2, shift to divide. (Use CL for 4, 8, etc.)
div <op>	186+
`shr accum, n`	When <op> resolves to a power of 2; use shifts to divide.
enter imm16, 0	286+

`push  bp`
`mov   bp, sp`
`sub   sp, imm16`
	ENTER is always slower and 4 bytes in length. If **imm16** = 0, then **push/mov** is smaller.

enter imm16, 0   386+

```
push  ebp
mov   ebp, esp
sub   esp, imm16
```

inc reg16   16-bit CPU modes

lea reg16, [reg16 + 1]   Use to preserve flags for BX, BP, DI, SI.

inc reg32   32-bit CPU mode

lea reg32, [reg32 + 1]   Use to preserve flags for EAX, EBX, ECX, EDX EDI, ESI, EBP.

int nn   Real mode

```
pushf
call dword ptr mem
```
int takes many cycles, 16–82 cyc depending on CPU mode. **CALL DWORD PTR** takes 4. You must previously save a copy of the vector knowing that it will not change. Can cause problems for memory managers that need to get control of all interrupts.

jcxz <dest>   486+

```
test cx, cx
je   <dest>
```
JCXZ is faster and smaller on 8088–286. On the 386 it is about the same speed.

```
test ecx, ecx
je   <dest>
```
Never use **JCXZ** or **JECXZ** on 486 or Pentium except for compactness.

lea reg, mem   8088–286

mov reg, OFFSET mem   **MOV reg, imm** is faster on 8088–286. 386+ they are the same.

Note: There are many uses for **LEA**, see: **add, inc, dec, mov, mul**

leave   486+

```
mov sp, bp
pop bp
```
LEAVE is only 1 byte long and is fastest on the 186-386.
The **MOV/POP** is much faster on 486 and Pentium.

```
mov esp, ebp
pop ebp
```

`lodsb`	486+

```
mov al, [si]
inc si
```

LODS is only 1 byte long and is faster on 8088-386, much slower on the 486. On the Pentium **LODS** is 2 cycles. **MOV/INC** or **MOV/ADD** pair to 1 cycle.

`lodsw`	

```
mov ax, [si]
add si, 2
```

Note: Use **LEA SI, [SI+n]** to advance **LEA** without changing the flags.

Note: Use **DEC** or **SUB** when DF is set.

`lodsd`	

```
mov eax, [esi]
add esi, 4
```

`loop <dest>`	386+

```
dec cx
jnz <dest>
```

LOOP is faster and smaller on 8088-286. On 386+ **DEC/JNZ** is much faster.

`loop <dest>`	

```
dec ecx
jnz <dest>
```

| `loopXX <dest>` | 486+ |
`( XX = e,ne,z or nz)`	

```
je    $+5
dec   cx
jnz   <dest>
```

Conditional loop instructions are much slower on the 486+. They are smaller and faster on 8088–286. The speed is about the same on the 386.

`loopXX <dest>`	

```
je    $+5
dec   ecx
jnz   <dest>
```

| `mov reg2, reg1` | 286+ |
| followed by one of: | |
`inc/dec/add/sub reg2`	

```
lea reg2, [reg1+n]
```

Faster, smaller and preserves flags. This is a way to do a **MOV** and **ADD/SUB** of a constant, *n*.

`mov acc, reg`	**All CPUs**

`xchg acc, reg`

Use **xchg** for smaller code when one register can be ignored.

`mov mem, imm`	**Pentium**

```
lea bx, mem
mov [bx], imm

mov ax, imm
mov mem, ax
```

Displacement/immediate does not pair. **LEA/MOV** can be used if other code can be placed inbetween to prevent AGIs. **MOV/MOV** may be easier to pair.

`mov [bx+2], imm`	**Pentium**

```
mov ax, imm
mov [bx+2], ax
```

Better pairing.

```
lea bx, [bx+2]
mov [bx], imm
```

Better pairing.

`movsb`	**486+**

```
mov al, [si]

inc si
mov [di], al
inc di
```

MOVS is faster and smaller to move a single byte, word or dword on the 8088–386. On the 486+ the **MOV/INC** method is faster.

REP MOVS is always faster to move a block.

Note: Use **DEC** or **SUB** when DF is set.

`movsw`

```
mov ax, [si]
add si, 2
mov [di], ax
add di, 2
```

`movsd`

```
mov eax, [esi]
add esi, 4
mov [edi], eax
add edi, 4
```

`movzx r16, rm8`	486+
`xor bx, bx` `mov bl, al`	**MOVZX** is faster and smaller on the 386. On the 486+ **XOR/MOV** is faster. Possible pairing on the Pentium. (Source can be reg or mem.) Disadvantage: modifies flags.
`movzx r32, rm8`	
`xor ebx, ebx` `mov bl, al`	
`movzx r32, rm16`	
`xor ebx, ebx` `mov bx, ax`	
`mul n`	8088+
`shl ax, cl`	Use shifts or **ADDs** instead of multiply when *n* is a power of 2.
`mul n`	Pentium
`add ax, ax`	**ADD** is better than single shift because it pairs better.
`mul`	32-bit CPU modes
`lea`	Use **LEA** to multiply by 2, 3, 4, 5, 7, 8, 9
`lea eax, [eax+eax*4]`	(ex: multiply EAX * 5)
	LEA is better than **SHL** on the Pentium because it pairs in both pipes; **SHL** pairs only in the U pipe.
`or reg, reg`	Pentium
`test reg, reg`	Better pairing because **OR** writes to register. (This is for src = dest.)
`pop mem`	486+
`pop reg` `mov mem, reg`	Faster on 486+. Better pairing on Pentium.

push mem	486+
`mov   reg, mem` `push  reg`	Faster on 486. Better pairing on Pentium.
pushf	486+

`rcr reg, 1`
or
`rcl reg, 1`
	To save only the carry flag use a rotate (**RCR** or **RCL**) into a register. **RCR** and **RCL** are pairable (U pipe only) and take 1 cycle. **PUSHF** is slow and not pairable.

popf	486+

`rcl reg, 1`
or
`rcr reg, 1`
	To restore only the carry flag.

rep movsb	8088+
none	Always fast.
rep movsw	
rep movsd	
rep stosb	8088+
none	Always fast.
rep stosw	
rep stosd	
rep scasb	Pentium

`loop1:`
`  mov al, [di]`
`  inc di`
`  cmp al, reg2`
`  je  exit`
`  dec cx`
`  jnz loop1`
`exit:`
	REP SCAS is faster and smaller on 8088–486. Expanded code is faster on Pentium due to pairing.
	
	Note: See Chapter 14

`shl reg, 1`	Pentium
`add reg, reg`	**ADD** pairs better. **SHL** only pairs in the U pipe.

`stosb`	486+
`mov [di], al` `inc di`	**STOS** is faster and smaller on the 8088–286, and the same speed on the 386. On the 486+ the **MOV/INC** is slightly faster.
`stosw`	**REP STOS** is fastest on 8088–386. **MOV/INC** or **MOV/ADD** is fastest on the 486+.
`mov [di], ax` `add di, 2`	
`stosd`	
`mov [edi], eax` `add edi, 4`	

Note: Use **LEA SI, [SI+n]** to advance **LEA** without changing the flags.

`xchg`	All CPUs
	Use **xchg acc, reg** to do a 1 byte **MOV** when one register can be ignored.

`xchg reg1, reg2`	Pentium

`push reg1`
`push reg2`
`pop reg1`
`pop reg2`
	Pushes and pops 1 cycle faster on Pentium due to pairing.
	
	Disadvantage: Uses stack.

`xchg reg1, reg2`	Pentium

`mov reg3, reg1`
`mov reg1, reg2`
`mov reg2, reg3`
	Faster and better pairing if reg3 is available.

xlatb	486+

```
mov bh, 0
mov bl, al
mov al, [bx]

xor ebx, ebx
mov bl, al
mov al, [ebx]
```

XLAT is faster and smaller on 8088–386. **MOVs** are faster on 486+. Best to rearrange instructions to prevent AGIs and get pairing on Pentium. Put zeroing of high part outside of loop.
Disadvantage: Modifies flags.

Optimization Guidelines by CPU

C

This Appendix contains optimization guidelines and information arranged by CPU.

8088

The maximum sustained execution rate is one code byte per four cycles, because of pre-fetching. It is actually less because of memory read/writes, DRAM refresh, etc.

Real execution time is the maximum of pre-fetch time (four cycles per byte) or "official" execution time in documentation.

Avoiding memory accesses in your code allows the prefetch to run faster (i.e., use registers).

Every 8088 bus access is four cycles—prefetching, data read or write (word accesses are eight cycles).

Sixteen-bit accesses are better than two 8-bit operations because there is only a four-cycle penalty for the second 8 bits. Two 8-bit operations have extra prefetch and execution time and result in larger code.

Keep values in registers (avoid memory accesses).

Use the shortest instruction forms because fetching is usually a bottleneck.

Avoid jumps since they flush the prefetch queue.

DRAM refresh can slow everything by about 5% to 7% from estimated times.

If you must use an instruction that takes a long time to execute (i.e., **mul**, **div**) in a loop, place it right after a frequently taken jump to allow the prefetch queue to refill.

Minimize quick instructions after a jump. Quick instructions (i.e., 2–4 cycles) do not give the prefetch queue time to refill. If there is an instruction that takes many cycles in a loop, try to position it near the top of the loop.

Avoid long effective address calculations—pull them out of loops because EA (effective address) calculations take 5 to 12 cycles.

When using BP to access the stack, make maximum use of the area within –128 to +127 bytes of BP because this takes one less code byte than accesses that are a greater distance from BP.

286

Align data that is accessed 16 bits at a time on even addresses. Word data on odd addresses causes two bus accesses and a minimum two-cycle penalty.

Each 16-bit bus access is two cycles, plus one for each wait state.

Align code labels on even addresses when they are the destination of loops. This is because it takes fewer fetch cycles to get the next instruction into the prefetch queue. Depending on the first instruction after the label, code at odd addresses can take two or more extra cycles.

Because of the memory board design and the display RAM speed, the IBM PC/AT display can be as slow as on an 8088. IBM PC/AT video cards are on an 8 MHz bus and generally add many wait states.

EA (effective address) calculations take 0 or 1 cycle. If the EA contains all three components (base, index and displacement), then it takes 1 cycle. Combine registers outside of a loop to eliminate this cycle.

Use new forms of shifts and rotates, allowing immediate counts of more than 1.

386

EA (effective address) calculations are the same as on the 286.

Memory architectures vary widely on the 386. Most have caches with main memory inserting one to five wait states. Video memory can have many wait states. Some boards have as many as 32 wait states.

Code and data should be aligned on dword boundaries for maximum performance. The 386SX accesses 32-bit data in two operations.

New 32-bit addressing for large segments in protected mode:

> base + scaled index + disp
> base   = EAX, EBX, ECX, EDX, EDI, ESI, EBP, ESP
> index= any of the same as a second register (not ESP) or any of the same as a scaled register
> displacement can be 1 or 4 bytes only, not 2

32-bit addressing in a 16-bit segment incurs a one-cycle prefix delay.

Using the scaled index inside a loop can cause slower code. For example:

```
loop1:
  add  eax, array[edi*4]     ;add dword from array
  inc  edi                   ;advance index to next array element
  dec  edx                   ;dec loop count
  jnz  loop1
```

Optimize to:

```
  shl  edi, 2                ;pre multiply by scale factor of 4
loop1:
  add  eax, array[edi]
  add  edi, 4
  dec  edx
  jnz  loop1
  shr  edi, 2                ;remove scale factor, if required
```

Because of the way that 32-bit operands work, there are some interesting code size quirks. 32-bit immediate moves always take 4 bytes. Other instructions, such as OR, perform sign extension:

1a. **sub** eax, eax	;eax = 0	2 cycles, 2 bytes
inc eax	;eax = 1	2 cycles, 1 bytes
1b. **mov** eax, 1	;eax = 1	2 cycles, 5 bytes

```
2a. or    eax, -1        ;eax = -1        2 cycles, 3 bytes
2b. mov   eax, -1        ;eax = -1        2 cycles, 5 bytes
```

486

Because of the internal cache, optimizations are repeatable across many more systems than with 286 and 386 systems.

Frequently called procedures or targets of jumps should be aligned on 16-byte boundaries because this is the size of a cache line. (At least use 4-byte boundaries.)

Data should be aligned on a boundary the same size as the data item; i.e., words on a word boundary and dwords on a dword boundary.

The 486SX has the same 32-bit bus and the same alignment criteria as the 486. The 486SX has no FPU.

EA (Effective Address) Calculations

using two registers (base + index)	1 cycle delay
using a displacement	1 cycle delay
using a scaled index	1 cycle delay

Use the simple instructions (defined as simple on the Pentium). These generally take one cycle on the 486. Complex instructions, such as **LOOP**, **XLAT** and **XCHG** are slow.

AGIs (Address Generation Interlocks)

2 cycle delay in real mode (1 cycle if 2 instructions away)
1 cycle delay in protected mode

SP (and ESP) AGIs are resolved internally for implied use of SP or ESP so there are no delays; i.e., **push**, **pop**, **call**, **ret**.

Using SP or ESP like a general register will still cause an AGI; i.e.:

```
add    esp, 10
```

The new **BSWAP** instruction is fast and doesn't change the flags. Note that **ROR** and **BSWAP** are not the same; both just allow the high word of EAX to be accessed via AX or AL and AH.

```
ror eax, 16          ;2 cycles AABBCCDD --> CCDDAABB
bswap                ;1 cycle  AABBCCDD --> DDCCBBAA
```

Immediate shift/rotate values of 2–31 are faster than a shift/rotate of 1. The third byte of a shift immediate can accept a value of 1, but the assembler does not generate this. This quirk is only true for the 486.

```
shl    eax, 1        ;3 cycles, 2 bytes
shl    eax, 2        ;2 cycles, 3 bytes
```

applies to: **shl**, **shr**, **sal**, **sar**, **rol**, **ror**

Pentium

Frequently called procedures or targets of jumps should be aligned on 32-byte boundaries because this is the size of a cache line. But this is not as important as on the 486 because of branch prediction. The importance can be seen because a small, frequently called procedure could all fit in one cache line if aligned properly, but would take two cache lines if misaligned. On the other hand, aligning every procedure and loop will waste many bytes filling the cache with many NOP bytes.

Data should be aligned on a boundary the same size as the data item; i.e., words on a word boundary and dwords on a dword boundary, etc.

All EA (effective address) calculations take zero cycles.

Use simple instructions—keep both pipelines working.

Follow the pairing rules in Appendices D and E.

Use one- or two-cycle forms of pairable instructions; three-cycle forms block execution slots. Two-cycle forms will block an execution slot unless paired with another two-cycle instruction.

No instruction pairing occurs with any instruction containing an address displacement and an immediate value, such as:

```
mov    mem1, 5       ;1 cycle, no pairing

add    array[bx], 1  ;1 cycle, no pairing
```

The following example shows how some displacement/immediate code can be optimized for pairing with an additional nearby instruction:

```
mov    mem1, 0        ; these two instructions do not pair
mov    mem2, 0        ; and take 1 cycle each
```

Replace with:

```
xor    eax, eax       ; 1 cycle (could pair with next instruction)
(pairable instruction) ; 0 cycle slot open
mov    mem1, eax       ; 1 cycle (pairs with below)
mov    mem2, eax       ; 0 cycle
```

Only optimize loops (running out of the cache) for pairing. If a loop won't run many times, it is probably best to optimize for size to keep other code in the cache.

Branch prediction means that a branch that frequently jumps to the same place takes only one cycle (i.e., the bottom on a loop returning to the top of the loop). The penalty for a misprediction is large; see the table.

Instruction	Penalty If in U Pipe	Penalty If in V Pipe
Jcc	4 cycles	5 cycles
call near	3 cycles	3 cycles
jmp near	3 cycles	3 cycles

Simple Instructions for Pentium Pairing

	Instruction Format			16-bit Example			32-Bit Example	
MOV	reg,	reg	mov	ax,	bx	mov	eax,	edx
MOV	reg,	mem	mov	ax,	[bx]	mov	eax,	[edx]
MOV	reg,	imm	mov	ax,	1	mov	eax,	1
MOV	mem,	reg	mov	[bx],	ax	mov	[edx],	eax
MOV	mem,	imm	mov	[bx],	1	mov	[edx],	1
alu	reg,	reg	add	ax,	bx	cmp	eax,	edx
alu	reg,	mem	add	ax,	[bx]	cmp	eax,	[edx]
alu	reg,	imm	add	ax,	1	cmp	eax,	1
alu	mem,	reg	add	[bx],	ax	cmp	[edx],	eax
alu	mem,	imm	add	[bx],	1	cmp	[edx],	1

where alu = add, adc, and, or, xor, sub, sbb, cmp, test

INC	reg		inc	ax		inc	eax	
INC	mem		inc	var1		inc	[eax]	
DEC	reg		dec	bx		dec	ebx	

Instruction Format			16-bit Example			32-Bit Example		
DEC	mem		dec	[bx]		dec	var2	
PUSH	reg		push	ax		push	eax	
POP	reg		pop	ax		pop	eax	
LEA	reg,	mem	lea	ax,	[si+2]	lea	eax,	[eax+4*esi+8]
JMP	near		jmp	label		jmp	label2	
CALL	near		call	proc		call	proc2	
Jcc	near		jz	lbl		jnz	lbl2	
NOP			nop			nop		
shift	reg,	1	shl	ax,	1	rcl	eax,	1
shift	mem,	1	shr	[bx],	1	rcr	[ebx],	1
shift	reg,	imm	sal	ax,	2	rol	esi,	2
shift	mem,	imm	sar	ax,	15	ror	[esi],	31

Notes:

- rcl and rcr are not pairable with immediate counts other than 1
- All memory-immediate (mem, imm) instructions are not pairable with a displacement in the memory operand
- Instructions with segment registers are not pairable

Instruction Pairing Rules for Pentium

1. Both instructions must be simple. (See Appendix D.)
2. Shifts or rotates can only pair in the U pipe. (**SHL**, **SHR**, **SAL**, **SAR**, **ROL**, **ROR**, **RCL** or **RCR**)
3. **ADC** and **SBB** can only pair in the U pipe.
4. **JMP**, **CALL** and **Jcc** can only pair in the V pipe. (Jcc = jump on condition code.)
5. Neither instruction can contain *both* a displacement and an immediate operand. For example:

```
mov     [bx+2], 3          ; 2 is a displacement, 3 is immediate
mov     mem1, 4            ; mem1 is a displacement, 4 is immediate
```

6. Prefixed instructions can only pair in the U pipe. This includes extended instructions that start with 0Fh except for the special case of the 16-vit conditional jumps of the 386 and above. Examples of prefixed instructions:

```
mov     ES:[bx], 1
mov     eax, [si]          ; 32-bit operand in 16-bit code segment
mov     ax, [esi]          ; 16-bit operand in 32-bit code seg
```

7. The U pipe instruction must be only 1 byte in length or it will not pair until the second time it executes from the cache.
8. There can be no read-after-write or write-after-write register dependencies between the instructions except for special cases for the flags register and the stack pointer (rules 9 and 10).

```
mov    ebx, 2          ; writes to EBX
add    ecx, ebx        ; reads EBX and ECX, writes to ECX
                       ; EBX is read after being written, no pairing

mov    ebx, 1          ; writes to EBX
mov    ebx, 2          ; writes to EBX
                       ; write after write, no pairing
```

9. The flags register exception allows an ALU instruction to be paired with a **Jcc** even though the ALU instruction writes the flags and **Jcc** reads the flags. For example:

```
cmp    al, 0           ; CMP modifies the flags
je     addr            ; JE reads the flags, but pairs

dec    cx              ; DEC modifies the flags
jnz    loop1           ; JNZ reads the flags, but pairs
```

10. The stack pointer exception allows two **PUSH**es or two **POP**s to be paired even though they both read and write to the SP (or ESP) register.

```
push   eax             ; ESP is read and modified
push   ebx             ; ESP is read and modified, but still pairs
```

Single-Byte Instructions

PAIRABLE ONE-BYTE INSTRUCTIONS

dec	**reg**	decrement register (16-bit or 32-bit)
inc	**reg**	increment register (16-bit or 32-bit)
nop		no operation
pop	**reg**	pop register (16- or 32-bit general-purpose register
push	**reg**	push register (16- or 32-bit general-purpose register

NON-PAIRABLE ONE-BYTE INSTRUCTIONS

aaa	ASCII adjust after addition
aas	ASCII adjust after subtraction
cbw	convert byte to word
cdq	convert double to quad
clc	clear carry flag

`cld`	clear direction flag
`cli`	clear interrupt flag (maskable interrupts disabled)
`cmc`	complement carry flag
`cmpsb`	compare string byte
`cmpsw`	compare string word
`cmpsd`	compare string dword
`cwd`	convert word to double
`cwde`	convert word to extended double
`daa`	decimal adjust after addition
`das`	decimal adjust after subtraction
`hlt`	halt
`in acc, dx`	input from port
`insb`	input from port to string byte
`insw`	input from port to string word
`insd`	input from port to string dword
`int 3`	software interrupt 3
`into`	interrupt on overflow
`iret`	interrupt return
`iretd`	interrupt return double
`lahf`	load flags into AH register
`leave`	high-level procedure exit
`lodsb`	load string byte
`lodsw`	load string word
`lodsd`	load string dword
`movsb`	move string byte
`movsw`	move string word
`movsd`	move string dword
`out dx, acc`	output to port
`outsb`	output string to port byte
`outsw`	output string to port word
`outsd`	output string to port dword
`pop sreg`	pop segment register (only DS, ES, SS)
`popa`	pop all
`popad`	pop all double
`popf`	pop flags
`popfd`	pop eflags
`push sreg`	push segment register (only CS, DS, ES, SS)

pusha	push all
pushad	push all double
pushf	push flags
pushfd	push eflags
ret	return from procedure
retn	return from procedure near
retf	return from procedure far
sahf	store AH into flags
scasb	scan string byte
scawsw	scan string word
scasd	scan string dword
stc	set carry flag
std	set direction flag
sti	set interrupt flag (enable maskable interrupts)
stosb	store string byte
stosw	store string word
stosd	store string dword
wait	wait for co-processor
xchg acc, reg	exchange accumulator with register (16- or 32-bit)
xlat	translate

PREFIX BYTES

26h	**ES:**	ES segment override
2Eh	**CS:**	CS segment override
36h	**SS:**	SS segment override
3Eh	**DS:**	DS segment override
64h	**FS:**	FS segment override
65h	**GS:**	GS segment override
66h		operand-size prefix
67h		address-size prefix
F0h	**lock**	lock the bus

lock only works with the following instructions when accessing a memory operand:

bts, btr, btc

```
add, or, adc, sbb, and, sub, xor
not, neg, inc, dec
cmpxchg, xadd
xchg (lock is automatic)
```

F2h	repne	repeat string while not equal (also **repnz**)
F3h	repe	repeat string while equal (also **repz**)
	rep	repeat string (same as **repe**)

0Fh — prefix for two-byte opcodes of newer instructions, such as **SETcc**, **LFS**, **LGS**, **CMPXCHG**, **XADD**, **Jcc** (16-bit), **SHLD**, **BSWAP**

D8h–DFh — floating-point instructions

Quick Reference for Important Instruction Timings

MOV

	8088	186	286	386	486	Pentium	
mov reg, reg	2	2	2	2	1	1	UV
mov mem, reg	19	19	9	2	1	1	UV
mov reg, mem	18	18	12	4	1	1	UV
mov mem, imm	20	20	13	2	1	1	UV*
mov reg, imm	4	4	4	2	1	1	UV

* = not pairable if there is a displacement and immediate

POP PUSH

	8088	186	286	386	486	Pentium	
pop reg	12	10	5	4	1	1	UV
pop sreg	12	10	5/20	7/21	3/9	3/12	NP

(cycles for: real mode/prot mode)

	8088	186	286	386	486	Pentium	
push reg	15	10	3	2	1	1	UV
push sreg	14	10	3	2	3	1	NP

MFSC

	8088	186	286	386	486	Pentium	
xchg reg,reg	4	4	3	3	3	3	NP
xchg reg,mem	31	17	5	5	5	3	NP
clc, stc	2	2	2	2	2	2	NP
cbw	2	2	2	3	3	3	NP
nop	3	3	3	3	3	1	UV
xlat	11	11	5	5	4	4	NP
lea	7	6	3	2	1/2*	1	UV

* = 486 **LEA** takes two cycles when EA contains an index register

ADD ADC SUB SBB AND XOR OR (alu)

alu reg, reg	3	3	2	2	1	1	UV
alu mem, reg	30	10	7	7	3	3	UV
alu reg, mem	18	10	7	6	2	2	UV
alu mem, imm	20	16	7	7	3	3	UV*
alu reg, imm	4	4	3	2	1	1	UV

* = not pairable if there is a displacement and immediate

SHL SHR SAL SAL RCL RCR ROL ROR (sh)

sh reg, 1	2	2	2	3	3	1	PU
sh reg, cl	8/4	5/1	5/1	3	3	4	NP
sh reg, imm	—	5/1	5/1	3	2	1	PU*
sh mem,1	29	15	7	7	4	3	PU
sh mem, cl	32/4	8/1	8/1	7	4	4	NP
sh mem, imm	—	8/1	8/1	7	4	3	PU*

cycles = base/per shift
* = not pairable if there is a displacement and immediate;
rcl, **rcr** not pairable with immediate counts other than 1

JUMP LOOP CALL RET

jmp short/near	15	13	8	8	3	1	PV
jmp reg	11	11	8	8	5	2	NP
jmp mem	23	17	12	11	5	2	NP
Jcc	4/16	4/13	3/8	3/8	1/3	1	PV
jcxz	6/18	5/16	4/9	5/10	5/8	5/6	NP
loop	5/17	5/15	4/9	11	6/7	5	NP
loope	6/18	6/16	4/9	11	6/9	7	NP

(cycles for: no jump/jump)

call near	23	14	8	8	3	1	PV
call reg	20	13	8	8	5	2	NP
call mem	35	19	12	11	5	2	NP
ret near	20	16	12	11	5	2	NP

String							
	8088	*186*	*286*	*386*	*486*	*Pentium*	
String							
rep movs	17	8	4	4	3	1	NP
rep stos	10	9	3	5	4	1	NP
repecmps	22	22	9	9	7	4	NP
repescas	15	15	8	8	5	4	NP
lodsb	16	10	5	5	5	2	NP
stosb	15	10	3	4	5	3	NP

IMPORTANT COMBINATIONS FOR THE PENTIUM

	8088	*186*	*286*	*386*	*486*	*Pentium*	
dec reg/Jcc	7/19	7/16	5/10	5/10	2/4	1	pair

(cycles for: no jump/jump)

mov r, m/inc reg	21	21	14	6	2	1	pair
mov m, r/inc reg	21	21	11	4	2	1	pair
push reg/pop reg	27	20	8	6	2	1	pair
xchg reg,reg	4	4	3	3	3	3	NP

Undocumented Pentium Registers

T he sophisticated nature of the Pentium architecture led Intel to develop a number of internal registers and counters for various purposes such as checking for errors and performance monitoring. For unknown reasons Intel has elected to not widely publicize this information.

These "secret" registers are accessed via the RDMSR and WRMSR instructions. The following is what Intel documents about the RDMSR instruction in the *Pentium Processor User's Manual, Volume 3:* Architecture and Programming Manual:

> "RDMSR is used to read the content of Model-Specific Registers that control the functions for testability, execution tracing, performance monitoring and machine check errors. Refer to the Pentium Processor Data Book for more information. The values 3h, 0Fh and values above 13H are reserved. Do not execute RDMSR with reserved values in ECX."

RDMSR   Read machine-specific register
inputs: ECX   register number

ECX	Name	Description
0	Machine check address	Address of cycle causing exception
1	Machine check type	Cycle type of cycle causing exception

For other values used to perform cache, TLB and BTB testing and performance monitoring, see Appendix H.

Note: The Appendix H referred to is the Appendix H of the *Intel Pentium Processor User's Manual, Volume 3.*

The Appendix H of the *Intel Manual* is one paragraph in length. It states that "non-essential information regarding the Pentium processor are considered Intel confidential and proprietary and have not been documented in the publication."

Sure, this information is non-essential—until you find out your competitors have it. I have not seen and do not know what is in the Intel Appendix H. You may contact Intel to obtain this information by signing a non-disclosure agreement.

Thanks to the work of Terje Mathisen, a software developer in Norway, some of the information required for performance optimization has recently become publicly available, as published in the July 1994 issue of *Byte* magazine.

The values of two counters can be accessed at one time. MSR 11h controls which two counters are available. The two counters are then read as MSR 12h and MSR 13h. Only the lower 32 bits of MSR 11h are used. The first 16 bits control MSR 12h and the next 16 bits control MSR 13h. The encodings for each 16 bits are the same, as follows:

bits	Description
0–5	counter number (see Table H.1)
6	1=count in rings 0,1,2
7	1=count in ring 3
8	0=count events, 1=count cycles
9–15	reserved, do not change

For example, to count the number of instructions executed in each pipe you would need to use counter numbers 16h and 17h, as follows:

```
        cn_1 equ 16h          ; total instructions executed
        cn_2 equ 17h          ; total V pipe instructions executed
        ev3  equ 80h          ; count ring 3 events

        mov  ecx, 11h
        rdmsr
        and  eax, 0FE00FEh    ; save reserved bits
        or   eax, (cn_1+ev3) + ((cn2+ev3) shl 16)
        wrmsr

; save initial counter values

        movecx, 12h
        rdmsr
        mov  ctr_12, eax
        mov  ctr_12[2], edx

        mov  ecx, 13h
        rdmsr
        mov  ctr_13, eax
        mov  ctr_13[2], edx

; << place test code here >>

; determine elapsed difference

        mov  ecx, 12h
        rdmsr
        sub  eax, ctr_12
        sbb  edx, ctr_12[2]
        mov  ctr_12, eax
        mov  ctr_12[2], edx

        mov  ecx, 13h
        rdmsr
        sub  eax, ctr_13
        sbb  edx, ctr_13[2]
        mov  ctr_13, eax
        mov  ctr_13[2], edx
```

The RDMSR and WRMSR instructions are privileged. They must be executed from ring 0 in protected mode or in real mode. It is possible that there is a way to enable execution of these instructions while in protected mode rings 1, 2 or 3, or in virtual 8086 mode, but, of course, it is undocumented.

Table H.1 Undocumented Pentium Counter Registers

Counter Number	Name
0	data read
1	data write
2	data TLB miss
3	data read miss
4	data write miss
5	write (hit) to M or E state lines
6	data cache lines written back
7	data cache snoops
8	data cache snoops hits
9	memory accesses in both pipes
A	bank conflicts (may cause machine to hang)
B	misaligned data memory references
C	code read
D	code TLB miss
E	code cache miss
F	any segment register load
12	branches
13	BTB hits
14	branch taken or BTB hit
15	pipelines flushes
16	instructions executed
17	instructions executed in the v-pipe
18	bus utilization (clocks)
19	pipelines stalled by write backup
1A	pipeline stalled by data memory read
1B	pipeline stalled by write to E or M line
1C	locked bus cycle
1D	I/O read or write cycle
1E	noncacheable memory references
1F	AGI
22	floating-point operations
23	breakpoint 0 match
24	breakpoint 1 match
25	breakpoint 2 match
26	breakpoint 3 match
27	hardware interrupts
28	data read or write
29	data read miss or data write miss

DEBUG32 Command Summary

T he following address formats can be used based on the CPU mode:

segment:offset	is a real mode segment plus offset.
selector¦offset	is a protected mode selector plus offset.
linear+offset	is a protected mode linear address plus offset.

Segment addresses (":" identifier) refer to a segment address in both real and protected mode. Selector addresses ("¦" identifier) must be used in protected mode to refer to a selector+offset value.

"|" in command syntax separates choices
<> indicates an optional parameter

Assemble <address>
Assembles instructions to memory.

BP <address> <R|W|RW|I>
Sets a breakpoint. If no **R/W/RW/I** is specified, then the breakpoint is for execution only.

R   causes a break on reading data.
W   breaks on writing data.
RW   breaks on reading or writing.
I   uses the debug registers to break on execution (works with ROM).

BC <address|*>
Clears a breakpoint (**<*>** for all breakpoints).

BL
Lists breakpoints. Format is:

> **n) e address t=n**

"**t=n**" is total executions.

CLS
Clears the screen.

CPU
Displays CPU types, operating mode, A20 status, and prefetch length.

Compare <address_1 <address_2> <L length>>
Compares data at **<address_1>** to data at **<address_2>** for length **<L length>**.

DA <address>
Dump data at **<address>** in ASCII format.

DB <address>
Dump data at **<address>** in byte format.

DD <address>
Dump data at **<address>** in doubleword (32-bit) format.

DF <address>
Dump data at **<address>** in far pointer (16:32) format.

DP <address>
Dump data at **<address>** in pointer (16:16) format.

DW <address>
Dump data at **<address>** in word (16-bit) format.

Dump <address>
Dump data at **<address>** in the current format.

Enter <address <byte<,byte>>> 'character_string'
Enters data into memory.

Fill <address <end_address <byte<,byte<...>>>>> <L length>
Fills memory with a repeating value.

FLip ON|OFF
ON (default) causes switching to the application screen on **T** and **P** commands. **OFF** does not switch on **T** and **P** commands, and thus may confuse the application and debugger screens.

Go <=address> <temp_breakpoint <temp_breakpoint2 <...>>>
Resumes execution.
<=address sets new IP value
<temp_breakpoint> sets breakpoints temporary breakpoint(s).

HELP <initial_command_letters>
HELP or **?** commands alone produce the full help text.
The help output can be limited by specifying the first letter(s) of the command(s) to be described.

Hex value1 value2
Calculates the hexadecimal sum and difference of value1 and value2.

In <address>
Inputs a byte from port **<address>** and displays it in hex.

Load <program_name <address>>
Loads the specified program.
An address may be specified for non-EXE format files.

Load <address>
Loads the file identified by a **NAME** command.
An address may be specified for non-EXE format files.

Load address drive_number first_sector number_of_sectors
Loads data on a sector basis from the specified disk.
drive_number is 0 for A, 1 for B, 2 for C, etc.
first_sector is the starting sector on the disk (in hex).
number_of_sectors is the number of 512 byte sectors (in hex).

LOG <filename>
Copies all command window output to the specified file.
LOG without a filename closes the logging file.
Use of the logging facility is limited to non-DOS, non-interrupt areas of code. Use inside DOS or interrupt handlers does not work.

MEMory
Shows memory control block allocations.

MORE ON|OFF
ON (default) pauses command output on each screenfull.
OFF allows scrolling to proceed uninhibited. This is useful when the data is simply being logged to a file, rather than being read. When the **MORE** prompt is issued, any key continues for another full window. **ESC** cancels the command, and a digit allows that many more lines output.

Move <address_1> <address_2> <L length>
Copies data at **<address_1>** to **<address_2>** for length **<L length>**.

Name <program name | parms>
Sets the program name for a subsequent **Load** command.
Sets the command line parameters for an already loaded program.

Out <address> <value>
Outputs **<value>** to port **<address>**.

PRegs
Displays the privileged registers.

`Ptrace <=address <count>`

Traces a single inline instruction or procedure.

`<=address>` sets resume location.

`<count>` specifies the number or instructions to trace.

`Quit`

Quits the debugger and returns to DOS.

`R <register_name <new_value>>`

`R` alone displays all of the registers in the current (16/32) mode.

`R <register_name>` displays the current value of `<register_name>` and prompts
   for input of a new value.

`R <register_name> <new_value>` sets a register to a new value.

`R16/R32 ...`

`R16` sets 16-bit register mode.

`R32` sets 32-bit register mode.

Both commands perform the same as the "`R`" command, with the additional function of
   setting the 16/32 bit mode.

`RC`

Displays the changed registers.

`Read <file_name <address>>`

Reads the specified file. An address may be specified, or defaulted to the prefix area +
   100h. EXE formatting is read as ordinary data (it is not interpreted).

`REAson`

Displays the reason for entry into the debugger.

`Search <address <end_address <byte<,byte<,...>>>> <L length>`

Searches for the specified byte or character values.

`SELector value`

Displays the linear address active for the specified selector.

`SKIPCR`

Disables access to the control and debug registers for operating environments that do
not allow such access.

Trace <=address> <count>
Traces a single instruction.
<=address> overrides the resume address.
<count> sets the number of instructions to trace.

Unassemble <address>
Interprets memory at **<address>** as assembly language instructions.

USE32
USE16
Forces assemble/unassemble commands to assume the specified format.

Viewswap
Swaps the display to the application screen. Any key returns. See also the **FLIP** command.

Write address drive_number first_sector number_of_sectors
Writes data on a sector basis from the specified disk.
drive_number is 0 for A, 1 for B, 2 for C, etc.
first_sector is the starting sector on the disk (in hex).
number_of_sectors is the number of 512 byte sectors (in hex).

XA page_count
Allocates **page_count** EMS pages.

XD handle
Deallocates specified EMS handle.

XM physical_page logical_page handle
Maps the specified EMS handle/logical page into a physical page.

XS
Displays the current EMS status.

* comment
Enters a comment.

Improving Performance

I n this Appendix I'll discuss two hardware methods for improving performance in future 80x86 designs:

- new CPU instructions
- new 80x86 architectures

NEW INSTRUCTIONS

One method to improve performance might be to add more instructions. I think that it is possible that RISC (i.e., the original idea of fewer instructions, not the simple load/store concept) is the wrong direction. Because chips have orders of magnitude larger transistor counts than they did when the first RISC designs were conceived, there seems to be a mental block against adding new instructions. Of course, compatibility is always an issue, but I'm sure that many readers have always wondered, "Why isn't there an instruction to do X?"

When you think of the applications of the future you probably think about graphics, live motion video, and voice and handwriting recognition. Although special instructions could boost performance of these applications, it is probably more efficient to use special hardware, such as graphics accelerators. However, handheld devices and other low-cost systems will need to contain as much capability in the CPU as possible.

If you'd like a challenge, try to design several instructions that could be implemented as simple (one-cycle), pairable Pentium instructions. These instructions should be usable in many, if not most of present day applications and should provide a performance gain of at least 100% over alternate methods of execution.

Here are a few simple instructions I have designed.

The first instruction is the Compare-Ignore-Case (**cmpi**). If you haven't noticed, all CPUs seem to be ASCII-illiterate. Ostensibly, all CPUs know nothing about ASCII in fear of another standard emerging. The penalty has been hundreds of millions of chips with no concept of the character data type other than it is the same as a byte. A 256-byte table could be loaded in the CPU so that other character sets could be used. Instructions could also convert between cases, check case and other ASCII attributes.

The next instruction is the Compare-List, (**cmpl**).

Instead of writing this code:

```
cmp    al, 10
je     1f
cmp    al, 13
je     cr
cmp    al, 32
je     space
cmp    al, 0
je     null
```

you would write:

```
cmpl   ebx, al
je     match
```

Each byte in EBX is compared with AL. This instruction would be four times as fast as the current method. Other forms would be:

```
cmpl   ebx, ax
cmpl   bx, al
```

The **cmpl** instruction could be combined with the cmpi instruction forming **cmpli**— Compare-List-Ignore-Case.

Another instruction is the Compare-Or. This instruction would compare each byte in a register until a match is found, if any. This allows four bytes to be compared at once. (The regular CMP instruction is a logical AND of the compare of the bytes.) The following code compares four bytes in a sequential manner:

```
cmp     al, bl
je      found
cmp     ah, bh
je      found
ror     eax, 16
ror     ebx, 16
cmp     al, bl
je      found
cmp     ah, bh
je      found
```

Using the Compare-Or:

```
cmpor   eax, ebx
je      found
```

Ignore-case could also be added, creating **cmpori**.

These are just a few instructions I came up with related to processing text with variants on the CMP instruction. An important aspect of these instructions is that they allow the use of the full power of 32-bits on 8-bit data. Although microprocessors have gone from 8-bits to 16-bits to 32-bits in the past 20 years, text and character processing is still primarily done with instructions that process only eight bits at a time.

OTHER PENTIUM-CLASS MACHINES

As this is being written there have been many news releases about Pentium-class CPUs being designed by other companies—the AMD (Advanced Micro Devices) K5, the Cyrix M1 and the NexGen Nx586. There is no doubt that this extra competition will do at least two things: provide more choices and lower prices. The question for performance-minded programmers is: How will these CPUs handle Pentium-optimized code? Probably, no one knows except the designers of these chips.

NexGen claims that the Nx586 will outperform a Pentium when running integer instructions, at the same clock speed. It is not difficult to see how this could be done. Just make more instructions to be defined as simple or pairable in both pipes. Of course there are many other details that chip designers can optimize, such as cache performance, branch prediction, I/O buffer throughput, etc. Since all these things may be different, it is wise to test your time-critical code on every major platform.

The internal architecture of the Nx586 is quite different from the Pentium. When each 80x86 instruction is fetched it is converted into one or more RISC86 instructions. RISC86 instructions are RISC-like load/store instructions that can be executed in the pipelines. From the description of the Nx586, it appears that it should run Pentium-optimized code at the same or better speeds than the Pentium.

Few details are currently known about the AMD and Cyrix chips. But they are both claiming increased performance over the Pentium. The Cyrix M1 is reported to use speculative execution for part of its performance edge.

Finally, IBM is reportedly working on a PowerPC that includes an 80x86 instruction decoder. This CPU, the PowerPC 615, would decode 80x86 instructions and convert them to native PowerPC instructions for execution.

Glossary of Terms

Address

Location of a data item in memory. Also see Linear Address, Physical Address.

Address Generation Interlock (AGI)

A delay caused by the fact that a register required for an address calculation is being calculated by a previous instruction. Occurs on pipelined processors (the 486 and above).

Address-Size Prefix

An instruction prefix that overrides the default size for the size of address operands. Address operands may be 16-bits or 32-bits. The default for each code segment is set in the GDT or LDT for each segment.

AGI

Address Generation Interlock.

Alignment

The placement of data or code on a specific address boundary (i.e., a 2-, 4-, or 8-byte evenly divisible address).

ALU

Arithmetic Logic Unit.

Arithmetic Logic Unit

The portion of the CPU that performs the integer operations such as **ADD**, **SUB**, **AND**, **OR** and **CMP**.

ASCII

American Standard Code for Information Interchange. A standard code for representing English characters and symbols with various extensions for foreign characters.

Assembler

A program that translates an assembly-language program to machine language (or object code).

Assembly Language

A programming language, based on the architecture of a particular machine, where each statement translates into one machine instruction.

Base Address

The address at the start of a structure or of data array.

Base Register

A register that contains a base address. Usually BX (EBX) or BP (EBP) is a base register.

Base

Also see Base Address. In number systems, used to specify the number of digits in a system, i.e., base 10 has 10 digits, base 2 has two, etc.

BCD

Binary Coded Decimal. See also Packed BCD. This is a format for encoding base 10 numbers where the low order 4 bits are used to store the numerical value.

Big-Endian

A method of storing multi-byte data types where the low-order byte is stored at the highest address and the high-order byte is stored at the lower address.

BIOS

BASIC Input/Output System. Built-in software (usually stored in ROM) that starts up the computer and controls hardware such as the keyboard, screen and disks.

Bit

A binary digit. Can be a zero or a one.

Branch Prediction

A feature of the Pentium CPU where the CPU attempts to predict the branch destination based on previous branches from the same instruction.

Branch Target Buffer

A small buffer used to store a history of branches for the Branch Prediction feature of the Pentium.

Byte

A data type consisting of 8 bits.

Cache

A small fast memory buffer that holds a copy of the most recently used or most active portions of the larger slower memory. Also see Disk Cache.

Central Processor Unit (CPU)

The main processing unit in a computer. Sometimes referred to as the processor, the chip or the computer.

Character String

A data type that is an array of characters. Usually followed by a byte of 0 in assembly language or C.

Character

A data type that is the same as a byte.

Checksum

A simple error detection scheme where values are added (summed) into a variable to be compared with a similar previously calculated value.

Chip

A small piece of semiconducting material on which an electronic circuit is placed. A CPU chip is also known as a microprocessor.

CISC

Complex Instruction Set Computer.

Clock Speed

The speed that a processor executes instructions, usually in MHz.

Code Segment

The addressable area of memory defined by the segment in the CS register.

Code Segment Selector

In protected mode, the segment selector in the CS register.

Compiler

A program that translates a high-level language (such as C, Pascal or Fortran) into machine language or sometimes into assembly language.

Complex Instruction Set Computer

Computers designed with many complex and sometimes irregular instruction sets. The 80x86 architecture is considered CISC. See RISC.

CP/M

Control Program for Microcomputers. An operating system originally designed for 8080 and Z-80 based computers.

CPL

See Current Privilege Level.

CPU

See Central Processor Unit.

CRC

Cyclic redundancy check. A complex error detection scheme, similar to a checksum, but each value is operated on in a position-dependent manner. This increases the reliability of the error detection.

Current Privilege Level

The privilege level of the code that is currently executing. This applies to protected mode code only and is the same as the lowest 2 bits of the code segment selector.

Cycles

Periodic pulses created by an electronic clock that causes CPU activity.

Data Segment

The addressable area of memory defined by the segment in the DS register.

Data Structure

A scheme for organizing related data items.

Debugger

A program that allows executing, monitoring and modifying a program's code and data to enable a programmer to locate program errors (or bugs).

Descriptor Privilege Level

The privilege level that is applied to a segment, found in the segment descriptor.

Descriptor Table

An array of segment descriptors. There can be one Global Descriptor Table (GDT) and many Local Descriptor Tables (LDT). There can be one Interrupt Descriptor Table (IDT).

Directive

An assembler statement that contains information for the use of the assembler rather than an instruction to be assembled and executed as part of the program.

Disassembler

A program that attempts the difficult task of reconstructing an assembly language source file from machine language.

Disk Cache

A program and/or areas of memory set aside keep frequently used or most recently used data from a disk for quicker access.

Displacement

The constant part of an effective address (EA).

DMA

Direct Memory Access. A method for a device to transfer data to/from memory without using the CPU.

DOS

Disk Operating System. Also called MS-DOS or PC-DOS.

DPL

See Descriptor Privilege Level.

DR-DOS

Digital Research DOS. (Now Novell DOS).

DRAM

Dynamic RAM. The type of memory chip used in most computers. It is called dynamic because it must continually be refreshed or the contents will be lost.

Dword

A data type consisting of a double word or 32-bits.

EA

Effective Address

Editor

A program that allows the user to create and edit files.

Effective Address

The combination of any or all of a base register, index register and displacement used to produce an offset within a segment.

Emulator

A program that attempts to emulate, or work the same as, another program or machine.

Endian

Little-endian and big-endian.

Exception

A forced call to an interrupt routine that handles error conditions.

External Cache

A memory cache not physically located on the same chip as the CPU.

Extra Segment

The addressable area of memory defined by the segment in the ES register.

Far Pointer

A reference to memory consisting of a segment and an offset. In real mode the segment is the upper 16 bits of a 20-bit segment starting address. In protected mode the segment is a selector.

Fault

An exception that is called with the return address on the stack of the instruction that caused the fault.

File

An organized collection of data or information, usually stored on a disk with a specific name or filename.

Flat Model

A program model where all segment registers are the same and are usually set to be larger than 64K segments.

Floating-Point Unit

The portion of the 80486 or Pentium that performs the floating-point operations like the floating-point processor.

FPP

Floating-Point Processor.

Floating-Point Processor

A floating-point math processor. The processing unit that performs IEEE 754 floating-point arithmetic on 32-bit, 64-bit and 80-bit signed numbers with exponents.

FPU

Floating-Point Unit.

Gate Descriptor

A special segment descriptor that is the destination of a call or jump. The gate descriptor is used to change the CPU privilege level. There are four types: Call gates, Interrupt gates, Trap gates and Task gates.

GB

Gigabyte.

GDT

Global Descriptor Table.

Gigabyte (GB)

2^{30} or 1,073,741,824 bytes.

Global Descriptor Table

An array of segment descriptors for all programs in the system. The GDT is controlled by the operating system.

Hertz

A frequency of one cycle per second.

HLL

High-Level Language, such as C, BASIC, Pascal and Fortran.

Hz

Abbreviation for hertz.

IDT

Interrupt Descriptor Table.

IEEE

Institute of Electrical and Electronic Engineers. An organization best known for developing electrical and electronic standards for the computer industry.

Integer

A positive whole number, negative whole number or zero. On computers integers have a limited range—for example, byte integers have a range of −128 to +127.

Interpreter

A program that executes another program by reading each program statement and interpreting the actions to be taken.

Interrupt Descriptor Table

An array of gate descriptors used to call handlers for interrupts and exceptions in protected mode.

Interrupt Handler

A routine specifically designed to respond to an interrupt.
Interrupt Vector Table   An array of 256 far pointers to interrupt handlers. Located at address 0000:0000 (in real mode).

I/O

Input/Output.

IVT

Interrupt Vector Table.

KB

Kilobyte.

Kilobyte (KB)

2^{10} or 1,024 bytes.

Label

An identifier used in assembly language programs to specify a memory address by name rather than by its actual numerical address.

LDT

Local Descriptor Table.

Library

A collection of programs or subroutines stored in object file format, usually in a .LIB file.

Linear Address

A 20-, 24-, or 32-bit address into a large unsegmented memory space. With paging (virtual memory) disabled, the linear address is the physical address. With paging enabled, the paging mechanism translates the linear address to a physical address.

Link

The complex process of combining object files and hooking, or linking together, subroutines or data in one file that are referenced in another file.

Linker

A program that links one or more object files into an executable program file, usually an .EXE file.

Little-Endian

A method of storing multi-byte data types where the low-order byte is stored at the lowest address and the high-order byte is stored at the highest address. The Intel 80x86 processors use this format.

Local Descriptor Table

An array of segment descriptors for an individual program.

Logical Address

A segment and offset combine to generate a logical address. The segmentation unit translates the logical address into a linear address.

Long Integer

See integer. An integer data format consisting of 32 bits.

Machine Language

The binary codes that a machine (CPU) can execute.

Mask

A bit pattern constructed to be logically combined with a data value to allow only some bits of the original data value to show through (i.e., the others are masked out).

Math Coprocessor

A floating-point math processor.

MB

Megabyte.

Megabyte (MB)

2^{20} or 1,048,576 bytes.

Megahertz

A million hertz; 1MHz is a million cycles per second.

MHz

Megahertz.

Microprocessor

A computer processor fully contained on one integrated circuit (or chip).

Module

Part of a program, usually one file, containing one or more procedures or subroutines and/or data values.

MS-DOS

Microsoft DOS.

Near Pointer

A reference to memory containing only the offset portion of the address. The offset must be combined with a segment or selector in one of the segment registers.

Nibble

4 bits. There are two nibbles in a byte.

NPX

Numerical Processor Extension. Original name for the 8087 FPP.

Numeric Coprocessor

A floating-point math processor.

Object Code

An intermediate form of machine language produced by assemblers and compilers that is structured so that it can be linked together.

Offset

A 16-bit number that specifies the byte number beyond the start of a segment. On the 80386 and above segments may have 32-bit offsets.

Operand-Size Prefix

An instruction prefix that overrides the default size for integer operands. Operands may be 8- and 16-bits or 8- and 32-bits. The default for each code segment is set in the GDT or LDT for each segment.

Operand

Data provided in a register, in memory or immediately with an instruction to be used in the processing of the instruction.

Operating System

The program(s) that load applications and control access to memory, disk files, I/O ports, etc., such as DOS, Windows, OS/2 and UNIX.

OS

Operating System.

P-system

UCSD p-system.

Packed BCD

Packed Binary Coded Decimal. A data format that stores one decimal digit in each nibble of a byte.

Page

A 4K-byte block of memory. This is the size of memory block used for paging.

Paging

A method of managing memory, by an operating system, to implement a virtual memory system. Pages of memory are stored on a disk when not in use and recalled later when needed.

Pairing

The process of issuing two instructions at the same time to two different CPU pipelines. On the Pentium, these are the U and V pipelines.

Paragraph

16 bytes of memory, aligned on an even 16-byte boundary.

Parity

An error detection system commonly used in data communications where the sum of the set bits in a data packet is odd or even.

PC-DOS

Personal Computer DOS. IBM's version of MS-DOS.

Physical Address

The actual hardware address of memory issued by the processor. The maximum physical address is determined by the number of address pins on the processor.

Pipeline

A series of stages that an instruction passes through to complete its function.

Port

A channel, or connection, for data to enter or leave the CPU.

Prefix

One of several machine-language codes that can be placed in front of other instructions to modify their actions or default conditions.

Privilege Level

Protection codes for each segment when in protected mode. They range from 0 (most privileged, OS code) to 3 (least privileged, applications).

Processor

Short for microprocessor. The part of the computer that actually performs the arithmetic, logical and control functions of a computer.

Protected Mode

A CPU mode where memory address ranges are protected from being read and/or written to by unauthorized segments of code.

Pseudo-op

Another term for assembler directives.

Quadword

A data type consisting of 8 bytes or 64 bits.

RAM

Random Access Memory. The read/write memory used by the computer, usually consisting of DRAM chips.

Re-entrant

A property of a procedure or program that allows it to be interrupted and called or run again and both logical instances remain intact and properly execute independently of each other.

Real Mode

The only CPU mode of the 8088 and 8086 and the startup mode for the 80286 and above. There is no memory protection in real mode.

Reduced Instruction Set Computer

Computers designed with (relatively) a few simple instructions, a load/store architecture and a regular instruction set that can be easily pipelined.

Register

A storage area in a CPU. Each register usually has a number of operations that can be directly performed on it by the CPU, unlike a memory storage location.

RISC

Reduced Instruction Set Computer.

Segment Descriptor

An entry in a descriptor table that describes the starting address, length and attributes of a segment in protected mode.

Segment Override

A prefix for an instruction that causes a segment register, other than the normal default segment register, to be used during the execution of the instruction.

Segment

In real mode a segment is a portion of memory specified by a 20-bit starting address of which the low 4 bits are always zero and whose length can be up to 64K. In protected mode a segment is a portion of memory described by a descriptor table entry.

Selector

In protected mode, a pointer to a segment descriptor. A selector is a 16-bit value and is used in protected mode instead of a paragraph address in a segment register.

SRAM

Static RAM. Faster and more stable than DRAM, but requires more power and is more expensive. Usually used in memory caches.

Stack Segment

A portion of memory pointed to by the stack segment register for use as the system stack.

Stack

A last-in, first-out data structure in memory used for saving return addresses, temporary variables and system status information. A system can have any number of stacks, but only one may be in use at any time.

String

Any consecutive bytes of memory can be a string. HLLs specify rules for defining strings. In the C language strings must end with a byte containing a value of zero.

Superscalar

A CPU that can complete more than one instruction per machine cycle.

Task

One of many programs currently executing or waiting to execute in a multi-tasking system.

Task State Segment

A segment used to store the state of the CPU during a task switch.

Task Switch

The transfer of execution from one task to another.

TSS

Task State Segment.

Trap

An interrupt, usually generated as a result of an illegal instruction or condition.

Twos Complement

A mathematical operation where a binary value is multiplied by
−1. Each bit is changed to the opposite value and then one is added to the entire value.

UCSD P-system

University of California San Diego pseudo-code system. A system based on languages that are semi-compiled (to p-code or pseudo-code).

Unsigned Integer

A positive whole number or zero. On computers unsigned integers have a limited ranged; for example, an 8-bit unsigned integer has a range of 0 to 255.

V86 Mode

Virtual-8086 Mode.

Virtual Memory

A scheme used that allows programs to logically allocate and use more memory than is physically available by moving and swapping portions that are not currently needed or infrequently used to a hard disk.

Virtual-8086 Mode

A mode on 386 and above processors that provides for the emulation of the 8086 architecture. An operating system may run a mix of protected mode tasks and virtual-8086 mode tasks.

Word

A data type consisting of two bytes or 16 bits.

APPENDIX

Products
Mentioned

L

TASM & Borland C++
Borland International
1800 Green Hills Rd.
Scotts Valley, CA 95067-0001
(408) 438-5300   (800) 336-6464

Cloaking Developer's Toolkit
Helix Software Company
47-09 30th Street
Long Island City, NY 11101
(718) 392-3100

Pentium Processor User's Manual
Intel Literature
P.O. Box 7641
Mt. Prospect, IL 60054-7641
(800) 548-4725

Kedit (Editor)

Mansfield Software Group
P.O. Box 532
Storrs, CT 06268
(203) 429-8402

MASM & Microsoft C/C++ and Visual C++

Microsoft Corp.
One Redmond Way
Redmond, WA 98052-6399
(206) 882-8080   (800) 426-9400

Soft-Ice and Bounds Checker

Nu-Mega Technologies, Inc.
P.O. Box 7780
Nashua, NJ 03060-7780
(603) 889-2386

Periscope Model IV

Periscope
1475 Peachtree St. Suite 100
Atlanta, GA 30309
(404) 888-5335   (800) 722-7006

PentOpt Professional and ASMFLOW Professional

Quantasm Corp.
19672 Stevens Creek Blvd. Suite 307
Cupertino, CA 95014-2465
(408) 244-6826   (800) 765-8086

Sourcer (Disassembler)

V Communications
4320 Stevens Creek Blvd., Suite 275
San Jose, CA 95129
(408) 296-4224

Index

$75 Discount

Name_____

Company_____

Address_____Apt._____

City _____State _____Zip_____

Country_____

Phone _____

Visa/MC # _____Expires _____

Signature for charge orders_____

Send or fax a copy of this page to receive PentOpt Professional, the Pentium optimization program, for $124.95 (normally $199.95). See the description on the enclosed disk for full details.

SEND TO:
Quantasm Corp.
19672 Stevens Creek Blvd. #307-B
Cupertino, CA 95014-2465

Phone: 408-244-6826
         800-765-8086
Fax: 408-244-7268